Law and Philosophy Library

Volume 134

The Law and Philosophy Library, which has been in existence since 1985, aims to publish cutting edge works in the philosophy of law, and has a special history of publishing books that focus on legal reasoning and argumentation, including those that may involve somewhat formal methodologies. The series has published numerous important books on law and logic, law and artificial intelligence, law and language, and law and rhetoric. While continuing to stress these areas, the series has more recently expanded to include books on the intersection between law and the Continental philosophical tradition, consistent with the traditional openness of the series to books in the Continental jurisprudential tradition. The series is proud of the geographic diversity of its authors, and many have come from Latin America, Spain, Italy, the Netherlands, Germany, and Eastern Europe, as well, more obviously for an English-language series, from the United Kingdom, the United States, Australia and Canada.

More information about this series at http://www.springer.com/series/6210

Thomas Søbirk Petersen

Why Criminalize?

New Perspectives on Normative Principles of Criminalization

Springer

Thomas Søbirk Petersen
University of Roskilde
Roskilde, Denmark

ISSN 1572-4395 ISSN 2215-0315 (electronic)
Law and Philosophy Library
ISBN 978-3-030-34689-8 ISBN 978-3-030-34690-4 (eBook)
https://doi.org/10.1007/978-3-030-34690-4

Cover illustration: eStudio Calamar, Berlin/Figueres

This Springer imprint is published by the registered company Springer Nature Switzerland AG.
The registered company address is: Gewerbestrasse 11, 6330 Cham, Switzerland

Acknowledgments

Many people and organizations have supported me in my research, especially with the parts of it presented in this book, and it is a pleasure to thank all those I can remember for their kind support, comments, and inspiration. First, my clever and dear colleagues of Philosophy and Science Studies at the University of Roskilde have always been willing to discuss the topics of this book. Among those colleagues, I would like to offer a special thank you to all the members of our Research Group for Criminal Justice Ethics. Our group has been fortunate to consist of philosophers like Fatima Sabir, Frej Klem Thomsen, Jakob v. H. Holtermann, Sebastian Holmen, Kasper Mosekjær, Rune Klingenberg, Sune Læggard, Ditte Marie Munch-Jurisic, Søren Sofus Wichmann, Jesper Ryberg, Kira Vrist Rønn, and Kasper Lippert-Rasmussen. Thanks to all those members who have read my work and made important comments at our monthly research meetings. Without your comments, this book would certainly contain many more errors than it does. I would like to acknowledge that Jesper Ryberg and Kasper Lippert-Rasmussen have been extraordinarily helpful in making many very valuable comments and suggestions about most chapters in this book. I wish every person could have the benefit of such clever, inspiring, and thoughtful colleagues and friends.

I have presented parts of this book at several seminars and conferences, and at all these meetings I have received valuable comments. Drafts of Chap. 2 were presented at a seminar at Oxford University. Thanks to Roger Crisp for the invitation and the audience for the inspiring comments. My views on hedonism, expressed in the Appendix, benefited from two seminars, one of which was held at the University of Edinburgh. Here I would like to thank Eli Mason for the invitation and the audience for the inspiring comments. Another was held at the University of Gothenburg. This also helped to improve the ideas on hedonism expressed and argued for in this book, and I must thank Ingmar Persson and Christian Munthe for the original invitation and for some very valuable comments. I would also like to thank Anthony Duff for inviting me to present a paper on criminalization, punishment, and dignity at a seminar on this topic hosted by the Minnesota Law School.

I would like to thank the Uehiro Centre for Practical Ethics in Oxford and all its staff members for their hospitality and interest in my research during my stay as a visiting academic in the second half of 2009. I have benefited from discussions with many people in addition to those mentioned so far. I hope I will be forgiven if I do not mention all those who have contributed to my work or thinking on the topics presented and critically discussed in this book. I have tried my best to scan my brain and to mention those I can remember: Gustaf Arrhenius, Ludwig Beckmann, Christopher Bennett, David Birks, Lene Bomann-Larsen, Bart Bremmen, Christoph Bublitz, Krister Bykvist, Roger Crisp, Jens Damgaard Thaysen, Katrien Devolder, Tom Douglas, Göran Duus-Otterström, Søren Flinch Midtgaard, Nils Holtug, Niklas Juth, Karsten Klint Jensen, Kevin McNish, Heidi Maibom, Morten E.J. Nielsen, Nikolaj Nottelmann, Toby Ord, Paul Robinson, Raffaele Rodogno, Julian Savulescu, Wayne Sumner, Victor Tadros, Torbjörn Tännsjö, and Martin Westergren. I would also like to thank all the students who attended my seminar on criminalization theory in the autumn of 2010 and spring of 2018. I remember many helpful discussions.

I would also like to acknowledge a valuable but often overlooked influence on research, namely, the administrative staff surrounding researchers. The motivational and administrative support provided by people at our Department of Communication and Arts at Roskilde University has meant a lot to me, and I would like to thank those I have been assisted by the most over the years: Alberto Nielsen, Martin Bayer, Tania Brask, Camilla Lomholt, Hanne Løngreen, Vibeke (Skipper) Mortensen, Ib Poulsen, Anya Strøm, Tina Nielsen, Kirsten Høffding, Vibeke Olsen, Elsebeth Olsen, Marianne Sloth-Hansen, and Marie Brobeck. Furthermore, I would like to thank Springer Nature and editor Anja Trautmann for their patience and support, and Paul A Robinson and Ad Hoc Translations for professional proofreading.

Thanks to my beloved father, the late Henning Anker Petersen, who taught me much about morality and showed me how the way we deal with moral issues defines us as the persons we are, or become, and shapes the relationships we have with other people and the society in which we live and die.

Finally, this book is dedicated to the loves of my life: to Helle Søbirk, whom I have had the pleasure to know and love since I was 17 years old, and to our two children, Amanda and Malthe, whom we have always loved and will always love. All three of you have given my life meaning, and more than I can ever put in words.

Roskilde, Denmark
September 2019

Thomas Søbirk Petersen

Sources

Parts of some of the chapters in this book have appeared in print elsewhere. The following list indicates where. However, all these chapters in this book are, in several ways, significantly different, and I would say significantly improved too, from the following publications.

Chapter 2: Petersen TS (2014) Being Worse Off: But in Comparison with What? On the Baseline Problem of Harm and the Harm Principle. Res Publica: A Journal of Moral, Legal and Social Philosophy 20(2):199–214.

Chapter 3: Petersen TS (2016) No Offense: On the Offense Principle and Some New Challenges. Criminal Law and Philosophy: An International Journal for Philosophy of Crime, Criminal Law and Punishment 10(2):355–365.

Chapter 4: Petersen TS (2011) What is Legal Moralism? SATS: Northern European Journal of Philosophy 12(1):80–88 and Petersen TS (2010) New Legal Moralism: Some Strengths and Challenges. Criminal Law and Philosophy: An International Journal for Philosophy of Crime, Criminal Law and Punishment 4 (2):215–232.

Chapter 6: Petersen TS (2019) A Soft Defense of a Utilitarian Principle of Criminalization. Res Publica: A Journal of Moral, Legal and Social Philosophy https://doi.org/10.1007/s11158-019-09426-3 (First online): 11 March 2019.

Appendix: Petersen TS (2009) What Is It for a Life to Go Well (or Badly)? Some Critical Comment of Wayne Sumner's Theory of Welfare. Journal of Happiness Studies: An Interdisciplinary Forum on Subjective Well-Being 10(4):449–458.

Contents

Chapter 1
Introduction

1.1 What Is This Book About?

I take it for granted that most of us firmly believe, and would indeed insist, that murder, violent attacks on innocents, and rape are kinds of conduct the state ought to criminalize. Living in a society where these kinds of conduct were not criminalized would probably lead to breakdown of civil order and a huge increase in human misery.[1] However, when it comes to practices such as: abortion, alcohol consumption, euthanasia, colouring rabbits and birds, prostitution, selling sex toys, sex between half-siblings, selling and smoking marijuana, wearing a burkini or using reptiles in religious services, public attitudes as well as the attitude of scholars to criminalization are often less firm and generally fall short of a consensus.[2] These observations about what to criminalize, naturally gives rise to at least two normative questions, the first more theoretical than the second:

(a) By what moral principle(s) should criminalization decisions be guided?
(b) What kinds of conduct should be criminalized?

There are some important connections between these two questions, which make it natural to answer both questions, once you begin to answer one of them. For instance, if the state or its citizens have to decide or discuss whether a kind of conduct C should be criminalized (question b), they will usually, as a matter for fact, be guided by some principles that can justify whether C should be criminalized or not. And this requires an answer to question (a). However, to what extent this proposed connection is genuine can only be based on empirical evidence. Moreover, it is at least possible that, in certain cases, there is no such connection at all although there are good reasons, as will be made clearer in Sect. 1.2, for thinking that a state

[1] Duff (2018), p. 8.

[2] For references to the fact that e.g. bird and rabbit colouring and using reptiles during religious services are prohibited in certain states in the US, see e.g. Husak (2008), p. 35.

T. Søbirk Petersen, *Why Criminalize?*, Law and Philosophy Library 134,
https://doi.org/10.1007/978-3-030-34690-4_1

will always try to come up with a principled justification of why it wants to criminalize certain kinds of conduct. In addition, when it comes to such important matters as which conduct to criminalize, it seems *morally right* to present a justification for why certain kinds of conduct ought to be criminalized.[3] Furthermore, instead of letting decisions about the criminalization of conduct C be guided by a principle (or several principles), it is also possible that the principle or principles are and should be guided by what the state wants to criminalize. If, for instance, it does not follow from a principle P (or a set of principles) that slavery should be criminalized, one could use this as a counterexample that would disqualify P as a plausible principle of criminalization. In this sense, answers to question (a) can be guided by answers to question (b).[4]

The primary focus of this book is on critical discussion of answers to question (a). So instead of going into detailed analysis of whether or not euthanasia, cannabis or prostitution, for example, should be (or remain) criminalized, which would be a branch of applied ethics, the focus will be on a critical discussion of answers to question (a). In other words, the aim of this book is a critical discussion of some central normative principles of criminalization, rather than a discussion of specific kinds of conduct the state ought to criminalize.[5] That being said, and alluded to above, we shall often see that a standard way of criticizing a principle of criminalization is to focus on the implication it would have for the kinds of conduct that should be criminalized.

Over the last 150 years or so,[6] it has been standard, within criminal justice ethics, to answer question (a) with reference to *versions* of one or more of the following five principles: the harm principle, legal paternalism, the offense principle, legal moralism and the dignity principle of criminalization.[7] These principles, which are here only presented by their names, will be specified and critically discussed at length in this book, with some receiving more attention than others. However, as the literature on principles of criminalization is enormous and ever-expanding, and because furthermore that lierature touches upon many different issues within political science, law, legal philosophy, metaphysics, meta-ethics, moral and political philosophy and

[3]In Sect. 1.3 (on methodology), it will be explained why we ought to justify our criminalization decisions and what characterizes some of the minimum requirements for a plausible justification.

[4]In Chap. 5, for example, we will discuss a reasoning like this where the 'case of the happy slave' is used to argue in favour of the attractiveness of a Kantian Dignity Principle of Criminalization over harm principles.

[5]Concerning terminology, one can also say that the subject of this book is 'theories of criminalization' instead of 'principles of criminalization'. I will not enter a discussion on the possible differences between a theory of criminalization and principles of criminalization. I here follow Duff (2018), p. 11 when he says that the purpose of a normative theory of criminalization it to give 'an account of the principles by which deliberations about what to criminalize should be guided'.

[6]Or at least since the publication of John Stuart Mill's *On liberty* in 1859.

[7]See e.g. Feinberg's four volumes (1984, 1985, 1986, 1988), where each volume contains a specification and critical discussion of one of the first four principles mentioned above. See also Simester and von Hirsch (2011) and Murphy (2007) for this overall categorization of normative principles of criminalization.

applied ethics, it is impossible for one person, in one book, to do justice to it on this important subject. I do hope that the reader will bear all this in mind when reading the book. Furthermore, I believe that the issues I have tried to focus on are in some ways neglected or undeveloped in the literature (at least at the time of writing), and that the following chapters will represent an interesting advance of the field.

One central goal of this book is to argue that all five principles (or, more precisely, standard versions of them) generate important problems that point in the direction of rejections (or at least a rethink or replacement) of the standard principles of criminalization. In the chapters to come, I will argue that one of the reasons why we should reject or revise standard principles of criminalization is that versions of the harm principle and legal paternalism that have been offered so far, are rendered redundant by general moral theories. We should resort to general moral theories in order to give a more plausible and applicable answer to our initial research question. Furthermore, I will argue, that versions of the offence principle can be reduced to harm principles, thus making these principles redundant too. Alternatively, it will be demonstrated how versions of legal moralism and dignity principles either rests on unacceptable assumptions (e.g. that versions of legal moralism are based on speculative and wrong empirical assumptions), or have implausible implications. Therefore, there is reason to move beyond the traditional principles of criminalization, and instead try to investigate alternative principles which the state (or we, the people) should be guided by when we deliberate about which kinds of conduct should be criminalized.

In Chap. 6, I try to defend one such principle, namely a utilitarian principle of criminalization. Since the days of Jeremy Bentham and John Stuart Mill, there have been very few defenders of a utilitarian principle of criminalization. I hope that, by rattling an intellectual orthodoxy from its complacency, this last part of the book is worthwhile, if only to force non-utilitarians to think harder about their positions. If nothing else, I try to take some steps in the direction of showing that the so-called beast of a utilitarian principle of criminalization is not as scary as we have often been told.[8]

1.2 Why Is This Book Important?

I hope it is obvious why the answers that we arrive at, and live by, when it comes to criminalization decisions are very important. To give just two examples. First, for the freedom and well-being of all people in a society, it matters what kinds of conduct are criminalized and what kinds are not. Imagine two societies, which we can call 'Libertaria' and 'Prohibitia'. In Libertaria, only violent crimes like murder, assault, rape, and some lesser crimes like fraud and stealing are prohibited. So, in Libertaria, for example, abortion, alcohol consumption, assisted reproduction,

[8]See e.g. Husak (2008), p. 188.

affirmative action, the cloning of animals and humans, a free market for selling organs, driving without a seatbelt, duelling, euthanasia, gambling, homosexuality, music piracy, nakedness in public spaces, pornography, prostitution, recreational drug production (plus distribution, selling, buying and use), the use of performance-enhancing drugs in sports and in education and research, sex between siblings, sex with animals, smoking tobacco, women driving cars and weapon possession are all legal activities. In Prohibitia, by contrast, all these above-mentioned activities are criminalized.

It is obvious that whether you live in Libertaria or in Prohibitia you will find yourself facing a state-enforced background with a huge impact on your freedom and well-being—affecting not only your opportunities to engage in different kinds of conduct with or without the threat of state punishment, but also concerning the risk of being punished. For the more acts that are criminalized, the higher the risk of transgressing the criminal law will usually become; and a higher risk of being punished will normally follow that. Furthermore, the risk of being a victim of a crime also depends on which kinds of conduct a state decides to write into the criminal law. We must add to this the financial cost to the state and its citizens of enforcing criminal laws like those mentioned in our two imaginary societies.[9] The economic resources required could be used to prevent harm in other areas of our society—for example, in the health care service or programmes for crime prevention.

Secondly, if a type of conduct is criminalized and detected, punishment will usually follow. And when punishment is inflicted, it will have a huge impact on many people's lives. When it comes to imprisonment, for example, the latest figures from 2015 tell us that an estimated 11 million people worldwide are held in penal institutions.[10] In the US, which has the highest documented incarceration rate in the world, there were a total of 1,570,300 adults in federal and state prisons and local jails in 2017.[11] This is about 0.6% of people over 16 years of age in the US resident population. Moreover, it is no secret that life in prison can be very tough. At its best, it might be boring, but assaults from guards and other inmates, e.g. homosexual rape, are not uncommon.[12] Furthermore, ex-offenders face huge difficulties in finding employment, and especially well-paid jobs, at least partly as a consequence of their criminal records, as most employers do not wish to employ them and because ex-offenders are banned from many public jobs (e.g. in the police force, prison service, etc.).[13] Apart from such 'collateral consequences', ex-offenders in some states lose their right to vote and may be excluded from social benefits like public

[9]For example, in 2010 the US spent $261,1 billion on the direct cost of crime including expenditure on federal, state and local correction, police protection and judicial and legal services. See Kyckelhahn and Martin (2013) for these data.

[10]Walmsley (2018).

[11]United States Bureau of Justice Statistics (2019). The same bureau has collected data which show that in 2016 about 6,615,500 adults were under correctional supervision (probation, parole, jail, or prison), equivalent to about 2.8% of the resident adult population of the US.

[12]See e.g. Struckman-Johnson and Struckman-Johnson (2000).

[13]See e.g. Holzer (1996), Thomas (2007) and Petersen (2016).

housing and student loans. Moreover, punishment will not only have a huge direct impact on the individuals being punished; it will, of course, also have an indirect effect on the well-being of relatives, including parents, spouses and children, and the well-being of friends. On top of that, the number of inmates, the kinds of punishment they receive (e.g. community service, prison, being fined or public shaming) and how harshly they are punished (e.g. for how long they are incarcerated) will affect the cost of the criminal justice system.[14] Imprisonment, for example, will also have a direct negative impact on the number of people available to participate in the education system and the labour market.[15]

On the other hand, one might, as a second thought, wonder whether, just as it is obvious that these normative questions are important, their answers are equally obvious. If this is true, not only the whole project of this book but also the field of criminalization theory would be an unnecessary time-wasting academic exercise. But although there might be some immediate and obvious answers to questions like those about what principles or criteria we should apply when deciding whether to criminalize a certain kind of conduct, these allegedly obvious answers, as we shall see in the next paragraph, do not appear to be suited to cover all kinds of conduct when criminalization is properly discussed. In any case, immediate, apparently obvious answers or opinions might not always be the right or best answers.

Take a look at the questions about what the state ought to criminalize and why. As was said at the beginning of this introduction, it seems obvious that most of us have a clear conception that certain kinds of conduct ought to be criminalized by the state. Few would doubt, for instance, that assault, murder, and rape should count as criminal acts. Similarly, nobody would argue that acts like drinking a glass of water in public or counting stars in the sky should normally be considered criminal offences. But when we scratch beneath the surface, we readily see that there are very different opinions about exactly what conduct should be criminalized and punished by the state and why. If we take the differences between Libertaria and Prohibitia as a background, we will see that while some countries in today's world do not prohibit acts such as abortion, alcohol consumption, homosexuality, prostitution, marijuana, and artificial reproduction, others do. Such variation can also be seen across time within many countries. What was once a criminal act, e.g. homosexual sex between consenting adults, is now perfectly legal in states like the UK, the US and the Scandinavian countries. Again, what was once legal in a country may come to be criminalized again, as has happened with homosexual sex in India.[16] So what might be counted as a criminal act in one country might not be so in another country, and

[14]See note 9 above.

[15]For a resent, and very good and critical overview of the collateral consequences of punishment, see e.g. Hoskins (2019).

[16]In India, homosexual sex was legal between 2009 and 2013, then criminalized from 2013 to 2018 and then decriminalized again in September 2018. For the latter claim see https://www.bbc.com/news/world-asia-india-45429664 (assessed August 12, 2019).

what was once criminalized within one country might come to be decriminalized in the very same country, and vice versa.

But even if (as is very unlikely) all states agreed on the kinds of conduct to be criminalized, this would not necessarily show that what they agree over is, morally speaking, the right thing to do. For it is possible that many states (and people) are mistaken. What kinds of conduct the state should punish, and why such conduct should be punished, needs independent argument. It is the primary aim of criminalization theory to provide and critically assess arguments of this sort.

It goes without saying that those engaged in criminalization theory need to develop not just answers, but answers that they can justify. This, at least, is one of the basic methodological requirements imposed in this book. When it comes to important ethical challenges for our society, like those presented by the various parts of the criminal justice system, I take it for granted that we, as citizens, as politicians and as decision-makers, should give arguments in favour of the policy we want to adopt. I imagine most readers of this book would agree with the following view, which we can call the *'justification requirement'*: in support of policy suggestions about important ethical questions, those who suggest such policies must also present a justification (offer an argument or arguments) in support of their views. However, the mere provision of such justification is not the only methodological requirement, for we should also strive to give a justification that is clear and well founded.

However, what does a clear and well-founded justification amount to? How can moral principles be defended in a plausible way? Are not moral opinions, attitudes and the acceptance of normative principles just a matter of taste? To answer these questions in detail would take us deep into the discipline of *meta-ethics*—a discipline which, in broad terms, deals with the ontological, semantic and epistemological nature of moral judgement. However, because this is a book about *normative ethics*, and more precisely normative principles of criminalization, it would be inappropriate to tackle meta-ethics at length.

On the other hand, it does seem like a good idea to provide a thumbnail sketch of the way in which moral attitudes and principles are taken to be justified in this book. For, when one is doing criminalization theory, one is usually trying to criticize or defend normative principles of criminalization; and when we do this we already (more or less consciously) have views about what criticizing and defending moral principles involves. Therefore, in what follows, I will very briefly, and in no sense claiming to do anything original, describe some further methodological requirements of moral reasoning besides the justification requirement just mentioned. These requirements are employed by most other contemporary philosophers working in the field of criminalization theory, at least, within the contemporary tradition that is sometimes called Anglo-American, or analytical, philosophy.[17] However, instead of

[17]See e.g. Kagan (1998), Tadros (2011), Holtug (2010) and Lippert-Rasmussen (2005). However, it is fair to underline that the justification requirement and the four requirements that will be presented in the next paragraphs, are all requirements that any respectable intellectual or scientific enterprise not only should accept but also usually does accept.

engaging in a lengthy description and defence of these requirements, something that would not do justice to the enormous meta-ethical literature on moral reasoning and justification that already exists,[18] I will try primarily to show how the methodology is applied in the chapters to come. Thus each chapter in this book can be seen as an application and exemplification of the methodology that will, very briefly, be described in the next section.

1.3 Methodology

Below, four methodological requirements will be described and illustrated. These revolve around: conceptual clarification; empirical evidence; consistency, and the appeal to moral intuitions. I will not go into the heated debate over how, exactly, we should understand these requirements, or whether all of them are necessary or sufficient in the proper evaluation of moral arguments. I will simply ask the reader to consider whether it would be a good idea, or something that we would value from an epistemic point and moral point of view, for an argument in favour of an important public policy to rest on unclarified concepts, no empirical evidence, and inconsistency, and to be such that it does not appeal to anyone's considered moral intuitions. I imagine, and take it for granted that most rational people would answer 'No', and that we ought to accept the requirements I am imposing, or most of them, when discussing and making decisions on important social issues—including the issue of what kinds of principles should guide our deliberations about what to criminalize. Let us now look at the four requirements in a little more detail.

1.3.1 Conceptual Clarification

A large part of the book is concerned with the clarification of central concepts, distinctions, and principles that are used in the justification of accounts of the kinds of conduct which merit criminalization. It seems obvious that, in order to make progress in any academic field, we have to clarify the central concepts involved in the problem and the arguments being employed to solve it. If we do not, we could easily be talking at cross purposes, and then the prospect of our having a fruitful discussion would be, to say the least, limited. So we shall strive to specify what we mean by the central terms being used, and to explain how they deviate from common usage or from standard philosophical use.[19]

---

[18]See e.g. Miller (2003) and Thomson (2002).

[19]See e.g. Hansson (2006) for detailed analysis of how to construct conceptual clarity; for a strong defence of the use of conceptual analysis, see Jackson (1998).

In Chap. 2, for instance, the concept of *being harmed* by another person is specified as follows: a person P1 is harmed by another person P2 doing C, if and only if P1 is made worse off in terms of well-being because of C. Such a specification, combined with a further analysis of the terms 'worse off' and 'well-being', is very important if we want to understand central principles in criminalization theory, such as versions of the harm principle. The harm principle, in one version, says that the only plausible reason for the state to prohibit conduct of type C is to prevent C harming (or there being a risk that C will harm) individuals. However, although in many cases it seems obvious that a person is being harmed (or at risk of harm), we must aim to clarify what it means to say that someone is harmed. Without such clarification, we cannot hope to characterize fully the acts that, according to versions of the harm principle, are candidates for criminalization. Furthermore, the clarification of what it means to be harmed by another individual is essential when our aim is to evaluate the implications, and hence the plausibility, of principles which claim that the harming of others (and of oneself, as legal paternalism would emphasize) matters morally in criminalization decisions.

Another of the many examples of this enterprise can be found in Chap. 4, where one of the aims is to clarify and map out different versions of the principle of criminalization, already mentioned above, known as 'legal moralism'. It is argued that the core claim of legal moralism is that if conduct of type C belongs to a certain class of immoral conduct C∗, then the state has, all things considered, sufficient reason to criminalize C even if C-type conduct does not cause (or risk causing) someone to be harmed. However, there is huge disagreement in the literature over how to specify legal moralism, and in Chap. 4 (Sect. 4.2) I therefore aim to unpack this diversity and to carefully distinguish different ways to understand legal moralism. If progress is to be made in the normative discussion of the principles of criminalization, a vital preliminary task is to identify clearly which principle and which specific version is under discussion.

1.3.2 Empirical Evidence

There is no doubt that empirical evidence can play a significant role in the justification of moral claims. Given this, it seems reasonable to impose a methodological requirement that we ensure that the justification of our moral beliefs rests on empirical evidence that is as solid as possible. In some parts of this book, the empirical premise of an argument in favour of a normative conclusion is questioned or rejected. An example of this way of challenging a normative viewpoint can be drawn from Chap. 4 (Sect. 4.3), where it is argued that Patrick Devlin's empirical premise—that activities, such as abortion, bigamy, euthanasia and homosexuality, pose a threat to the cohesion of society, in the sense of threatening to bring about a breakdown of law and order—is factually inaccurate. The chapter points to empirical evidence that several stable liberal states have not disintegrated in the way Devlin anticipated, although abortion, euthanasia and homosexuality have been legal in these states for decades.

Another example of empirical data being involved in a critical discussion of a normative principle of criminalization can be seen in Chap. 6, where I try to defend a utilitarian principle of criminalization (UPC). There, I refer to empirical data to show that we can safely assume that UPC can justify the criminalization of core cases of criminal conduct such as murder, rape and assault. I base my claim that we can do that on empirical studies showing that murder, rape and assault flourish where they are not criminalized and punished by the state, or where detection and conviction rates are very low, say because, there is a police strike or the country is at war. In the same chapter (Sect. 6.5), I also try to show why one of Victor Tadros's arguments against UPC is difficult to evaluate because it relies on an empirical assertion, that is follows from UPC that sacrificing oneself for the lesser good should be criminalized, as this would maximise the total sum of well-being).

1.3.3 Consistency

At several points, when I am discussing arguments or positions, I strive to show that a set of propositions is inconsistent (or consistent), and that we therefore cannot (or can) hold on to the entire set. Like the previously mentioned requirements, this is hardly a controversial methodological demand. Let me give a few examples of it from the chapters to come.

In Chap. 4, I is argue that when legal moralists (1) claim that legal moralism and the harm principle are different principles of criminalization *and* (2) specify moral legalism as the view that 'if the conduct of type *a* is regarded as immoral (or is immoral), then the state has *a reason* to criminalize *a*', (1) and (2) *can* be interpreted as being inconsistent. The problem in a nutshell is this: several versions of the harm principle hold that it is only the prevention of *morally wrongful harm* that counts as a necessary condition for criminalization. In other words, the moral wrongfulness of the kinds of conduct to be criminalized do play the one and only part for adherents of a harm principle. However, if this is true, then there is no difference between legal moralism and harm principles. There is no difference because most adherents of harm principles (e.g. Feinberg) agree with the above-mentioned specification of the structure of legal moralism, i.e. they agree that it is only immoral acts that we have a reason to criminalize. So one must either give up the idea that the two principles are distinct or give up this definition of legal moralism. It can, as I have shown, be inconsistent to hold both views. In Chap. 4, I duly defend the view that we should give up the above-mentioned specification of legal moralism and argue for a specification ensuring that legal moralism explicitly differ from standard versions of the harm principle.

Again, furthermore, in Chap. 5, where I discuss a Kantian dignity principle of criminalization (KDPC), I want to show that adherents of such a principle are inconsistent when they claim that harm principles should be rejected because it follows from them that not all types of slavery (i.e. so-called happy enslavement) should be criminalized. And as will be shown in detail in Chap. 5, defenders of KDPC are inconsistent when they reject a class of theories (harm principles) because they give the so-called wrong answer in the case of happy enslavement, and then at the same time, favour a theory (KDCP) from which it follows that it too delivers the wrong answer in the very same type of case.

1.3.4 The Appeal to Moral Intuitions

Throughout the book, I also appeal to moral intuitions in order to defend or criticize moral theories and principles. The general structure of the reasoning here is often as follows: a case is used to show that an implication of a moral theory, moral principle or value theory is counterintuitive and because of the requirement of consistency, one ought to reject or modify the principle so that counterintuitive implications do not follow. In Chap. 2, for example, I use some cases to show that certain baseline specifications of harm are problematic when they imply that one person's intentional prolonging of another person's headache is not, all else being equal, an example of doing harm. Likewise, in Chap. 6 where several intuitions against a utilitarian theory of criminalization are presented and criticized. I try to show how any appeal to intuitions can be problematized. I also suggest that if we want to use intuitions as a way of criticizing moral claims, then for example Victor Tadros's non-consequentialist critique of a utilitarian theory of criminalization has counter-intuitive implications of its own (e.g. as shown in Sect. 6.5, that we should criminalize car driving).

Another example of appealing to intuitions appears in the Appendix, where it is argued, by means of a counter-example, that the view that a person cannot have positive or negative well-being if they are deceived or mistaken about reality has counterintuitive implications. Such a value-theoretical view of well-being would imply, for example, that you cannot experience real negative well-being through the fear and discomfort of a fake threat. I point out that a value theory which implies *that* is simply counterintuitive, and that we therefore have a reason to reject it.

Of all the requirements that have been described so far, the appeal to intuitions is by far the most controversial. Let me therefore explain my view on this requirement in a little more detail. There are three views on the employment of intuitions to justify claims about value or morality. Some have argued that intuitions should not be used to defend or criticize such claims.[20] Others appear to hold that intuitions (or some small set of evident intuitions) alone are sufficient to reject or accept a moral principle or claim.[21] In this book like most other philosophers, I occupy the middle ground

[20]See e.g. Hare (1981), p. 12; Singer (2005).

[21]Audi (1998).

between these two extremes.[22] When I appeal to intuitions, claiming, say, that a moral principle has counterintuitive implications and is therefore questionable, I will generally stress that I do not take myself to be offering a knockdown argument against the principle. Instead, my point is that we have *a reason* not to accept a moral principle if it fails to fit with some of our *considered intuitions*, and similarly, that a fit with such intuitions can give us a reason to adopt a principle. This we can affirm with the proviso that the intuitions must be considered, in the sense that they should be based on the aforementioned requirements in order to eradicate, or more realistically minimize, any intuitions that are the result of misinformation or cultural indoctrination. Such intuitions will reflect explicit as well as implicit bias or superstition. For example, if a sexist has the intuition that women should not be given the same salary as men because he believes women to be stupid and lazy, his intuitions should be ignored, because they rest on empirical assumptions that are false. Further, if two intuitions are inconsistent, one should be jettisoned, or they should be modified in such a way as to render them consistent. In this sense, considered moral intuitions when combined with the requirement for consistency, are corrigible.

I offer one further observation about the methodology of intuition. I believe, like Norman Daniels, that we cannot give a plausible justification of a substantial moral claim or value theoretical claim without an appeal to some intuitions. At some point in the justificatory process of a moral principle or assertion we must refer to moral intuitions.[23] Imagine a hard-core utilitarian who does not believe the appeal to intuitions has any bearing on the justification of her choice of theory. How could she justify the idea that we ought to be utilitarians? Why should we try to maximize well-being? Her answer may be that we should do so because well-being is valuable. But why is well-being valuable? Is it valuable because it is good in itself? But the notion that well-being is good in itself, and that we ought to maximize it, seems to play the role of a moral axiom that well-being is good in itself and that we ought to promote what is good. However, if this is right, utilitarians, and indeed advocates of other theories of morality and value, will at some point have to appeal to intuitions, too.[24]

1.4 Overview of Chapters

I now present a brief overview of the chapters to come. The starting point of Chap. 2 is a critical discussion of versions of what is called ‘the harm principle’. But, and this is a central preoccupation of Chap. 2 (and the Appendix), what is harm? According

[22]See e.g. Holtug (2010), Lippert-Rasmussen (2005) and Tadros (2011).

[23]Daniels (2016), p. 11.

[24]One could, of course, argue that our moral views ought to be guided by things other than our moral intuitions (e.g. by the logic of moral concepts, or by human rationality, or by God). Again, however, one could here claim that these prescriptions are themselves moral intuitions about how we ought to reason when we discuss moral issues.

to one general specification, a person P1 is harmed by another person P2 doing C, if and only if P1 is made worse off in terms of well-being because of C. Two concepts here stand in need of clarification. First of all, what is the baseline against which we assess whether someone is 'worse off'? When a person is harmed we can agree that he is worse off, certainly, but what is he worse off than? What is the depletion in well-being a variation from? Secondly, what exactly is well-being? The first question is the subject of Chap. 2. An attempt to answer the second is made the Appendix and in part of Chap. 3. A central part of Chap. 2 critically discusses a range of answers to the first question, mobilizing versions of what I call 'temporal baselines', 'baselines from mankind', and 'counterfactual baselines'. It is argued that the counterfactual baseline leaves us with a better understanding of when an individual is being harmed by another individual than the other baselines discussed, even though it has problematic implications of its own. The counterfactual baseline says, roughly, that a person P1 is harmed by another person P2 doing C, if and only if P1's well-being, because of C, is worse, compared to the closest world *where P2 did not do C*.

The final part of Chap. 2 describes some of the implications of this investigation, for the view that harm matters in the justification of which kinds of conduct should be criminalized by the state. The overall conclusion of the chapter is that most adherents of a harm principle face a devastating problem. In their effort to narrow down the scope of harms that the state ought to prevent through criminalization, they resort to moral theory. However, once they do that, there is no need for harm principles, as the whole job of justifying what to criminalize can be done by moral theory. In the last part of Chap. 2, I discuss some possible objections to the claim that standard versions of the harm principle are redundant when set beside what can be specified as grand moral theory.

Besides the endeavour of specifying what harm is, an important discussion within criminalization theory is whether the state may only criminalize kinds of conduct that are harmful. Whereas some advocates of a harm principle, like J. S. Mill or H. L. A. Hart do indeed believe that the prevention of harm is a necessary condition of criminalization, those who champion versions of the offense principle or legal moralism usually believe this is incorrect. A critical discussion of these two views is presented in Chaps. 3 and 4. Chapter 3 critically evaluates the offense principle. In Joel Feinberg's version, this principle is formulated as follows:

> It is always a good reason in support of a proposed criminal prohibition that it would probably be an effective way of preventing *serious offense* (as opposed to injury or harm) to persons other than the actor, and that it is probably a necessary means to that end (i.e., there is probably no other means that is equally effective at no greater cost to other values).[25]

The offense principle claims, then, that harm prevention is not the only thing that matters in the justification of which acts the state ought to criminalize. The position I defend in Chap. 3 is that the conduct referred to by the offence principle, depending on one's theory of individual well-being, can easily be interpreted as a subset of the conduct referred to by another principle of criminalization—namely, the standard

[25]Feinberg (1985), p. 1.

formulation of the harm principle given by Mill and Hart. This finding is contrary to both the formulation of the offense principle itself and the belief, held by prominent advocates of the principle, that the two principles are distinct principles of criminalization. Furthermore, I argue that the definition of harm, deployed by leading proponents of the offense principle such as Feinberg, A. P. Simester and Andreas von Hirsch, as a 'setback to interests' is both difficult to apply to the distinction between harming and causing offence and in itself inadequately supported.

Chapter 4 deals with another theory that represents harm as far from being the only factor that matters in the legitimization of criminalization, namely legal moralism. Legal moralism can be specified as a group of theories of criminalization all of which holds that the immorality of a type of conduct gives us a reason to criminalize that conduct, even where it is causing no harm (or offense) to others. A central aim of the first part of Chap. 4 is to distinguish, and analytically characterize, some important variations in the way legal moralism is specified in the literature. The goal here is to provide not so much a normative evaluation of legal moralism as a properly differentiated picture of it. The first part of Chap. 4 is devoted to a critical examination of some of the leading specifications that have been presented in writings designed to tell us what legal moralism is. Unfortunately, these definitions have not always been carefully distinguished. I end this part of the chapter by identifying a specification that seems to capture the essence of what many philosophers are referring to when they talk about legal moralism—one which, as presented, I hope, affords greater clarity.

It is in the second part of Chap. 4, I turn to critical assessment of the plausibility of legal moralism, with an emphasis on some leading and recent presentations of the view. First, I defend the thesis that recently developed varieties of legal moralism promoted by Robert P. George, John Kekes, Michael Moore and Antony Duff are more plausible than Lord Devlin's traditional, well-discussed account. The main argument for this thesis is that, in its more modern versions, legal moralism is immune to some of the forceful challenges to Devlin made by Hart, Dworkin and Feinberg, among others. As an example of this, it is shown that, while it follows from Devlin's position that the state should enforce the shared morality of a society no matter how evil that morality is, the new generations of legal moralists (apart from Duff) are invulnerable to this kind of 'moral relativism' criticism. Second, however, Chap. 4 also challenges the new generation of legal moralists. I argue, for example, that some of the new generation views are susceptible to the *no difference objection*, according to which there is no difference between their versions of legal moralism and the harm principle. Additionally, and alternatively, I make a case for saying that the legal moralists under discussion (with the exception Kekes) need to overcome what I call *the criminological levelling-down challenge* (CLDC) and *the weighing challenge* (WEC).

Dissatisfied with traditional principles of criminalization, including versions of the harm principle and the offence principle, some theorists, who would not categorizes themselves as legal moralists, have proposed an alternative approach to criminalization based on respect for human dignity. Chapter 5 discusses this approach. The relevant dignity principle is captured by the general idea that violation of human dignity is either a necessary condition of criminalization or a sufficient condition to criminalize conduct (or both). Although it is easy to sympathize with this idea, the primary aim of Chap. 5 is to argue that recent attempts to justify it fail. Two Kantian interpretations of the dignity principle of criminalization are outlined and criticized. A non-Kantian interpretation of a dignity principle of criminalization is also introduced and critically discussed.

In the sixth and final chapter, I argue that the utilitarian principle of criminalization (UPC) is sounder than its poor reputation suggests. The chapter begins by describing three possible answers to the research question: to what extent should the consequences of criminalization matter morally in a theory of criminalization? I then explain why I propose to discuss only two of these answers. Following this, a detailed and critical specification (UPC) is presented. Further, I argue that criticisms of UPC associated with the recent work of philosophers like Douglas Husak and Victor Tadros are far from convincing. I end the chapter by developing a positive reason for accepting UPC as a principle of criminalization, namely, that UPC is consistent with what I call the 'counterproductive criminalization principle' (CCP), while non-consequentialist theories of criminalization are not necessarily so.

The Appendix is closely connected with Chap. 2 in the sense that if harm consists in being worse off in terms of well-being, we also have to specify what well-being is in order to fully understand, apply and evaluate harm principles. This specification is the subject of the Appendix. What is well-being? In other words, what is personal welfare? Although there is currently a huge range of theories of well-being, I confine myself to the defence of a traditional and familiar theory of well-being called 'welfare hedonism'. Welfare hedonism is, broadly speaking, the view that well-being consists solely of the presence of pleasure and the absence of pain experienced by an individual. I devote much of the Appendix, to the defence of welfare hedonism from some challenging objections raised by, among others, the Canadian philosopher Wayne Sumner and the Indian economist and philosopher Amartya Sen. In his critique of welfare hedonism, Sumner imposes two requirements on the kinds of experience that are to count as well-being: the information requirement and the autonomy requirement. I argue that both requirements are problematic, and that pleasurable experiences can give an individual well-being even if they are not well informed or experienced by an autonomous being. In sum, if one accepts that harm is relevant to the state's justification of the kinds of conduct it criminalizes, one has a reason to understand well-being (in a specification of harm) in terms of welfare hedonism.

It may be helpful to summarize the key conclusions of the book here. In Chap. 2, I (1) defend a counterfactual baseline for harm, and (2) argue for the view that harm principles and principles of legal paternalism are redundant, given general moral theories. In Chap. 3, I argue for the view (3) that plausible interpretation of offense principles indicates that they are not distinct from harm principles, making offense principles redundant too. In Chaps. 4 and 5, I argue (4) that versions of legal moralism, and dignity principles of criminalization, have serious problematic implications of their own. My evaluation of standard criminalization theory is therefore negative. It implies that we should abandon these theories (or at least rethink them) and instead try to justify which kinds of conduct a state should criminalize by means of a general moral theory. In the final chapter, Chap. 6, I defend (5) a utilitarian principle of criminalization. In the Appendix, I (6) defend a welfare hedonistic theory of well-being.

References

Audi R (1998) Intuitionism and the epistemology of moral judgement. Ethical Theory Moral Practice 1(1):14–34

Daniels N (2016) Reflective equilibrium. In: Zalta EN (ed) The Stanford Encyclopedia of philosophy. Center for the Study of Language and Information (CSLI), Stanford. (Oct. 2016 edition)

Duff A (2018) The realm of criminal law. Oxford University Press, Oxford

Feinberg J (1984) Harm to others. Oxford University Press, Oxford

Feinberg J (1985) Offense to others. Oxford University Press, Oxford

Feinberg J (1986) Harm to self. Oxford University Press, Oxford

Feinberg J (1988) Harmless wrongdoing. Oxford University Press, Oxford

Hansson SO (2006) How to define – a tutorial. Principios Natal 13(19–20):5–30

Hare RM (1981) Moral thinking. Clarendon Press, Oxford

Holtug N (2010) Person, interests, and justice. Oxford University Press, Oxford

Holzer H (1996) What employers want? Job perspectives for less-educated workers. Sage, Thousands Oaks

Hoskins Z (2019) Beyond punishment? A normative account of the collateral consequences of conviction. Oxford University Press, Oxford

Husak D (2008) Overcriminalization: the limits of the criminal law. Oxford University Press, Oxford

Jackson F (1998) From metaphysics to ethics: a defence of conceptual analysis. Clarendon Press, Oxford

Kagan S (1998) Normative ethics. Westview Press, Boulder

Kyckelhahn T, Martin T (2013) Justice expenditures and employment extracts, 2010 - Preliminary, Table 1. Bureau of Justice Statistics, Office of Justice Programs, U.S. Department of Justice, Whasington, DC

Lippert-Rasmussen K (2005) Deontology, responsibility, and equality. Museum Tusculanum Press, Copenhagen

Mill JS (1859/2003) On liberty. In: Warnock M (ed) Utilitarianism and on liberty. Blackwell Publishing, New Jersey

Miller A (2003) An introduction to contemporary metaethics. Polity Press, Cambridge

Murphy MC (2007) Philosophy of law: the fundamentals. Blackwell Publishing, New Jersey

Petersen TS (2016) Some ethical considerations on the use of criminal records in the labor market: in defense of a new practice. J Bus Ethics 139(3):443–453

Simester AP, von Hirsch A (2011) Crimes, harms and wrongs: on the principles of criminalisation. Hart Publishing, London

Singer P (2005) Ethics and intuitions. J Ethics 9(3–4):331–352

Struckman-Johnson C, Struckman-Johnson D (2000) Sexual coercion rates in seven midwestern prisons for men. Prison J 80(4):379–390

Tadros V (2011) The ends of harm: the moral foundations of criminal law. Oxford University Press, Oxford

Thomas T (2007) Criminal records: a database for the criminal justice system and beyond. Palgrave Macmillan, Basingstoke

Thomson A (2002) Critical reasoning in ethics. Routledge, London

United States Bureau of Justice Statistics (2019) Correctional population in the United States office of justice programs

Walmsley R (2018) World prison population list, 12th edn. International Centre for Prison Studies, University of Essex, Essex

Chapter 2
Harm and Criminalization: On Why Harm Principles Are Redundant

2.1 Introduction

I believe that it goes without saying that the most well-known and discussed principle of criminalization is the harm principle, or more correctly, as we shall see in the next paragraph, versions of the harm principle.[1] The one who initially formulated it and who is the most obvious exponent of a harm principle is J. S. Mill. In his formulation, he declares that the state is *only* morally justified in interfering with the conduct of any of its citizens (e.g. by means of criminalization and punishment) against their will if the intervention would *prevent harm to others* or risk of harm to others, i.e. people other than the agent of the conduct.[2] In other words, the state does something morally wrong if the criminalization of certain types of conduct C will not prevent harm to others who are not the agents of conduct C.[3]

[1]Several philosophers have shown that there is not only one harm principle, but several versions of it, see e.g. Edwards (2014) and Holtug (2002).

[2]Mill (1859), Chapter 1, paragraph 7. Note that the Harm Principle in Mill's formulation describes a *necessary*, but *not sufficient*, condition of state intervention. So although we can identify kinds of conduct that the criminalization of will prevent harm-doing, it does not follow from Mill's harm principle that every time the state can prevent harm-doing (or risking harm) by criminalizing a kind of conduct, then it should be criminalized (or otherwise interfered with by the state or the public), since the enforcement required to avoid the harm may be even more harmful. See e.g. Mill (1859), Chapter 5, paragraph 3; Crisp (1997), pp. 180–181.

[3]It should be noted that it is important to talk about types of acts instead of single acts (tokens). It is easy to imagine single acts that do not, all things considered, harm people but which nevertheless are (or should be) considered criminal because such acts usually harm others or risk harming others. These acts might be termed "criminal right-doing". For example, if Peter's reckless driving results in Paul breaking his leg on the way to the airport to catch a plane, causing him to miss a plane that he would have otherwise died on as a result of a fatal crash, then Peter's reckless driving did not, all things considered, harm Paul; in fact we might say that he benefited from Peter's reckless driving. For a case like this see Parfit (1984), p. 372.

T. Søbirk Petersen, *Why Criminalize?*, Law and Philosophy Library 134,
https://doi.org/10.1007/978-3-030-34690-4_2

Just to mention a few well-known variations of what we could label as a harm principle, legal philosophers like H. L. A. Hart, Joseph Raz, A. P. Simester and Andreas von Hirsch have, contrary to Mill and Feinberg, for instance, argued that prevention of *harm to oneself* could also be used as a legitimate reason for criminalization.[4] In other words, scholars like Hart, Raz and Simester and von Hirsch would also accept that a harm principle should be combined with or entail legal paternalism. So when a philosopher such as Hart and Raz accepts that both harm to others and the agent herself are what matters in criminalization decisions, this view could be characterized as a version of a broader harm principle than the one favoured by Mill and Feinberg.[5]

Harm principles may also differ according to whether, for example, it is only humans or also non-human animals whose harm we should prevent or whether or to what extent we should criminalize kinds of conduct in order to prevent harm to future generations.[6] Finally, and just to mention one more, out of further complexities, it has also become standard to differentiate between what Edwards has called *'act-centred versions*' and *'instrumental versions'* of harm principles.[7] Act-centred versions emphasize the fact that the state only have reason to criminalize conduct C *if C is harmful*, whereas instrumental versions (e.g. Mill's and Feinberg's versions of the harm principle) emphasize that the state only has a reason to criminalize a kind of conduct C *if this will prevent harm*. That there is a difference between act-centred and instrumental versions of harm principles should be obvious. On the one hand, adherents of an act-centred version could argue, that because alcohol consumption is often harmful, we have a reason in support of its criminalization, irrespectively of whether criminalization of alcohol consumption will prevent harm. On the other hand, adherents of an instrumental version could argue that even though alcohol consumption is harmful, the state ought not to criminalize alcohol consumption if this, all things considered, would not prevent harm all things considered.[8] But apart from all the different versions of the harm principle, there are several legal philosophers, then, who all believe that harm prevention to others or oneself ought to

[4]See e.g. Hart (1963), Feinberg (1984), Simester and von Hirsch (2011) and Raz (1986).

[5]In what follows, I will use the categorization 'harm principle's to also cover 'principles of legal paternalism', however for stylistic reasons and because I believe one can interpret some harm principles as also entailing harm to the agent I will leave out the terms 'legal paternalism'. In what follows, however, we shall bear in mind that legal paternalism, is also subject to the same kind of objection from redundancy that target harm principles (whether or not versions of harm principles include harm to the agent herself).

[6]See e.g. Baker (2011), pp. 56–61 for a defence of the view that harm principles should also include harm to non-human animals.

[7]Edwards (2014). Duff (2018), pp. 237–39 uses other words ('responsive' and 'preventive') to capture the same distinction as Edwards.

[8]In what follows, I will stick to the instrumental/preventive version of harm principles. This I will do for stylistic reasons but also for the reason that all prominent adherents of harm principles explicitly formulate their versions of a harm principle in these terms.

matter and should play a central, if not the only role, when the state makes decisions and tries to justify which kinds of conduct it should criminalize.

However, adherents of a harm principle have been under various kinds of attack for many years. Just to give a few examples: some have used *empirical* observation to argue that the use of a harm principle by legislators in their decisions on what to criminalize leads to over-criminalization by failing to live up to the liberal motivation behind that principle—the motivation being to limit the reach of the criminal law and make sure that citizens can choose how to live as long as they do not harm others. As an example, Harcourt mentions laws against public drinking, public urination, loitering, panhandling, graffiti spraying, and so on, that have been enforced, not because these kinds of conduct are very harmful in themselves, but because some legislators believe that these minor offences of disorder contribute causally to more serious crimes (and therefore indirectly to more harm) that can be prevented if the minor harms are criminalize.[9] An obvious criticism of this empirical objection is that if it is true that, by using a harm principle to justify what should be criminal, the criminalization decisions made by the state will imply over-criminalization, thereby doing more harm than good, then one can argue that it is the *use* of the harm principle that is wrong, not the principle itself.[10]

Others have argued that harm principles or some versions of it are wrong because they cannot be used to justify the criminalization of harmless but wrongful conduct that ought to be criminalized (e.g. harmless kinds of conduct like happy slavery, non-harmful rape or non-harmful trespassing of private property). This type of objection has been called '*the objection from under-inclusiveness*'.[11] Still others have argued that harm principles are morally wrong because, given certain empirical conditions, it follows from these principles that they can be used to criminalize conduct that ought not to be criminalized (e.g. adultery or sacrificing oneself for the lesser good). This type of objection has been called '*the objection from over-inclusiveness*'.[12]

The aim of this chapter, however, is primarily to criticise harm principles and legal paternalism along another route that has not often been taken. I want to argue that harm principles (and legal paternalism) should be considered *redundant* to grand moral theories, like versions of deontology or consequentialism.[13] By 'grand moral

[9]See e.g. Harcourt (1999), p. 113.

[10]See e.g. Baker (2011) for a critique of the empirical objection similar to this.

[11]See e.g. Edwards (2014). This type of objection is posed by e.g. Dan-Cohen (2002), Ripstein (2006), Duff (2007) and Stewart (2010). For a critique of this objection, see e.g. Edwards (2014). This type of objection will be dealt with in more detail in Chap. 5.

[12]This type of objection against the harm principle is posed by e.g. Husak (2008), Duff (2007) and Stewart (2010). For a critique of this objection, see e.g. Edwards (2014). We will discuss examples of this type of objection in Chap. 6.

[13]The few exemptions from this kind of criticism are Holtug (2002) and Petersen (2010). However, Holtug does only write a few sentences about this objection, and I will therefore (in Sect. 2.6) reconstruct, specify and critically discuss what I believe to be Holtug's argument for the conclusion that certain (moralized) versions of the harm principle are redundant compared to grand moral

theories' I mean moral theories that give us answers about what is morally right to do in every situation.[14]

As the concept of harm runs through all versions of the harm principle (and legal paternalism) and can be understood in many different ways, we begin Sect. 2.2 with a specification of the concept of harm. This is followed, also in Sect. 2.2, by a clarification of some important distinctions, like those between local/global harm, non-moral/moral harm and non-comparative/comparative conceptions of harm. All of this is done in preparation for one of the central foci of this chapter, which is to clarify the concept of harm. If a person is harmed and this roughly means that she is worse off in terms of well-being, then we need to know at least two things before we can have a firm grasp of what harm is. First, what is 'worse off' a variation from? In other words, compared to *what* is a person worse off when she is harmed? This question raises a challenge we can call 'the baseline problem of harm'. Secondly, what is well-being (which is the sole subject of the Appendix)? In Sect. 2.3, we shall discuss what might be called '*temporal baseline views*'. In these views, the proper baseline is the situation *prior* to the alleged harm. We shall here critically assess two different versions of this view; it will be argued that neither can explain the fact that someone is harmed in some of the cases where it seems obvious that a person actually has been harmed. In addition, and importantly for our discussion, we are talking about harms that obviously ought to be criminalized if this could prevent those harms from occurring.

In Sect. 2.4, different versions of what might be called the *'baseline from mankind'* will be discussed. In these views, the proper baseline is the *well-being of mankind*. This is a type of baseline which, to my knowledge, has not yet been critically discussed within the philosophical literature. One focus here will be on Shlomit Harrosh's current view that a person is harmed if they are worse off relative to the potential of our *species* to live a fully human life.[15] Even though these species-based theories do a better job by giving the right answers to the cases presented against the temporal baselines, they fail to give the right answer in other cases where

---

theory. Stanton-Ife, in his 2016 paper titled 'What is the Harm Principle For?', argues that Simester and von Hirsch, who are in favour of a harm principle, 'would lose little of any significance were their Harm and Offense Principles simply excised' (p. 1). This may sound very much like the conclusion that Holtug and I have also reached, but it is not. Whereas Stanton-Ife argues that Simester and von Hirsch's view on a harm principle is redundant to legal moralism (see e.g. Chap. 4 for a critical discussion of this class of criminalization theories), Holtug and I claim that moralized (and, from my point of view, also non-moralized) versions of harm principles are redundant to grand moral theories that can guide us in all situations and not only when it comes to criminalization decisions, as is the case with legal moralism. Furthermore, Stanton-Ife's critique is based on the idea that Simester and von Hirsch's understanding of harm is very broad and includes harms (e.g. moral harm to one's character if one watches pornography) that do not relate to the well-being of individuals. However, as we shall see in what follows, I only focus on harm as something that is related to and affects individual well-being.

[14]See e.g. Kagan (1989) for an understanding of moral theories like this. Hereafter, I will just write 'moral theory' for short instead of 'grand moral theory'.

[15]Harrosh (2012), p. 493.

harm seems to be involved. In addition, it follows from these versions of a baseline for harm that some kinds of conduct that we would call 'harms', and which obviously ought to be criminalized, cannot even be classified as harms.

In Sect. 2.5, we move on to a critical discussion of what might be called a '*counterfactual baseline*' (CB). In these views, the proper baseline for harm is said to be *the closest possible world* in which the harm did not occur. I will here argue that although a CB is the most plausible baseline, because it can deal with the cases all the other theories fail to cope with, it is evident that it has serious problems of its own. However, as we shall see in more detail, a CB, like the other baseline views, seems to be able to describe certain kinds of conduct as non-harmful (e.g. torture of person P in situations where the closest possible world to torture of P is even worse for P) even though it seems obvious that they are harmful (e.g. torture). So, it seems to follow from a CB that some kinds of conduct C that we would call 'harms' and which obviously ought to be criminalized cannot (given a certain specification of what would happen if C did not take place) even be classified as harm, and therefore cannot be used as a reason for criminalization if we combine harm principles with a CB.

In Sect. 2.6, I will first describe some of the implications of our investigation for the application and evaluation of harm principles. But, more importantly, it will be argued that there is no need for harm principles, as the whole function of justifying what to criminalize can and should be fulfilled by applying a general moral theory. This conclusion is easy to reach when adherents of harm principles, in their effort to specify the scope of harmful conduct, employ the well-used claim that it is only *morally wrongful harms* that are candidates for criminalization. In this case, it is obvious that the justificatory work for criminalization could not be done without a reference to the moral theory, which should specify which harms are morally wrong. Furthermore, I will argue that even if adherents of harm principles do not accept a moralized concept of harm, they too ought to resort to moral theory in order to be able to justify which kind of conduct the state ought to criminalize. However, the harm principle will then once again be redundant compared to a moral theory.

2.2 A Further Specification of the Concept of Harm and Some Key Distinctions

But what is harm? Although in many cases it seems obvious when a person, for example, is being harmed by another individual or a group of individuals, adherents of a harm principle who believe that harm matters in the justification of legal sanctions must try to clarify what it means to be harmed. Without such clarification, which I shall be concerned with in the main part of this chapter, we cannot hope to characterize fully the acts, which we have reason to criminalize. In other words, we need to specify the scope of harm principles. Furthermore, the clarification of what it means to be harmed is essential if our aim is to evaluate the implication, and hence the plausibility, of harm principles.

I start by specifying a common-sense general claim that a person P1 is harmed by another person P2 when P1 is made worse off in respect to well-being in the following way[16]:

Being Harmed by Another Person
A person P1 is harmed by another person P2 doing C if and only if P1 is made worse off in terms of well-being because of C.[17]

This description seems to capture the observations that murder, rape and violent attacks are clear cases in which one individual is harmed by another person or a group of persons. These acts are usually harmful because they make the victim worse off in terms of well-being.[18] In the next paragraph, I will specify some elements of the above-mentioned specification of harm. Thereafter, some key distinctions will be presented in order to make the focus of the chapter clearer.

First, in order to understand what it is for someone to be harmed, given this specification, we need to analyse what constitutes *well-being*. Prominent contenders in theories of well-being are variants of well-known theories like hedonism, preference theory, and the objective-list theory.[19] The whole Appendix and a small part of Chap. 3 will be devoted to a critical discussion of some of these theories; more precisely, objective theories of well-being will be criticized (Chap. 3) and a subjective theory of well-being will be defended (Appendix). However, even if we know what the best theory of well-being is, we still need to specify what it means to be made *worse off* (in terms of well-being) in order to know when a person has been harmed.[20] One central question here involves the *baseline* against which we assess whether someone is 'worse off'. In other words, when a person is harmed he is worse

[16]Being harmed need not be confined to cases of reduction of the currency of *well-being*; instead, it might involve the reduction of *autonomy* or *moral character*. For an autonomy-based conception of being harmed, see e.g. Raz (1986), p. 420. For a critical discussion of the idea that 'moral harm' (e.g. watching pornography) can harm the moral character of a person, though the person is not made worse off in terms of well-being, see Sumner (2004), pp. 35–50. However, these differences over the currency of harm have no role in our discussion of the baseline problem, as this problem (as we shall see) exists whether you relate harm to reductions in well-being, autonomy or moral character.

[17]For an understanding of being harmed in this way, see e.g. Holtug (2002), p. 364; Kagan (1998), p. 84; Feldman (2010), p. 165; Tadros (2011), p. 177.

[18]I write 'usually' here because even murder and rape can, in some rare circumstances, benefit a person by preventing even greater harm (e.g. by ending a person's life, you can terminate their intense and untreatable pain).

[19]See e.g. Griffin (1986), Sumner (1996), Feldman (2004) and (2010) for philosophical work on what constitutes well-being.

[20]In what follows, the focus will be on the search for the baseline governing harm. As far as I know, the problem of identifying the baseline governing *benefit* is just as neglected in the philosophical literature.

off, certainly—but what is worse off a variation from? This question raises a challenge that in the introduction was labelled 'the baseline problem of harm'.

The question of what constitutes well-being will be put aside for now. However, when reading this chapter you can have your favourite theory of well-being in mind. Compared with the quantity of literature on the nature of well-being, philosophical discussion of the proper baseline for harm (or benefit) is limited.[21] This is rather peculiar, as these areas of enquiry will presumably be equally important in any effort to determine when a person has been harmed.[22] As we shall see, different views on what constitutes the proper baseline of harm can give conflicting answers to the question of whether an act is harmful. Therefore, while clarifying the baseline of harm is of importance in applying the concept of harm, we shall also see that this clarification is of importance in applying and evaluating criminalization theories that fall under the umbrella concept of what has been labelled 'harm principles'. This is because whether or not the state has a morally plausible reason to criminalize a certain kind of conduct C depends on whether the criminalization of C will prevent harm.

Second, an individual can, of course, also be harmed by events like an earthquake or a tsunami, by non-human individuals like animals or by themselves. Nevertheless, because our subject matter is criminalization, which very often has to do with what some people do to others, I will focus on the harm that individuals inflict on others. Thirdly, the terms 'person P1 is harmed' refer to *beings* that can be made worse off in terms of well-being like humans and some animals. Fourthly, although it might be controversial, let us accept that this specification entails that harms can be brought about both by *doing* and *allowing harm*. In the latter case, if a person does not help the victim of a traffic accident, it is an involvement in another person's harm that makes it obvious that allowing harm is covered by all plausible specifications of the concept of harm and by most explicit adherents of a harm principle.

Our definition of harm also leaves us with some distinctions that need to be clarified before we can identify when someone is harmed by another individual. First, the specification is neutral concerning whether we should adopt a *global* or *local interpretation* of being harmed. In a global interpretation, a person is only harmed by an act if that act makes the person worse off *overall*. Alternatively,

---

[21]Feinberg (1984), pp. 136–145; Raz (1986), p. 416; Petersen (2001), p. 415; Holtug (2002), pp. 368–371; Norcross (2005), pp. 149–150; Bradley (2012) are some of the few exceptions. Although Nozick (1974) and his critics, e.g. Cohen (1995), Kymlicka (2001) and Wolf (1991), were engaged in a baseline discussion relating to 'worsening', the scope of their discussion is confined to the special kind of worsening that may occur for others when one or more people come by an initial acquisition of external and formerly unowned resources. Instead, our discussion concerns harming/worsening in a much wider perspective, including harms that come about by any type of act or omission.

[22]One reason for this lack of interest may be due to the observation that the most obvious kinds of harm can easily be described as harm, almost no matter what kind of baseline for harm you favour. However, as will be shown in the following sections, what we would consider as harm, or harm in some specific situations, cannot be considered as harm according to certain theories of the baseline for harm.

however, one could delete the last word in the latter sentence and insist on a local interpretation according to which a person is harmed if he is made worse off in some regard. To see the difference between these two interpretations we can turn to an example originally given by Shelly Kagan: 'suppose that George is trapped beneath a fallen tree, and will die unless we free him by cutting off his trapped leg.'[23] Depending on the specification you adopt, you will be guided to different answers to the question of whether you would harm George by amputating his leg. According to the global interpretation, we can say that if we save his life by amputating his leg, we have not harmed George, as we can presume that it is better for him to lose his leg than his life. If, on the other hand, we accept a local interpretation of harm, George is harmed by the amputation. For, seen in isolation (or locally), losing his leg adversely affects his well-being. Whether or not being harmed is interpreted globally or locally is, of course, very important in identifying when someone is being harmed, but this question will not be settled in this chapter, as the problem we shall focus on—the baseline problem—arises no matter which of these two interpretations one accepts.

Second, our definition of harm is initially phrased in a *morally neutral* way. I have chosen a morally neutral understanding of being harmed in order not to complicate things further for the moment. However, I am well aware that advocates of a harm principle can demand that the only type of harm to others (or oneself) that the state should try to prevent through criminalization are harms that are morally wrong. This is a separate issue, and one that will be dealt with in Sect. 2.6 of this chapter.[24]

Third, a distinction between non-comparative and comparative accounts of harm is usually made in philosophical discussions of harm. Non-comparative accounts of harm may, for instance, say that an action harms a person if it causes that person to be in a bad state. Bad states are understood as states that are in themselves bad, not bad because they are worse than the state the person would otherwise have been in.[25] According to this account, whether an act harms a person does not depend on a comparison with how things would have been had the harm not been inflicted, or how things were before the harm took place. However, for reasons of relevance and because there seem to be some huge problems for a non-comparative account of harm, I want to sidestep the debate about non-comparative and comparative accounts of harm, and instead focus entirely on comparative accounts.[26] Therefore, in what follows, the topic will be on comparative accounts of harm.

---

[23]Kagan (1998), pp. 86–87.

[24]Philosophers and penal theorists like Feinberg (1984), Husak (2008) and Simester and von Hirsch (2011) who believe that the prevention of harm-doing is a relevant reason to criminalize, all claim that it is only harm-doing or allowing harm that is *morally wrong,* that the state has a reason (among others) to prevent through criminalization.

[25]See Harman (2009).

[26]For defenders of a non-comparative account of harm, see Harman (2009) and Shiffrin (1999). For a critique of these views, see Bradley (2012). The main problem for non-comparative accounts of harm is that, although they can recognize that dying can be harmful, they cannot account for the view that death can be harmful for a person, because death or being dead is not something a person can experience.

2.3 Temporal Baselines

Let us begin our investigation with a type of act that most sane individuals would consider an example of harming. Rape is a clear such case, as it usually causes pain, anxiety, fear for one's life, humiliation, future problems with one's sexuality, indirect harm to relatives, and so on. One obvious suggestion about the baseline of being harmed that captures this initial case is the following:

The Temporal Baseline
A person P1 is harmed by another person P2 doing C if and only if P1's well-being, because of C, is lower than it was *prior* to C.

This definition entails that rape is harmful because the person being raped is worse off during and after the rape than she was before.[27] That it follows from a temporal baseline of harm that rape, murder, etc. are harmful acts initially speaks in favour of this baseline. However, as for example Nils Holtug has argued, there are clear counterexamples to this baseline.[28] Imagine the following case:

The Headache
Julia has had a terrible headache for 8 days. Although Julia is not aware of this, the headache is about to stop. Just before the moment in time when it will stop by itself, Julia orders a glass of water in a bar. Peter, the bartender who serves Julia, adds a drug to the glass of water he hands over to Julia. The drug causes Julia's headache to continue for another 8 days. Had Peter not added the drug to the water, Julia's headache would have ended at the time the drug was absorbed and acted on Julia. In addition, let's say that this is true because Peter would then just have served Julia a glass of pure water.

Peter's act does not make Julia worse off compared to the situation *immediately* prior to Julia drinking the glass of drugged water. But clearly Peter harms Julia by causing her headache to persist. Therefore, the temporal baseline above seems incorrect.[29]

---

[27] A good example of a temporal baseline is Nozick's proviso for just initial acquisition of unowned resources. Compare Kymlicka (2001), p. 117: 'Nozick's proviso says that an act of appropriation must not make others worse off than they were when the land was in common use.'

[28] Holtug (2002), p. 368. The structure of the case we shall now imagine resembles that in a case provided by Holtug.

[29] See Norcross (2005), pp. 149–150 for another case which shows that this kind of baseline is problematic. For more cases, see Kahane and Savulescu (2012), who point out that if harm implies that you were better off before the harm, we cannot say that a child born blind and deaf is harmed by the blindness and deafness, because such a child would not exist prior to the harm in question. This, however, does not seem right, especially if the harm involved is deliberately caused by the parents—e.g. during the pregnancy.

However, one could still hold a temporal view and try to revise the baseline in order to obtain the right answer in cases like the one above. Like Joel Feinberg, for example, one could claim that the proper baseline is not a matter of the person's well-being *immediately prior* to the harmful act but rather involves a *normal baseline* 'where a person's interests-line [or well-being-line] usually is'.[30] However, precisely what such a normal baseline refers to is not obvious. In one interpretation, it would refer to the average well-being level of the specific person in question. If we accept this, we can say that Peter harms Julia by ensuring her headache continues, since Peter does render Julia worse off if the comparison is with Julia's average well-being level prior to the headache. In order to reach this conclusion, we will here assume that the headache is a non-average condition for Julia, and that Julia's life on average contains more well-being than that involved when Julia is having a headache.

Although this revision of the temporal baseline can give the right answer in the headache case, it too has problems of its own. Imagine the following counterexample:

The Chronic Disease

Suppose Paul has always been in severe pain with a chronic disease, but that, suddenly, one day his pain is about to stop. But then, again Peter steps in, out of the blue, and just before the moment in time before Paul's pain is about to stop, Peter injects Paul with a toxic substance that will make Paul suffer from a new chronic disease. Although the new chronic disease is painful, it is not quite as painful as the old chronic disease of Paul's.

By injecting Paul, Peter causes Paul less pain than Paul used to experience in the normal course of his life. However, to claim that Peter has thereby *not* harmed Paul because he has not made Paul worse off compared to his average baseline seems wrong. If Peter injects Paul with a substance that causes a painful and chronic disease, Peter has harmed Paul. Without Peter's injections, Paul would not suffer from a chronic and painful disease.

One straightforward line of defence for adherents of temporal views would be to argue that in the headache case and the chronic disease case, Julia as well as Paul, everything else being equal, were better off before Peter intervened. An argument in favour of such a view could build on the premise that Julia and Paul were, in one sense, better off prior to the intervention, as before the intervention, they were living a life with the *potential* of having their pain end in a short time. But this potential is lost as soon as Peter intervenes. However, I believe we should reject this defence, as the alleged loss of potential pain reduction because of Peter's intervention can only be argued to make Julia and Paul's lives better in an objective sense, as neither of them will experience the alleged loss of potentiality. However, if you are in favour of a theory of well-being where an individual, in order to have their well-being changed

[30]Feinberg (1984), p. 143. Note, however, that Feinberg only seems to accept this 'normal baseline' in situations where a person has a moral duty to assist someone who, say, is drowning.

by X, must experience X, we cannot here meaningfully say, that Julia and Paul are better off before Peter's intervention. In the Appendix (and more indirectly in Sect. 3.3), I will argue in favour of a non-objective theory of well-being.

In what follows, we shall therefore investigate some other suggested baselines, the hope being that one of these might give us the right answers to the two cases discussed in this section: the headache case and the chronic disease case.

2.4 Baselines from Mankind

Instead of connecting the baseline to the well-being of a specific person (the victim) prior to the alleged harm, we can relate it more generally to the well-being of *mankind*. Here is one initial suggestion of the main idea:

> **The Mankind Baseline**
> A person P1 is harmed by another person P2 doing C if and only if P1's well-being, because of C, is *lower than the well-being for mankind*.

As we shall see in a moment, several versions of this baseline can give the right answers in the chronic disease case, and to a certain extent in the headache case. First, however, we need to be aware that this type of baseline can be interpreted either as a *relative baseline* or as an *objective baseline*. If it is relative, the baseline may be relative to the well-being of mankind at different times in history; and if it is objective, the baseline may be a rigid designator that will refer to the same level of well-being. In what follows, I will elaborate on both of these possibilities and examine how plausible they are.

According to one view, the level of well-being for mankind is relative to the *average level of well-being* for humans in the world over a specific time-span in which they live. So, for example, the average level of well-being might be relative to a specific year, such as 2019 or 2020. Let us call the basic idea behind this view the *'relative average view'*. Although it is difficult, if not impossible, to determine average well-being at a given time for the human population with any precision, let us accept that we have an idea what this amounts to. If we accept such a version of the mankind baseline, the right answer to the chronic disease case can easily be derived. Intoxicating a person, as happens in the chronic disease case, could easily be identified as an instance of being harmed—for it seems fair to say that such acts will make the victim worse off in comparison with the average level of well-being for humans living in the world of, say, 2019. It is fair to say this, at least, if we believe the plausible claim that, on average, people in that year did not suffer at the level they would with a painful chronic disease.

However, in other cases things are not so clear. Imagine Brian who, in 2019, is well above the average well-being level for humans living during that year. But then Peter shows up on New Year's Eve. By stealing Brian's car and crushing his legs, Peter brings Brian in alignment with the average level of well-being for mankind in

2019. On the relative average view, Peter has not harmed Brian. This, however, does not seem right. Similar reasoning can be applied to the headache case. If Julia's well-being is well above the average level for humans living in 2019, Peter's adding the drug to Julia's drink will not—if it brings Julia's well-being in alignment with the average well-being for humans in the year 2019—harm Julia. Again, this does not seem right. Furthermore, the relative average baseline has the repugnant implication that nobody has been harmed by an event even if everybody was worse off because of the event. Imagine everybody in the world in 2019 is at a well-being level of 100, which means they are very well off. However, on New Year's Eve 2019, just as the clock signals that a new year has begun, a huge meteor hits the earth. A lot of people die. The people who survive will, from the first day in 2020, have an average well-being level of 10. So, after the meteor has hit the earth the relative average well-being in 2020 for the remaining population is 10. Relative to this new baseline, nobody has been harmed by the meteor, since overnight the baseline has dropped from 100 to 10. This, however, seems wrong.[31]

Confronted with such counterexamples, one might be tempted to revise this type of mankind baseline. Shlomit Harrosh has presented a baseline account that is, in effect, an endorsement of the mankind baseline. At the same time, however, her view seems to deal well with the counterexamples just mentioned, and would also allow her to handle the headache case and the chronic disease case. Harrosh's conception of the baseline of being harmed is well captured in the following quotation:

> Harm shall therefore be viewed as a state in which a person is worse off relative to the human potential to fully engage with a *specific basic human good*. 'Fully' engage here means engage with that good through the relevant dimensions of a fully human life: experiencing, finding meaning and value, setting ends, participation in activities and maintaining/being in certain states. . . . In short, harm is identified relative to one of the goods necessary for a fully human life to obtain.[32]

In this passage, Harrosh seems to specify harm by declaring both a baseline and a currency of harm. I am not sure how, exactly, we should identify the baseline proposed. But an initial suggestion is this: when an individual is harmed, the harmful event or act makes the individual worse off in respect of one of the goods necessary for living a fully human life. Turning to the currency of harm, the basic goods necessary for a fully human life, Harrosh mentions several dimensions in which we can be harmed. It will suffice to mention three of these in order to understand the basic idea: (1) negative experiences (e.g. pain, sadness, anxiety, anger, humiliation); (2) compromise with our bodily integrity (e.g. disease, improper functioning of the body's organs, loss of body parts, dehydration); and (3) the non-promotion of interests (e.g. property destroyed, losing a long-term loving relationship). So, for

[31]Notice that temporal baselines can deliver the right answer in these cases. For example, that Brian is harmed by Peter's crushing and stealing (since Brian is worse off than he was before Peter stole his car and crushed his legs) or that people hurt by the meteor are harmed since they were all better off before the meteor hit Earth.

[32]Harrosh (2012), p. 397. In this 2012 article, Harrosh does not discuss different types of baselines, as the focus of the article is a presentation of her own idea of how we should identify harms.

example, if you feel pain you are worse off compared to one of the goods necessary for a fully human life to obtain. Let us call the version of the mankind baseline theory that is implicit in this quotation the *'fully human life view'*. Furthermore, we can call it an objective version of the baseline from mankind, if we conceive of a fully human life as an ideal life, up against which we can compare and know when an act is harmful or not.

This version of the mankind baseline, unlike the relative average view, makes it clear that stealing a person's car and crushing his legs or being hurt by a meteor, as mentioned in the above-mentioned cases, are always instances of harm. Such acts are harmful because they make the victim's life less than fully human, and they do this because at least one basic human good (e.g. absence of pain or protection of property) is not fully realized. So, in this respect the fully human view fares better than the relative average view that we have just discussed. A further advantage of Harrosh's approach is that it can also explain why the headache case and the chronic disease case are clear cases of harm-doing. Irrespective of the victim's well-being beforehand, causing a headache or intentionally causing a person to have a painful chronic disease are instances of harm-doing because this makes the victim's life less than fully realized. This is the case, at least, when it comes to aspects of human good such as mental and physical health.

However, this objective version of the mankind baseline seems to have problems of its own. First, the baseline in question is very difficult to identify. Imagine that you are far from living a fully human life in two of the dimensions referred to by Harrosh—say, that you suffer from anxiety and unemployment, and that on the other hand you are living a fully human life in a third dimension, in that you have a very good friendship with me—actually, let's say that I'm your only friend. Then consider a situation where I help you to get a fully human life in the first two dimensions (e.g. I talk you out of your anxiety and make sure you get a good job). However, in doing that, I somehow cause that you are far from living a fully human life in the third dimension (our friendship is lost). Have I, all things considered, harmed you? Although there are some cases where it is obvious that you have harmed a person according to Harrosh, the latter case also makes it clear that it is sometimes no easy task to determine if harm has been done. Unfortunately, however, Harrosh does not make any suggestions as to how one should weigh the different dimensions in order to identify the baseline in specific cases. Secondly, the following case seems to show that the baseline under discussion sometimes gives the wrong answers. Imagine the following:

Wonder Woman

Serena is born with a genetic mutation, M1, which makes her life fully human in the sense that she will be able to enjoy all human goods for the rest of her life. Unlike every other human, she is immune to a range of diseases, including malaria, AIDS, cancer, muscular sclerosis, diabetes, typhus, and cholera. Her IQ is 200, and she is able to take pleasure in almost anything, and she is extremely helpful and benevolent to other people. Furthermore, because of another genetic mutation, M2, affecting the ageing process in her cells, it is estimated that she will live 30 years longer than the average person in her country. Last, but not least, she is unaware that she is genetically different from other human beings.

If a doctor 'treats' Serena for her genetic mutation M2 by means of genetic intervention, it seems fair to say that the doctor has not harmed her on the fully human view. This is true; at least, if we accept that the treatment does not make her life less than fully human. In other words, according to Harrosh, the doctor has not harmed Serena, because the reduction in the well-being of her life (missing out 30 years of high quality life) will not make her worse off in comparison with a fully human life. However, it does not seem right to claim that the doctor has not harmed Serena. Instead, it seems fair to say that the doctor has harmed Serena by making her worse off in the sense that she will now have less well-being (because she will miss out 30 pleasant years) than she would have had, had the doctor not intervened in the way he did.

So, generally, even though the versions of what constitutes the baseline of harm looked at in this section, contrary to temporal baselines, can give what seems to be the right answers in the cases with Julia's headache and Paul and the chronic disease, we are still in search of a baseline view that gives what seems to be the right answers to all the counterexamples discussed so far (including the case of Wonder Woman).

In what follows, I will describe and defend a baseline theory of harm that many philosophers adhere to and which, at the same time, is consistent with what I take to be right answers to the cases that have already been dealt with in this chapter.

2.5 Counterfactual Baselines

The criticisms of the baselines set out in previous sections points to the following conclusions:

- There are situations in which an individual is harmed by another's action even though they are *no worse off after* the action (see the headache case).
- There are situations in which an individual is harmed by another's action even though they are actually *better off after* the action than they were before (see the chronic disease case).
- Decreasing the life span of an individual that lives a fully human life is an action that, contrary to the fully human view, harms that individual (see the Wonder Woman case).

Several philosophers have argued for the view that the baseline for harming should be set counterfactually.[33] The initial description of this baseline might run like this:

[33]Compare e.g. Raz (1986), p. 416; Holtug (2002), p. 369; Norcross (2005); Bradley (2012).

The Counterfactual Baseline (CB)
A person P1 is harmed by another person P2 doing C if and only if P1's well-being, because of C, is worse, compared to the closest world *where P2 did not do C.*

Before discussing some of the challenges to this view, we can note that there is something appealing about CB. First, it can easily explain why paradigmatic cases of harming, such as murder and rape, usually are harmful. If I murder you, it seems fair to say that I have harmed you, as you probably would have been better off had I not murdered you. Second, this description can also explain, for example, that I did not, all things considered, harm you when I broke one of your fingers, if this avoided you having ten fingers broken by another person.[34] Because, in this strange situation, you would have been worse off had I not broken one of your fingers. Third, CB can deliver the right answers to all the cases we have discussed so far. It can explain that the headache inflicted upon Julia in our case is an instance of harm, because Julia becomes worse off in comparison with a situation where Peter simply served harmless water. According to CB, Paul in the chronic disease case is harmed when Peter acts to ensure that he feels pain, even though Paul feel less pain than he did before the act by Peter was carried out. And the reason for this is that, if Peter had not caused Paul to develop a new chronic disease, albeit one that was less severe, Paul would probably have lived the remainder of his life without chronic pain. Again, in the case of Wonder Woman, the right answer can be derived from CB. For the 'treatment' for Wonder Woman will make her worse off than she would have been had she not been treated, and this implies that it is harmful to 'treat' the patient in this case. But is CB a plausible view, even if it gives what seem to be the right answers in all these cases? I will now discuss what I and others take to be some of the most serious challenges.[35]

The first challenge relates to the application of CB. According to the initial specification, a person P1 is harmed by another person P2 doing C if and only if P1's well-being, because of C, is worse, compared to *the closest world where P2 did not do C*. But which world, in which C does not occur, is the closest one? To appreciate the importance of this question, imagine the following case: a psychopath has just kidnapped you, and he is considering the following two options. He can torture you to death, or he can break your arm and then release you. Imagine that the psychopath breaks your arm and then lets you go, has he harmed you?

One answer in the literature on harm, and one used in our specification of CB, is that we shall compare the actual conduct C (which, for the time being, we assume is the act of breaking your arm) with the *closest possible* world in which C does not occur.[36] But what is meant by 'the closest possible world'? Instead of the phrase 'the

[34]Assuming, of course, that the closest world to the one where I break one of your fingers is one where another person breaks all ten of your fingers.

[35]For a critical but defensive discussion of CB, see e.g. Bradley (2012) and Norcross (2005).

[36]See e.g. Norcross (2005) and Lippert-Rasmussen (2005).

closest possible world', I believe it would be more appropriate to use 'the set of closest possible worlds', as it is indeterminate which of several closest worlds would be realized if the actual world had not been realized. For instance, would the psychopath, instead of breaking your arm, hit you once with a whip and then kill you, or will he hit you twice with a whip and then kill you and so on? I cannot enter the extensive discussion of how to identify the set of closest possible worlds. But let us confine ourselves in a rough manner and say that, in the selection of possible closest worlds, we should give priority to those worlds that (a) avoid deviation from the laws of nature and (b) maximize the number of particular (and relevant) facts that we find in the actual world.[37]

Again, there seem to be different possible closest worlds in our case. Let us say that, relative to the actual world in which the psychopath broke your arm and then released you, the closest possible world is one in which the psychopath let you go after he has kidnapped you. The reason for this could be that the psychopath would let you go because he thought that he would be sexually turned on by breaking your arm—but when he was actually going to break your arm he was turned off because he discovered a tattoo on your arm that made him sick. If this is the closest possible world, it is clear that breaking your arm is to harm you (unless, not very plausibly, you would enjoy having someone break your arm), since the psychopath would have acted in a way that, everything else being equal, would not have harmed you. Therefore, instead of breaking your arm, the psychopath could have released you immediately after the kidnapping. If this is indeed the closest possible world, CB fits well with the idea that having your arm broken by the psychopath is a case of harming you.

However, the world in which you are released immediately after being kidnapped may not be the closest possible world. Imagine that the psychopath knows that to release you immediately after the kidnapping is not an option for him. It would not be an option because he has an intense urge, which he cannot stop, to harm you physically.[38] Instead, the closest possible world is one in which he tortures you to death. If this scenario is the closest possible world, the psychopath will not harm you by breaking your arm and then releasing you. In fact, he will *benefit* you, as you would have been worse off had he not broken your arm.

Where does this leave us? First, we might here have an answer to how we should apply CB. We should not expect that we can produce a strict formula (or, in other words, a non-contextual formula) by which we can identify the closest possible world. For the best we can say, when we want to identify the possible world that is closest to the actual world in order to say whether an act is harmful, seems to be the following: *relative* to one possible world, you have in the actual world been harmed by having your arm broken, but relative to another possible world you have not been harmed, but benefited, by having your arm broken by the psychopath. Although

[37]These conditions build on Lewis (1986).

[38]In other words, and if you believe that determinism and incompatibilism is right, he *could* not have released you and furthermore, he *could* also not have chosen not to kidnap you.

there is such a thing as *the objectively* closest possible world, we cannot for sure know what that world is like, as we cannot for sure know what would have happened instead of the actual conduct C, if C would not have happened in the past. I mean, what would have happened if Hitler had not been born or had died as a child? Would second World War happened anyway? We cannot know. We therefore have to relate our talk about harm to a specific possible world that we believe is the closest. In other words, when we talk about harm in the CB sense, we have to refer to a specific context, saying, for example, that by breaking your arm, the psychopath harmed you compared to a situation where he released you. Again, if the context of the possible world is specified, we can compare the actual world with the possible closest world in question, and describe why we believe that a person has been harmed.[39]

Secondly, a further challenge to CB is based on the observation that, by implying that omissions/allowing something to happen can be harmful, it can follow from CB that many types of omission are harmful even though intuitively we would not classify them as such.[40] In other words, it follows from CB that an individual P1 can be harmed by P2, if P2 omits to engage in a conduct C where P2's omission causes P1 to have *less positive well-being* than P1 would have had if P2 had not omitted to perform C. But do we really want to say that we have always harmed a person if we leave him slightly worse off than he would otherwise have been had we done something else instead? Suppose David spends his savings on a holiday in the Caribbean, and in doing so omits to buy a pleasant holiday for a stranger, Ben. It seems to follow from CB that David, by not paying for a holiday for Ben, harms him. That the word 'harm' can cover such cases seems a counterintuitive implication of CB: it simply does not agree with our ordinary usage of the word, where the notion of 'harming someone' is assumed to involve the pursuit of psychologically demeaning conduct, or the infliction of physical injury or death, and so on.

However, I am not convinced this objection is a knock-down argument against CB. First, all the baseline theories of harm that we have discussed are subject to strong counterexamples. Secondly, if we appeal to the closest possible world, as we did before, it could very well be the case that the closest possible world to that in which David buys a holiday for himself to the Caribbean is one in which David buys himself a holiday to New York. Therefore, again it seems to be an open question whether you have harmed a person by leaving him worse off than he would have been had you acted otherwise. It all depends on what turns out to be the closest possible world against which we compare the actual world or what to take the closest world to be. However, despite these observations, it remains true that CB, at least in certain situations, implies that you harm a person if you leave them slightly worse off than they would have been had you acted otherwise. Imagine that you give 5% of your salary to a charity organization, and that as a result of your donation, the charity can save 50 lives a year. Moreover, suppose that the closest possible world to the

[39]For a very critical discussion of some implausible ways to identify, the relevant counterfactuals of harm, than the one described above, see e.g. Bradley (2012) and Norcross (2005).

[40]Kagan (1998), pp. 84–85.

world in which you give 5% is one where you give 6% of your salary, and that with that donation the same charity organization can save 60 lives a year.[41] In this case, CB implies that you harm ten people by leaving them worse off than they would have been had you given 6% of your salary.[42]

In sum, despite these challenges, and because some fairly good responses can be made to them, let's accept that CB is the least bad theoretical account of the baseline of harm. That is the least bad theory, because it gives the right answer in counter-examples to both temporal baseline views and baselines from mankind. Furthermore, as will be presented in the following section, CB will not have any moral problematic implication as mentioned above if CB is combined with harm principles that are based on a moralized notion of harm. However, where does our investigation now leave us when it comes to the application and evaluation of normative principles that can be categorized as harm principles? We shall now turn to this question.

2.6 Why Harm Principles Are Redundant

Initially, we might notice that harm principles do not fit well with temporal baselines and the baselines from mankind that we discussed in Sects. 2.3 and 2.4. First, on an obvious understanding of a harm principle, it would follow that we at least have a reason for criminalizing kinds of conduct like Peter's in the headache case and the chronic disease case discussed in Sect. 2.3 in order to try to prevent such harms from occurring. Secondly, adherents of a harm principle would again say that we at least have similar reasons to prohibit kinds of conduct like Peter stealing Brian's car and crushing his legs, or like the doctor, in the Wonder Woman case, 'treating' Serena with the result that she is worse off, as we saw in Sect. 2.4.

However, although CB can explain why these acts are harmful—unlike the other baselines we have discussed, we saw in Sect. 2.5 that CB has at least two problematic implications. One is that there exist certain kinds of conduct C (e.g. a psychopath breaking P's arm instead of torturing P to death) that does not, compared to a specific interpretation of the closest possible world, involve harm. Secondly, it follows from CB that the notion of harm has been expanded in a problematic direction if certain kinds of omissions would count as harmful conduct. For instance, I harm people if I only donate 5% of my salary to charity organizations if the closest possible world is a world where I instead donate 6%. However, I take it for granted that most of us—including adherents of harm principles—would say that breaking other people's arms against their will should not only be classified as doing harm, but also be

[41]Imagine, for example, that when you consider how much you should donate, you are in doubt about whether to donate 5% or 6% of your salary. However, if the closest possible situation is one where you give 4% of your salary, you have not harmed anyone by donating 5%, quite the contrary.

[42]You might, of course, think that you have not done anything morally wrong by this kind of harm, but we should, for now, bear in mind that we are discussing non-moral views of harm.

criminalized. Again, no-one, and no adherent of a harm principle, would claim that we have any reasons to criminalize a 5% donation of ones salary to charity. So where does this leave us concerning the application and evaluation of harm principles which entail CB?

If we look at how adherents of harm principles have tackled the problem of demarking the scope of relevant harms, one main strategy has been as follows. They are typically motivated by their beliefs about which kinds of conduct the state *ought* not to criminalize; and as it is often liberal theorists who are attracted by a harm principle, the different versions of a harm principle have been invoked as a justification for the decriminalization or legalization of certain acts that are supposed not to be harmful in order to secure the liberty of citizens. A clear example of this strategy was the discussion in the UK in the late 1950s, in which Hart argued that homosexual acts between consenting adults that do not harm others should be decriminalized, so there is no harm to be prevented by criminalizing homosexual acts.[43] Liberals can also use harm principles to secure liberty rights for citizens, for example, in an attempt to show that certain omissions—like the one where you harm a person by not offering him a cruise to the Caribbean—should not be criminalized. So although a conception of harm like that delivered by CB may be plausible in its own right, it does not, if combined with a harm principle, render this cluster of theories sufficiently protective of liberty. In fact, this protection of liberty calls for a normative interpretation of harm.

And this is exactly what many adherents of a harm principle have done over the years by claiming that the state should only criminalize acts if this will prevent *morally wrongful harms* from occurring.[44] With this move, it can be argued that you do not do anything immoral if you do *not* give a stranger, who would like it, a cruise to the Caribbean. It is not immoral, one might claim, because you do not stand in a relationship with the stranger of the kind that would make you morally responsible for his well-being and especially not for increasing his well-being through an expensive cruise, and you should therefore be free to do as you wish. Again, it could be argued that you have not done anything morally wrong, as you have chosen to spend some of your money on fighting global poverty instead of spending it on a cruise for a stranger. Alternatively, it can be argued that the psychopath has done something that is morally wrong if he breaks your arm. For instance, because the psychopath, by doing that, does not maximize well-being, or because he violates a constraint on harm of the innocent or because he uses you as a mere mean for his interests. Therefore, our understanding of a harm principle depends not only on how we specify harm, but also on which kinds of harms a moral theory would classify as morally wrongful harms. Moreover, our evaluation of a harm principle would therefore depend on the

[43]Hart (1963), p. 14.

[44]See e.g. Feinberg (1984), pp. 34–35; Husak (2008); Simester and von Hirsch (2011), pp. 38–39. Another strategy to specify which types of harm are relevant to prevent through criminalization is to claim that it is only the prevention of non-trivial harm that matters in criminalization decisions. See e.g. Husak (2008) for this constraint on the justification of criminalization. For a splendid and convincing critique of this strategy, see Holtug (2002).

plausibility of the specification of harm and on whether we believe that the moral theory in question is the right or most plausible moral theory.

For now, however, we shall not be engaged in the evaluation of any underlying moral theory about which kinds of harmful conduct and omissions are immoral and which of these kinds of conduct ought to be criminalized, as this would take us deep into normative ethical theory. However, in Chaps. 4 (on legal moralism), 5 (on dignity-based principles of criminalization) and 6 (on a utilitarian principle of criminalization), I will critically discuss different moral theories that, in a more general vein, do specify when a type of act is morally wrong and when it ought to be criminalized. Moral theories, which we can use to answer the central question of this book, namely: by what moral principle(s) should the state's criminalization decisions be guided?

However, the result of our investigation seems to leave adherents of harm principles who accept the above-mentioned *moralized* version of a harm principle with a devastating problem. In their effort to narrow down the scope of harms that the state ought to prevent through criminalization, they resort to moral theory. However, once they do that, it is unclear what purpose principles of criminalization which fit under the umbrella of a harm principle actually serve.[45]

Very few philosophers have tried to describe what purpose harm principles serve if the types of harm that the state has reason to criminalize are only morally wrongful harms. As far as I understand him, Holtug's verdict is that moralized versions of harm principles should be replaced by a moral theory that, at the same time, can tell us when harm is morally wrong and, furthermore, when it should be criminalized. However, Holtug's argument concerning this point is not very detailed. Nevertheless, here is what Holtug has in mind:

> [Joseph] Raz also offers another baseline, namely, that a person is harmed if he is rendered worse off than he is entitled to be. . . . In order to apply the Harm Principle, we need to know what people are entitled to. And in order to know what people are entitled to, we need a theory of justice.[46]

> The Harm Principle is of no use without a theory of justice, but if we have this theory, it seems that we have no need for the Harm Principle. It would seem that the theory of justice will settle the issue of coercion [i.e. state coercion through criminalization and punishment] all by itself.[47]

I hope a fair reconstruction of Holtug's argument could be as follows.

P1: If a moral principle P presuppose a moral theory M (or a theory of justice) in order to apply P, and M can cover the scope of P too, then P is redundant compared to M.

P2: Harm principles, which rely on a moralized notion of harm (e.g. entitlement), presuppose a moral theory M in order to apply a harm principle, and harm principles can have their scope covered by M.

[45]For the same conclusion, see Holtug (2002) and Petersen (2010).

[46]Holtug (2002), p. 385.

[47]Holtug (2002), p. 386.

Conclusion: Harm principles, which rely on a moralized notion of harm, are redundant to a moral theory M.

A few comments follow before a more critical discussion of this argument. In his argumentation, Holtug's focus is on a specific class of harm principles, namely those who entail a moralized notion of harm. However, as we shall see in what follows, I believe that the kind of reasoning used by Holtug can also be used to criticize all version of harm principles that are not moralized versions (and, in fact, all kinds of criminalization principles that are not based on a general moral theory). Furthermore, I take '... M can cover the scope of P...' to mean that a moral theory M can entail all the moral implications of a moral principle P. For instance, given that moral theories such as several versions of deontology and consequentialism can specify when harm is morally wrong, and justify when the state ought to criminalize a type of conduct C, such moral theories do, by themselves, cover the scope of all harm principles. Therefore, if you accept a harm principle (whether in a version where harm is moralized or not), and if you also accept a CB, why not simplify your theory of criminalization in the following way: the only good reason for implementing a proposed criminal prohibition is that this would probably be an effective way of preventing morally wrongful conduct and there is probably no other means that is as effective as criminalization.[48]

If, for example, the maximization of utility or the protection of rights are appealed to in order to establish which kinds of conduct are morally wrong and when they ought to be criminalized, the important thing is not that such conducts are also harmful or *morally harmful*. What matters is that a given kind of conduct is *morally wrongful*, and that criminalization would probably be an effective way of preventing such wrongdoing. Imagine, for instance, that utilitarianism is the right moral theory. The only thing one should be concerned about, when considering which kinds of conduct should be criminalized, is whether it would maximize well-being if the kind of conduct in question were criminalized. In Chap. 6, a utilitarian principle of criminalization will be defended. An advantage with letting a full-blown moral theory justify which acts should be criminalized (both from a theoretical point of view and from a public policy point of view) is that such a theory can also give us—contrary to, for instance, the harm principle formulated by Mill and most other principles of criminalization that exist in the field—a necessary and sufficient reason for criminalization. So, again, the relevant justification for criminalization can be obtained entirely with reference to a preferred moral theory.

As a defender of the position that harm principles are not redundant to moral theory, one could, of course, object to the above-mentioned argument. One could claim that because several moral theories can accept that certain non-harmful kinds

[48] Adherents of a harm principle who also accept the offence principle (like Feinberg) or who accept other reasons for criminalization than harm—because they believe in the existence of harmless immoralities—could also simplify their theories according to the wording in the above-mentioned phrase. They could claim that it is not only morally wrongful harms but also morally wrongful offenses that the state has reasons to criminalize.

of conduct C are morally wrong, and therefore are plausible candidates for criminalization, such general moral theories covers too much, compared to what adherents of harm principles would accept. In addition, because of this difference, it is not fair to argue that harm principles are redundant to moral theories. There is at least one mitigating answer to this objection. According to all the versions of the harm principle that I have read about, this objection does miss the target for one obvious reason: no defenders of a harm principle would say that harm is all that matters in criminalization decisions. For example, if the prevention of harm is only a necessary condition for the moral justification of criminalization (following Mill), it will leave room for other conditions to play a part too. Moreover, the same happens if prevention of harm is only one reason among others for criminalization (following e.g. Feinberg, Simester and von Hirsch, and Husak, and the set of criminalization theories, which go under the umbrella concept of legal moralism). In addition, if these other reasons were also moral reasons, it would again be better to accept a moral theory, which could also tell us how to weigh the different moral factors against each other. An example would be how the prevention of wrongful harm should be weighed against the prevention of non-harmful wrongs in order to settle whether a kind of conduct C should be criminalized or not.

Another objection to the argument above would be to argue that there is still place for a harm principle within a moral theory. For instance, Wayne Sumner has argued that even if you were a consequentialist, applying a harm principle in the justification of what the state should criminalize would, as a rule of thumb lead to good consequences.[49] So in one, more practical sense, harm principles are not redundant. Again, however, this will not solve the problem of redundancy in question, which is of a more theoretical nature. If harm principles should only play an instrumental role, their plausibility will still be contingent on fulfilling the aim of the moral theory in question. For if, from an empirical point of view, it turns out that the use of a harm principle in criminalization decisions will not satisfy the purpose of the moral theory in question, the harm principle in question will be of little or no use.

A third objection would be to claim that this kind of criticism is unfair, as most adherents of a harm principle do favour a moral theory. Mill, for instance favours utilitarianism and Feinberg favours a liberal rights-based moral theory. However, I do not believe that it is unfair to argue that harm principles are redundant to moral theory even though adherents of harm principles do favour moral theories. If adherents of a harm principle do favour a moral theory, then we should use this theory directly on the question at hand—namely how we should justify what ought to be criminalized—and try to explicitly give us a specification of necessary and sufficient reasons for criminalization. It is far from obvious why we should use mid-level principles (like harm principles) of criminalization, when moral theory (contrary to mid-level principles) provides us with the answers we need in criminalization decisions.

---

[49] Sumner (2004).

In sum, we have a reason to reject the set of criminalization principles which fall under the umbrella of a harm principle simply because they are superfluous compared to moral theories that can explain when an act is wrong, when harm is wrongful and when the state ought to criminalize a kind of conduct. Therefore, instead of dealing with harm principles, which provide us with a necessary reason or one reason among others, we should go for a moral theory, which at the same time could provide us with both necessary and sufficient reasons for criminalization. If we want to answer the important question about which principle(s) should guide the state in criminalization decisions, because we want to know what kinds of conduct should be criminalized, we should not be satisfied with principles that only point to *a reason* for criminalization or *a necessary reason* for criminalization. If we were only content with non-sufficient reasons for our actions, we should, for example, be content to know that one reason to criminalize the use of a new medical technology is that it might be harmful to use. However, we want to know more in order to judge whether it is morally right to criminalize a new piece of medical technology because it might be harmful. What risk of harm is morally acceptable? Do the benefits of the technology outweigh the harm? And so on. In sum, only giving us non-sufficient reasons for how we should act in important areas of life, whether or not it has to do with criminalization, is not wholly satisfactory. You may say that this is not a fair criticism of harm principles, as adherents of such principles, as we know, do offer other moral reasons for criminalization than the prevention of harm. This is right, but what is happening, then, is that, once again, in order to weigh all these different reasons against each other, it seems obvious to shift to a moral theory. This would give more satisfactory answers to the question of which principle(s) should guide the state (and us, its citizens) in making criminalization decisions and which kinds of conduct the state (taking all relevant moral reasons into account) ought to criminalize.[50]

2.7 Conclusion

In order to understand, apply and evaluate harm principles, we need to know how we should understand the central notion of harm. I have tried to show that, although temporal baselines of different outlooks can be used to describe obvious harms like rape and robbery, they do not give the right answers to many other cases discussed in this chapter—for instance, the headache case and the chronic disease case. Alternative baselines, like the baselines from mankind, handled all these cases at least better than did the temporal baselines. However, adherents of baselines from mankind have problems of their own. In the relative average view, they were unable to recognize obvious cases of harm (e.g. crushing someone's leg). Alternatively, in Harrosh's

[50]For a splendid and critical discussion of the problems with applying mid-level moral principles like harm principles see e.g. Krom (2011).

objective view, no guidance for how to apply the baseline in question was explicated and her view could not give the right answer in a case such as Wonder Woman. Finally, the least bad theorization of the baseline for harm seems to be counterfactual.

However, when CB is applied in combination with a harm principle, this implies that the scope of harm relevant for criminalization can easily be too narrow or too wide. In other words, in applying a harm principle, we will get nowhere by clarifying the concept of harm along the lines of CB. For the most promising specification of harm implies some kinds of conduct that we would classify as harm (e.g. breaking an arm) but does not necessarily involve harm, or implies that some omissions can be interpreted as harmful that we would not consider instances of harm. We then saw that a well-known strategy for adherents of a harm principle to deal with these problems is to accept a moralized notion of harm.

However, the result of our investigation was to explain that adherents of a harm principle who accept a moralized version of harm (or not) face a devastating problem. In their effort to narrow down the scope of harms that the state ought to prevent through criminalization, they resort to moral theory. However, once they do that, there is no need for harm principles, as the whole job of justifying what to criminalize can be done by the use of a plausible moral theory. I have therefore argued for the view that people who sympathize with a harm principle do not need the principle—whether or not they believe in a moralized version of harm. Instead, we should consult a moral theory to justify which kinds of conduct are morally harmful or just morally wrong, and which type of conduct, in the final analysis, should be criminalized.

In Chaps. 5 and 6, we shall discuss some standard deontological and consequentialist moral theories of criminalization, but before that, in Chaps. 3, and 4, we shall investigate some well-known principles of criminalization which entail the idea that harm prevention is not a necessary reason for a state to use when they justify which kinds of conduct to criminalize. In Chap. 3, the focus is on the view that one reason for the criminalization of certain kinds of conduct C is to prevent people not from being harmed by C, but from *taking offense* at C. In Chap. 4, the focus is on legal moralism, which, in broad terms, is the view that the justification for criminalization of a kind of conduct C is that C is morally wrong. Moreover, as we shall see, adherents of legal moralism believe that harm and offense are not all that matters in criminalization decisions. In Chap. 3 I will argue that it follows from a plausible interpretation of offense principles that they are redundant to harm principles, and following the reasoning in the last part of this chapter, offense principles are therefore redundant to moral theory too. Moreover, as will be explained in Chap. 4 central versions of legal moralism has severe problems of its own.

References

Baker DJ (2011) The right not to be criminalized: demarcating criminal law's authority. Ashgate Publishing Limited, Abingdon
Bradley B (2012) Doing away with harm. Philos Phenomenol Res 85(2):390–412
Cohen GA (1995) Self-ownership, freedom, and equality. Cambridge University Press, Cambridge
Crisp R (1997) Mill on utilitarianism. Routledge Philosophy Guidebooks, Abingdon
Dan-Cohen M (2002) Defending dignity. UC Berkeley Shool Law Public Law Leg. Theory Reserach Pap. No. 92
Duff A (2007) Answering for crime: responsibility and liability in the criminal law. Bloomsbury Publishing, London
Duff A (2018) The realm of criminal law. Oxford University Press, Oxford
Edwards J (2014) Harm principles. Legal Theory 20(4):253–285
Feinberg J (1984) The moral limits of the criminal law. Vol. 1, Harm to others. Oxford University Press, Oxford
Feldman F (2004) Pleasure and the good life. Oxford University Press, Oxford
Feldman F (2010) What is this thing called happiness? Oxford University Press, Oxford
Griffin J (1986) Well-being: Its meaning, measurement and moral importance. Clarendon Press, Oxford
Harcourt BE (1999) The collapse of the harm principle. J Crim Law Criminol 90(1):109–194
Harman E (2009) Harming as causing harm. In: Roberts MA, Wasserman DT (eds) Harming future persons: ethics, genetics and the non-identity problem. Springer, Berlin, pp 137–154
Harrosh S (2012) Identifying harms. Bioethics 26(9):493–498
Hart HLA (1963) Law liberty and morality. Oxford University Press, Oxford
Holtug N (2002) The harm principle. Ethical Theory Moral Pract 5(4):357–389
Husak D (2008) Overcriminalization: the limits of the criminal law. Oxford University Press, Oxford
Kagan S (1989) The limits of morality. Clarendon Press, Oxford
Kagan S (1998) Normative ethics. Westview Press, Boulder
Kahane G, Savulescu J (2012) The concept of harm and the significant of normativity. J Appl Philos 29(4):318–332
Krom A (2011) The harm principle as a mid-level principle? Three problems from the context of infectious disease control. Bioethics 25(8):437–444
Kymlicka W (2001) Contemporary political philosophy: an introduction, 2nd edn. Oxford University Press, Oxford
Lewis DK (1986) On the plurality of worlds. Cambridge University Press, Cambridge
Lippert-Rasmussen K (2005) Deontology, responsibility, and equality. Museum Tusculanum Press, Copenhagen
Mill JS (1859/2003) On liberty. In: Warnock M (ed) Utilitarianism and on liberty. Blackwell Publishing, Hoboken
Norcross A (2005) Harming in context. Philos Stud 123:149–173
Nozick R (1974) Anarchy, state, and utopia. Basic Books, New York
Parfit D (1984) Reasons and persons. Oxford University Press, Oxford
Petersen TS (2001) Generocentrism: a critical discussion of David Heyd. Philosophia Philos Q Israel 28(1-4):411–425
Petersen TS (2010) New legal moralism: some strengths and challenges. Crim Law Philos 4 (2):215–232
Raz J (1986) The morality of freedom. Oxford University Press, Oxford
Ripstein A (2006) Beyond the harm principle. Philos Public Aff 34(3):215–245
Shiffrin S (1999) Wrongful life, procreative responsibility, and the significance of harm. Legal Theory 5(2):117–148
Simester AP, von Hirsch A (2011) Crimes, harms and wrongs: on the principles of criminalisation. Hart Publishing, Oxford

Stewart S (2010) The limits of the harm principle. Crim Law Philos 4:17–35

Sumner LW (1996) Welfare, happiness and ethics. Oxford University Press, Oxford

Sumner W (2004) The hateful and the obscene: studies in the limits of free expression. University of Toronto Press, Toronto

Tadros V (2011) The ends of harm: the moral foundations of criminal Law. Oxford University Press, Oxford

Wolf J (1991) Robert Nozick: property, justice and the minimal state. Stanford University Press, Stanford

Chapter 3
No Offense! On the Offense Principle and Some New Challenges

3.1 Introduction

As should be clear by now, the aim of criminalization theory is to give a plausible justification indicating what normative principle(s) should guide the state in its decisions about what kinds of conduct to criminalize. The aim of the last chapter was to specify and criticize some important principles of criminalization, all of which can be categorized as *harm principles*. However, even if we know how to specify harm, apply a harm principle, and object that harm principles are redundant to grand moral theory, a further question arises, namely: when the state argues in favour of criminalizing certain types of conduct, should it only criminalize conduct that is harmful or where the criminalization will prevent harm? In other words, is harm all that matters? In this and the following chapters, I will critically discuss principles of criminalization whose adherents argue that harm or harm prevention is not all that ought to matter when the state tries to justify its criminalization decisions.

One set of principles of criminalization which has been presented in the literature on legal philosophy, and which represents an alternative to the harm-based approach, contains variants of the offense principle.[1] The aim of this chapter is to discuss central versions of this principle critically. One scholar who has been extremely careful in his presentation and defence of an offense principle is the late Joel Feinberg. In his book *Offense to Others*, published in 1985, he gave the following formulation of the principle:

> **Feinberg's Offense Principle**
> It is always a good reason in support of a proposed criminal prohibition that it would probably be an effective way of preventing *serious offense* (as opposed to injury or harm) to persons other than the actor, *and* that it is probably a necessary

[1]See, for example, Feinberg (1985), Simester and von Hirsch (2006, 2011) and Duff (2014).

T. Søbirk Petersen, *Why Criminalize?*, Law and Philosophy Library 134,
https://doi.org/10.1007/978-3-030-34690-4_3

means to that end (i.e., there is probably no other means that is equally effective at no greater cost to other values).[2]

The plan of the chapter is as follows. In Sect. 3.2, the central components of the offense principle will be described in a little more detail, thus preparing the way for critical discussion. The task of Sects. 3.3 and 3.4 is critical evaluation of the first part of the offense principle in particular. Before we specify the content of this evaluation more precisely, it is important to keep in mind that some of the criticism of harm principles that we levelled in Chap. 2 can be extrapolated and applied to offense principles, too. If harm principles are redundant by grand moral theory, we can apply the same kind of reasoning to offense principles, as the most plausible versions of the offense principle are made redundant by harm principles. The reasoning will be as follows.

In Sect. 3.3, it will be argued that the conduct referred to in the offense principle, depending on one's theory of individual well-being, can easily be interpreted as a subset of the conduct referred to by harm principles. So in this sense, offense principles are shown to be redundant by harm principles. This finding is contrary to both the formulation of the offense principle itself and to the belief, held by prominent advocates of the offense principle, that the two principles are separate and distinct. In Sect. 3.4, it will be argued that the specification of harm given by leading advocates of the offense principle such as Feinberg, A. P. Simester and Andreas von Hirsch as a 'setback to interests' is both difficult to apply in a way that allows a distinction between harm and causing offense to be made, and poorly supported.

Some philosophical work has been done on some of the conceptual and moral issues raised by the interpretation and application of the offense principle.[3] In the present chapter, one theme is relatively new, however. This concerns the significance of theories of well-being in a critical assessment of the alleged difference between an offensive act and a harmful act.[4]

[2]Feinberg (1985), p. 1, my emphases. It is clear from Feinberg's writing that he interprets offensive conduct as conduct that causes unpleasant or disliked mental states (e.g. disgust or the feeling of insult) that are not in themselves necessarily harmful according to his specification of harm. Feinberg's specification of harm will be described in Sect. 3.4.

[3]For illuminating discussion of the metaphysics of disgust, see Husak (2006) and Tasioulas (2006). One central issue here is whether disgustingness is a property out there (e.g. a fact about a conduct such as urinating on one's food and then eating it) that exists independently of whether a particular person actually *feels* disgusted by it or only exists when someone experiences it.

[4]It is true that Thomson (1986), p. 386; Tasioulas (2006), pp. 164–165 have said, albeit briefly, that the theory of well-being you accept (or find least troublesome) can have a bearing on whether taking offense should be identified as a case of being harmed. At least, if we accept that an important element in the specification of harm is that it involves a reduction in well-being. However, they have not defended the view that taking offense can be reduced to harm in any detail. Tadros (2011), p. 42 also observes that 'it is a mistake to deny that offensiveness is harmful', but without engaging in more detailed discussion of why offensiveness is harmful.

3.2 The Offense Principle

When Feinberg writes, in formulating the offense principle, that the probable effective prevention of serious offense is 'always a good reason in support of a proposed criminal prohibition', he means (like other supporters of the principle such as Simester and von Hirsch) that there are other good reasons for criminalizing certain types of act. The *only* other principle of criminalization that Feinberg accepts is a particular version of a harm principle.[5] He describes this version as follows:

> **Feinberg's Harm Principle**
> It is always a good reason in support of penal legislation that it would probably be an effective way of preventing *harm* to persons other than the actor, *and* that it is probably a necessary means to that end.[6]

In Mill's classic statement of it, the harm principle can roughly be said to entail that the prevention of harm to others is a necessary condition of criminalization.[7] However, if we follow Feinberg's version of the harm principle, preventing harm to others is *not* a necessary condition for criminalization. For according to Feinberg, kinds of conduct ought only to be criminalized if it is probable that this is an effective way to prevent *either* harm *or* offense to others.

However, it is clear from Feinberg's formulation of the offense principle and the harm principle that preventing offense or harm to others, alone or together, is insufficient to justify criminalization. It is insufficient—as the last clause of the offence principle and Feinberg's version of the harm principle both indicate—because the negative impact of criminalization on other values (e.g. distribution of resources, economic cost, well-being, etc.) should be weighed against the effectiveness of criminalization before penal legislation is applied to kinds of conduct whose criminalization will prevent offense or harm to others.[8] However, in what follows I shall confine myself primarily to the investigation of the first part of Feinberg's version of the offense principle.

In order to clarify the offense principle and differentiate it from harm principles, one must first explain what taking offense at something involves. We are probably all acquainted first-hand with experiences such as feeling insulted by humiliating treatment that causes us offense, and most of us will have seen other people taking offense at something they see or hear about. The protests associated with the Danish

---

[5]Feinberg (1986), pp. 23–26. Feinberg rules out legal paternalism, i.e. the view that the state has reason to criminalize acts that are harmful to the very same people who perform these acts. Simester and von Hirsch (2011), on the other hand, accept legal paternalism, the offence principle, and a version of the harm principle too.

[6]Feinberg (1986), p. xiii.

[7]Mill (1859/2003).

[8]Again, as was argued in Chap. 2, how these different values should be weighed against each other must rely on a grand moral theory.

cartoon crisis were a clear case of many people taking offense.[9] But what is it, more precisely, to take offense at something? According to Feinberg, the common denominator in cases where someone takes offense at an act is that the act causes a *disliked mental state*[10] or an *unpleasant mental state*.[11] Taking offense includes states like affront to the senses, disgust, shame, anxiety, feeling insulted, and so on.[12] In order to get a clearer picture of different kinds of act that may cause offense, I will use and elaborate on Feinberg's own example. Imagine yourself seated on a crowded bus trying to get to an important meeting—say, a job interview—for which you are late.[13] Therefore, you cannot get off the bus without great cost to yourself. What is the bus ride like? You may feel *disgust* if the passenger next to you is malodorous, coughs loudly, sneezes openly, chews on rotten food, and vomits or farts. You might feel *shame* or *embarrassment* if the passenger next to you masturbates or if she or he is nude or tries to give sexual satisfaction to a dog. You might become *annoyed* if you have to listen to a loud and intimate conversation between the passenger next to you and someone on her or his mobile phone. You might feel *anger* or *insulted* if the person in front of you wears an anti-Muslim T-shirt with an offensive caricature of the prophet Mohammed and the message, written in large red letters, 'All Muslims are Terrorists', or if a person next to you begins to shout racist slogans like 'all blacks are criminals' or 'all whites are Nazis'.

Secondly, it is very important to notice that its adherents claim that the offence principle only covers offense caused by others' *morally wrongful conduct*—a condition clearly reflected in the final examples in the paragraph above. Thus Feinberg writes that only 'disliked mental states ... when caused by the wrongful conduct of others [which, Feinberg would add, *violates one's rights*] ... are intended in the offense principle as we shall understand it.'[14]

Simester and von Hirsch agree when they say that 'we treat offenses as not merely involving affront to others' sensibilities; an element of wrongdoing is also

[9]In 2005, a Danish newspaper published twelve cartoons, most of which depicted the Islamic Prophet Mohammed. The best known of these pictures is the one showing the Prophet with a bomb in his turban. The cartoons were considered offensive by many Muslims and non-Muslims, and for many reasons. Some objected, for example, to the satirical and insulting depiction of a religious minority in Denmark.

[10]Feinberg (1985), p. 1.

[11]Feinberg (1985), p. 2. I am not sure Feinberg is right about the psychology of these feelings. There might be some moralists who take offense at something, but who at the same time love to feel, say, disgust and share it with others. However, I will leave investigation of this possibility to one side and focus on some of the problematic implications of Feinberg's interpretation of what it means to take offense at an act performed by others.

[12]Feinberg (1985), pp. 1 and 10–13.

[13]The following examples are all from Feinberg (1985), pp. 10–13 or inspired by him.

[14]Feinberg (1985), p. 2. The same line of reasoning (that there is reason to criminalize only wrongful harms) applies also to Feinberg's and Simester and von Hirsch's version of the harm principle. See, for example, Feinberg (1984), pp. 34–35; Simester and von Hirsch (2011), pp. 38–39.

required.'[15] Wrongdoing, for Simester and von Hirsch, 'consists in treating other persons with a gross *lack of respect* or consideration'.[16] The reason these authors require the offence principle to have this wrongfulness condition is that, if the condition were absent, the principle could be used to justify the criminalization of many acts that no liberal would want criminalized. For, owing to their personal sensibilities, people can take offence at almost anything, from the colour of a person's hair to the way a teacher with a Scottish accent pronounces the word 'area'. A clear example of a disliked mental state which plausibly can be described as offence but was *not* caused by the wrongful acts of the person who directly caused it occurs when a person feels disgust, anger, and/or unpleasantness as he witnesses the victim of a traffic accident. For instance, we can imagine a situation where the victim lies in a pool of blood with a smashed skull. In such a case, it is clearly a gross mistake to claim that the victim of the traffic accident has offended the spectator in any sense that could justify a legal sanction being imposed on him or her.[17]

With this last observation in mind, I observe, *en passant*, that it is somewhat misleading of Simester and von Hirsch to claim that a missing element in Feinberg's elaboration of the offence principle is that it does not take 'wrongdoing' into account.[18]

Thirdly, one could, as Feinberg does, make a distinction between morally wrongful 'offense' using the ordinary or common-sense meaning of the word 'offense', and the same concept using the more technical specification of the word as it is used in the offence principle. In its ordinary use, the word 'offense' has a *narrow* sense and a *broad* sense. In the narrow sense it means that you (i) *suffer a disliked state*, (ii) attribute the state you experience to the *wrongful conduct* of another, and (iii) *resent* the other for his or her role in causing you the disliked state. In the broad sense, however, offense only requires (i) and (ii). Following Feinberg's more

[15]Simester and von Hirsch (2006), p. 119.

[16]Ibid, p. 120.

[17]The spectator of the traffic victim can, of course, be genuinely and morally offended if he knows that the victim was hit by a car driven in a morally blameworthy way.

[18]To demonstrate that it is a misleading interpretation by Simester and von Hirsch, compare, for example, 'the offense principle requires that the disliked state of mind . . . be produced wrongfully by another party' (Feinberg 1985), pp. 1–2 with the following quotation from Simester and von Hirsch: 'our objection, in short, is that Feinberg's portals to the offense principle are too wide. Affront to sensibility, by itself, should never suffice to invoke the Offense Principle' (2011), p. 97. Again, however, Feinberg has never said anything like this. Simester and von Hirsch argue for their point by observing that Feinberg sidesteps this (the wrongfulness requirement) with the assertion that 'there will always be a wrong whenever an offended state is produced in another without justification and excuse' (2011, p. 96, citing Feinberg 1985, p. 2). I think their interpretation is too strict. First, although the sentence referred to can be interpreted as a case of sidestepping the wrongfulness requirement, that requirement is mentioned several times in the introduction to Feinberg's presentation of the offense principle. Second, the quotation to which Simester and von Hirsch refer can be interpreted as entailing a wrongness requirement, since it seems right to claim that affront to a person's senses is morally wrong, for example, if it is, as Feinberg mentions, done without (or without plausible) justification or excuse.

technical understanding of the offense principle, the notion of wrongful offense specifies an objective condition in the sense that 'the unpleasant mental state must be caused by conduct that really is wrongful.'[19] Whether an individual takes offence at something or feels wronged is only part of the explanation in establishing whether an act is offensive in the sense invoked by the offense principle.

Following these clarifications, it might be informative to note that advocates of the offense principle add several *mediating principles* governing the criminalization of acts causing offense to others. Feinberg, for instance, argues that the decision to criminalize an act that causes offense should depend on (a) the seriousness of the offense, and (b) how widespread it is, as well as (c) the avoidability of the offensive act and (d) its social value. Moreover, we should remember the second part of the offence principle, which says that a prohibition should only be actualized if 'there is probably no other means that is equally effective at no greater cost to other values.'[20] However, the appropriate way to apply these mediating principles is not obvious; it requires clarification and elaboration. For instance, how widespread should a seriously offensive act be to warrant criminalization? When is a seriously offensive act unavoidable enough not to be criminalized? How do we measure the social value of an act that may be offensive to some, and exactly what social values are we talking about? Finally, how do we weigh these mediating principles against each other?

In what follows, we shall not dwell on these internal issues for those advocating the offence principle.[21] The questions are, of course, both relevant and important in normative evaluation of the offense-based strategy. However, the focus in this chapter is primarily on the relationship between the offense principle and other principles—e.g. whether the principle is just a subpart of a harm principle, or independent of it. This issue is independent of the way any mediating principles are formulated and should be applied. So, in what follows, the challenge mentioned in the last part of the introduction to this chapter will be presented and discussed. Our main question will be whether offence principles are different from harm principles.

3.3 Theories of Well-Being and the Distinction Between Offense and Harm

It is of paramount importance for those who support the offense principle that the experience of a wrongful 'serious offense' is not a specific case, or subset, of a wrongful 'harm'. So when Feinberg presents a number of examples where people are said to be taking offense, like those on the bus ride described earlier, it should be

[19]Feinberg (1985), p. 2.

[20]Feinberg (1985), p. 1. Furthermore, and according to Feinberg, these mediating principles also apply to the harm principle: see Feinberg (1984), pp. 187–217.

[21]Feinberg tries to answer some of these questions (1985), pp. 25–49. See also McKinnon (2006), pp. 82–89; Simester and von Hirsch (2011), pp. 123–140.

obvious (at least, according to Feinberg) that these examples are not examples of anyone being harmed. As Judith J. Thomson has observed, however, this is not obvious at all.[22] Why does Feinberg suppose that experiences of wrongful disgust, anxiety, and so forth differ from harm in the sense relevant to the harm principle? I believe most of us would agree that we have an interest in not experiencing morally wrongful acts that cause us feelings of insult, shame, embarrassment, or anxiety.[23] It also seems correct to say, for example, that racist or sexist proclamations usually harm people who listen to and are denigrated in them, and that some Muslims were harmed by the insult delivered by the Danish cartoons. Even if such proclamations or insults are not directly harmful to people, they could easily cause harm indirectly by creating, or supporting, an environment that is hostile to those targeted: blacks, women, or Muslims, for example. Therefore, when we want to know whether offenses are merely specific cases of harm, we need to clarify the crucial notion of *harm* itself.

To make a start, and as we saw in Chap. 2, several philosophers have claimed that a person is harmed by an event E or an act A if she or he is made worse off in terms of well-being by E or A.[24] In other words, harm is a reduction in a person's well-being. This means that, in order to clarify the notion of harm, we need, at the very least, a theory of well-being.[25] By adopting a particular theory of well-being, we might obtain a clear view of the alleged difference between offense and harm.

Let us consider the three main theories of well-being discussed in the philosophical literature: hedonistic theories, desire-satisfaction theories, and objective list theories.[26] In the standard version of hedonism, you fare better the more pleasant experiences you have, and you fare worse the more unpleasant experiences you have. Therefore, if hedonism is correct, then—since Feinberg writes that offense is constituted by *unpleasant mental states*—taking offense is a subset of being harmed.[27] Adherents of the offense principle do not do any better if we change the focus and concentrate on desire-satisfaction theories. These theories claim, roughly, that you fare better the more your desires are satisfied, and you fare worse the more your desires are frustrated. However, when the desire-satisfaction theory of well-

---

[22]Thomson (1986), pp. 385–386; see also Tadros (2011), pp. 39–42.

[23]At least, if we observe these experiences in isolation. I am well aware of the fact that feeling shame, for instance, in a situation X may cause you harm, but also, in the long run, make you behave in a way that increases your overall well-being because you have learned a valuable lesson from X.

[24]See, for instance, Bradley (2012), p. 396; Kagan (1998), p. 84; Lippert-Rasmussen (2005), p. 41; Norcross (2005), p. 150; Raz (1986), p. 414. Furthermore, and more relevant in our context, see Feinberg (1984), p. 34; Simester and von Hirsch (2011), p. 36.

[25]Apart from a theory of well-being, we also need to be clearer about the baseline from which the reduction in well-being is a variation. In other words, if being harmed is being made worse off, we need to know the baseline in comparison with which one is worse off. However, we shall not go into this in further detail. See Chap. 2 for a discussion of this problem.

[26]See, for example, Parfit (1984), Griffin (1986), Sumner (1996), Kagan (1998), Feldman (2004, 2010) and Bradley (2009).

[27]Feinberg (1985), p. 2.

being is spelled out, it seems obvious that causing people offense by making them feel embarrassed, insulted or humiliated is causing them to have experiences that people *normally do not desire*. Because of this, we usually fare worse when our desire to avoid the feelings caused by offence is not satisfied. Again, then, causing others offense can be characterized as a way of harming others.

Can an objective list theory help us to support a clear distinction between offensive and harmful acts? An objective list theory can contain things that make your life better whether or not you find them e.g. pleasant or an object of your desire. It might include, for instance, knowledge, health, love, having children, developing one's abilities, and appreciating beauty. Whether taken offense of a given conduct diminishes your well-being, and thereby harms you, will now depend on what is on the list. If pleasant experiences figure there, unpleasant experiences will, all else being equal, reduce your well-being, and that would mean that unpleasant feelings of humiliation caused by another's offensive conduct make your life worse. The same reasoning applies to desires if desire satisfaction is included on the list.

In short, then, whether you should accept the offense principle as a principle that differs from the harm principle depends on which theory of well-being you find most persuasive. If you are in favour of hedonistic theories or desire-satisfaction theories, at least in their standard formulations, you should accept that the offense principle is not a distinct principle that goes beyond the harm principle. If you accept an objective list theory with pleasant mental states and/or desire satisfaction on the list, then it will follow that offence is a specific case of harm, which means, in turn, that the offense principle is a subpart of the harm principle. So in order to keep the two principles distinct, you must accept an objective list theory of well-being in a variant that excludes pleasant mental states and desires from the list. In addition, this is, consistently enough, exactly what we find when we ask what theory of well-being is adopted by adherents of the offense principle such as Feinberg, Simester and von Hirsch. To evaluate the plausibility of the alleged distinction between offence and harm, then, we need to investigate the objective list theory accepted by Feinberg, Simester and von Hirsch.

3.4 Harm as Wrongful Setbacks to Interests

According to Feinberg, Simester and von Hirsch, your life goes well if your interests are satisfied; harm is accordingly defined as *setbacks to interests*. The kind of harm we should prevent through criminalization is wrongfully harming others,[28] but in order to apply this moralized concept of harm, we must first of all know what

[28]Feinberg (1984), Chapter 1. See also Simester and von Hirsch (2006), pp. 116–117, who believe that a setback to someone's interests occurs through the infringement of some physical resources, proprietary, or otherwise over which that person has a legitimate claim.

'setbacks to interests' means.[29] Consider Feinberg's use of the word 'interests'. A person's interests, according to Feinberg, can be divided into 'welfare interests' and 'ulterior interests'. The former, which are presumably shared by all human beings, include 'interests in one's own physical health and vigor ..., the absence of absorbing pain and suffering ..., emotional stability, the absence of groundless anxieties and resentments, the capacity to ... enjoy and maintain friendship, at least minimal income and financial security, [and] a tolerable social and physical environment'.[30] Welfare interests are necessary but not sufficient for a good life. 'They are "basic requisites of a man's well-being", but by no means the whole of that well-being itself.'[31]

When welfare interests are missing from your life, or, as Feinberg puts it, are blocked or damaged, your interests are *set back*, and you are therefore harmed. In that sense, welfare interests are the content of Feinberg's objective list theory of well-being. Ulterior interests, on the other hand, are of a more subjective nature (although they usually depend on the satisfaction of objective welfare interests) and therefore often differ from person to person. One person might have an ulterior interest in achieving goals like building a house, or solving a scientific problem. Another will have an ulterior interest satisfied if he or she advances a social cause or successfully raises a family. When these ulterior interests are set back, those with the interests are harmed. When neither your welfare interests nor your ulterior interests are thwarted, or set back, your life goes well. However, as our focus is on the question of how the state can legitimately justify which kinds of conduct ought to be criminalized, it is important to note that, according to Feinberg, it is primarily *welfare interests* that are, and should be, protected by the law.[32] Ulterior interests, such as having an interest in making an important scientific discovery, should not, for the most part, be directly protected by the law. They should be protected, at most, indirectly, as it is the task of the law to protect welfare interests that are essential to making an important scientific discovery (say, a minimal income and good health).

In what follows, then, we shall concentrate on the objective part of Feinberg's theory of well-being, the part involving welfare interests of the sort specified above.

---

[29] Adherents of an offence principle of criminalization sometimes use other words when they define harm. As Tasioulas (2006), p. 166 has remarked, it is not convincing when Simester and von Hirsch (2002), p. 288 claim that harming a person results in the diminution of that person's cognitive or evaluative powers. Semantically, and in terms of common sense, it seems right to claim that you can be harmed without having your 'cognitive or evaluative powers diminished'. Thus, as a counter-example, it seems to be true that I can be harmed by being declared bankrupt without any of my cognitive and evaluative powers being diminished. In fact, my evaluative powers may be increased by the personal insight into bankruptcy I gain, just as some of my cognitive powers such as memory and concentration may be enhanced by this experience.

[30] Feinberg (1984), p. 37. Compare ibid. p. 42, where Feinberg explicitly states that welfare interests are not framed within the terminology of a desire-satisfaction theory: 'but in respect ... to welfare interests, we are inclined to say that what promotes them is good for a person in any case, whatever his beliefs or wants may be.'

[31] Feinberg (1984), p. 37.

[32] Feinberg (1984), pp. 61–62.

As we shall see, there are at least four problems with Feinberg's use of the objective list theory to ground the offense principle. First, although we are presented with an objective list theory, it remains unconvincing that offensiveness should be characterized as something different from harm if we follow Feinberg's characterization of 'welfare interests'. At face value, it seems that causing offense by, for example, causing another wounded pride, hurt feelings, aroused anger, shocked sensibility, embarrassment, or feelings of guilt and shame *does* block or damage some welfare interests (e.g. 'emotional stability' or 'a tolerable social and physical environment'), at least, if the feelings are experienced intensely or at untimely moments. Remember the bus ride described above, or the insult felt by many Muslims at the publication of the infamous Danish cartoons of Mohammed.

Second, when reading Feinberg it is difficult to get a clear sense of how one should draw the line between causing offense, on the one hand, and harm that sets back welfare interests, on the other. Feinberg's idea is that offense constitutes harm when it is experienced *intensely*, or for a *long time*, or *recurs continuously*, or *occurs at strategically untimely moments*.[33] So, there seems to be a continuum running between cases of offense and cases of harm. At each end of the continuum, matters are pretty clear: at one end, offense is harmless; at the other, we have clearly harmful acts. However, between these clear-cut cases there is a grey area where it is not at all obvious whether causing offense to someone is also harmful. Given this, and following Feinberg, whether an act that causes offense also harms an individual is difficult to know. It is a matter of its intensity, duration, continuation, or occurrence at strategically untimely moments. Illustrating one of these factors, Feinberg writes that physical pain *below* an intolerable level should be characterized as a case of causing offence, but *above* that level, when it becomes intolerable, the pain should be characterized as seriously offensive, or as 'harm'.[34] However, when does an experience of offense reach that level for the offended person? How much physical pain are we talking about? And when are your interests (e.g. in 'emotional stability') set back? Suppose a person feels emotionally unstable watching two gays kissing each other. Should that count as a setback of interests?[35] Is it enough for you to feel emotionally unstable for 1 h for this to count as a setback to that specific welfare interest? We know that whether welfare interests are set back is, in part, a matter of duration: feelings of offense 'come to us, are suffered for a time, and then go, leaving us as whole and undamaged as before'.[36] This suggests that when someone takes

[33]See, for example, Feinberg (1984), p. 46: 'if the unpleasant experiences are intense or prolonged enough, however, or if they recur continuously or occur at strategically untimely moments, they can get in the way of our [well-being] interests.'

[34]Feinberg (1984), p. 46.

[35]We should, of course, always keep in mind that two conditions need to be satisfied if we are to have a plausible justification for criminalizing an act, according to Feinberg. First, the act must set back a person's interests (or, alternatively, cause serious offence to someone). Second, it must be a morally wrongful act. For now, however, we are trying to establish when an act causes harm or offence, not when it is wrongful.

[36]Feinberg (1984), p. 45.

offense at something for a long time, as happens when a person's experience of an insult or embarrassment darkens several months of his or her life, that should certainly count as a kind of harm. But again, for how long must you suffer from feelings caused by a wrongful offence for those feelings to be categorized as harm? Feinberg and his supporters are virtually silent on these issues. These shortcomings make it very difficult to know when taking offense turns into a serious taking of offense or being harmed.

Third, even if we could make a sharp distinction between causing offense and harming, e.g. by estimating the intensity and duration of different kinds of offense, we would still be left with a certain tension in Feinberg's use of the phrase 'serious offense'. Serious feelings of offense (i.e. those that are intense and prolonged) have two incompatible-looking properties. As we have just seen, they seem to be *no different* from harm; but at the same time, according to the wording of the offense principle, these unpleasant feelings *differ* from harm. This tension leaves us with a least two options: either we accept that the offence principle is a subpart of the harm principle, or we accept that the offense principle should be reformulated so that it encompasses only those acts we have a reason to criminalize as cases causing *non-serious feelings of offense*. However, it is clear that Feinberg cannot take either of these options. To opt for the first would be to make the offense principle no different from the harm principle, and to opt for the second would be to endorse a variant of the offence principle implying that there is a reason to criminalize forms of conduct causing mild (non-serious) offense. Acceptance that the offense principle is a subpart of the harm principle would be taxonomically problematic for its adherents, all of whom claim that the two principles are distinct. It would also be practically problematic, because supporters of the offense principle believe that it and the harm principle provide different reasons for criminalization. Again, it would be inconsistent with the liberal outlook of Feinberg, Simester and von Hirsch to accept that acts causing minor offence should be prohibited by law.[37] Alternatively, supporters of the offence principle could then argue that we should distinguish between serious offence that is also harmful and serious offense that is not harmful. However, this would be to use a vocabulary that is, as it were, 'messy'. It involves a considerable step away from the standard description of the distinction, used by Feinberg, as that between 'mere offense and 'serious offense.[38]

Finally, in order to distinguish causing offence from causing harm, those who advocate the offence principle and base their theory of harm on an objective list

[37]See, for example, Feinberg (1985), p. 49; Simester and von Hirsch (2011), p. 118.

[38]See, for example, Feinberg (1985), p. 25. This distinction should not be conflated with what Feinberg calls 'mere nuisance offenses' and 'profound offenses' (1985), pp. 57–60. The former involve personally disliked repulsive sensory stimuli which individuals experience and from which they may have a right to be free. In the latter, unpleasant states are caused not by the experience of disliked repulsive sensory stimuli, but rather by an affront to a higher-order moral sensibility from which people do not have a right to be free. So, for example, a mere nuisance offence can be a serious offense or a mere offense; it depends on, among other things, the intensity and duration of the mere nuisance offence in question and the number of people who are subjected to it.

theory of well-being should at least defend their theory of well-being against common objections to the objective list approach.[39] As they do not do so, their theory of setbacks to interests can seem to invoke an *ad hoc* theory of well-being designed to support the existence of the offence principle as an independent principle of criminalization. There are, it would seem, at least two important complaints about objective list theories of well-being that Feinberg, Simester and von Hirsch fail to address. First, it seems obvious that you are the primary authority on whether your life is going well for you, at least, if you are a well-informed and rational human being. Think of the opposite: that others are better equipped to make that kind of evaluation. This is an implication of at least some objective list theories, including the one endorsed by Feinberg. However, put simply, the tendency of Feinberg's and Simester and von Hirsch's objective list theories to exclude all reference to the subject's own evaluations of, or attitudes to, how well off they are is, to say the least, unattractive.[40]

Second, your life could, according to your-self, be full of joy and happiness even though it contains a setback to one of the items on the objective list. You could, to take one of the examples on Feinberg's list, be emotionally unstable, and that would count as a setback of your interests. However, are you always harmed when you are emotionally unstable? Let us say that when you are emotionally unstable, you are sometimes ecstatically happy and at other times a lot happier than you are when you are emotionally stable. If that were so, it would sound odd to suggest that you are being harmed just because one of your welfare interests—the interest in emotional stability—is not satisfied. Surely, if you believe that you are very happy, and that you are far better off in your life overall than you would be if you were emotionally stable, then emotional stability should not be of much importance for you.[41]

In sum, whether the distinction between harm and offense can be sustained in a plausible form depends on the theory of well-being in play. As we have seen, the theory of well-being that has been used to support this distinction is very special indeed (bear in mind that pleasurable experiences and desire satisfaction should not be allowed on the list, because if they were, then taking offence could easily be identified with harm).[42] Moreover, as has been argued, the theory is problematic for several other reasons. The points made in this section suggest that the offense principle should be interpreted as a subpart of a harm principle. However, we should note that the conclusions reached so far would not necessarily render the offense

[39]See, for example, Sumner (1996), pp. 42–44.

[40]As we have seen, however, Feinberg has room in his theory of well-being for subjective attitudes, because he believes that the satisfaction of the so-called ulterior interests is important for your well-being. When it comes to 'well-being interests', however, Feinberg's theory is purely objective.

[41]Objective list theories are defended in, for example, Sen (1999) and Moore (2000). For criticism, see Sumner (1996). For a critique, in turn, of Sumner's own theory of well-being, see the Appendix of this book.

[42]But (and this is a further problem for Feinberg), as the avoidance of suffering, for example, is on the list, and as offence can cause suffering, the difference between offence and harm as setbacks to interests is blurred.

principle useless. Even if one advocates a harm principle in an exclusive way—holding that it is the only principle we need to guide policy on which types of act ought to be criminalized—the offense principle could function under the umbrella of a harm principle. As Paul Roberts has suggested, the offense principle can be used under the umbrella of a harm principle to point out *specific forms of minor harm* that we should take less seriously in the discussion of what to criminalize and to separate these minor harms from severe harms.[43]

3.5 Conclusion

In this chapter it has been argued that, unless a rather special and implausible objective list theory of well-being is accepted, the offense principle should be subsumed within a harm principle. If we accept this, and if, furthermore, we endorse the reasoning in Chap. 2, this means not only that offense principles are redundant to harm principles (which again are redundant to grand moral theory), but also that offense principles too are redundant to grand moral theory. Again, the analysis in this chapter points in the direction of the conclusion that, in order for the state and its citizens to justify what kinds of conduct ought to be criminalized, it is necessary to refer to grand moral theory.

We shall turn to a critical discussion of such moral principles in Chaps. 5 and 6, where the subject of our investigation will be versions of dignity principles of criminalization and a utilitarian principle of criminalization. In what follows, however, in Chap. 4, we shall discuss versions of legal moralism, which have in common, or so it will be argued, that harm or offense is not all that should matter when the state tries to justify which kinds of conduct it ought to criminalize.

References

Bradley B (2009) Well-being and death. Oxford University Press, Oxford

Bradley B (2012) Doing away with harm. Philos Phenomenol Res 85(2):390–412

Duff A (2014) Towards a modest legal moralism. Crim Law Philos 8(1):217–235

Feinberg J (1984) Harm to others. Oxford University Press, Oxford

Feinberg J (1985) Offense to others. Oxford University Press, Oxford

Feinberg J (1986) Harm to Self. Oxford University Press, Oxford

Feldman F (2004) Pleasure and the good life. Oxford University Press, Oxford

Feldman F (2010) What is this thing called happiness? Oxford University Press, Oxford

Griffin J (1986) Well-being: its meaning, measurement and moral importance. Clarendon Press, Oxford

Husak D (2006) Disgust: metaphysical and empirical speculations. In: von Hirsch A, Simester AP (eds) Incivilities: regulating offensive behaviour. Hart Publishing, London, pp 91–113

[43]Roberts (2006), p. 23.

Kagan S (1998) Normative ethics. Westview Press, Boulder
Lippert-Rasmusssen K (2005) Deontology, responsibility, and equality. Museum Tusculanum Press, Copenhagen
McKinnon C (2006) Toleration: a critical introduction. Routledge, Abingdon
Mill JS (2003/1859) On liberty. In: Warnock M (ed) Utilitarianism and on liberty. Blackwell Publishing, New Jersey
Moore A (2000) Objective human goods. In: Hooker B, Crisp R (eds) Well-being and morality: essays in honour of James Griffin. Clarendon Press, Oxford, pp 75–89
Norcross A (2005) Harming in context. Philos Stud 123(1):149–173
Parfit D (1984) Reasons and persons. Oxford University Press, Oxford
Raz J (1986) The morality of freedom. Oxford University Press, Oxford
Roberts P (2006) Penal offence in question: some reference points for interdisciplinary conversation. In: von Hirsch A, Simester AP (eds) Incivilities: regulating offensive behaviour. Hart Publishing, Oxford, pp 1–56
Sen A (1999) On ethics and economics. Oxford University Press, Oxford
Simester AP, von Hirsch A (2002) Rethinking the offense principle. Legal Theory 8(3):269–295
Simester AP, von Hirsch A (2006) Regulating offensive conduct through two-step prohibitions. In: Hirsch A, Simester AP (eds) Incivilities: regulating offensive behaviour. Hart Publishing, Oxford, pp 173–194
Simester AP, von Hirsch A (2011) Crimes, harms and wrongs: on the principles of criminalisation. Hart Publishing, Oxford
Sumner LW (1996) Welfare, happiness and ethics. Oxford University Press, Oxford
Tadros V (2011) The ends of harm: the moral foundations of criminal law. Oxford University Press, Oxford
Tasioulas J (2006) Crimes of offense. In: von Hirsch A, Simester AP (eds) Incivilities: regulating offensive behaviour. Hart Publishing, Oxford, pp 149–171
Thomson JJ (1986) Feinberg on harm, offense, and the criminal law. Philos Public Aff 15 (4):381–395

Chapter 4
New Legal Moralism: Some Strengths and Challenges

4.1 Introduction

That murder, rape and child abuse are forms of conduct that ought to be and usually are criminalized, around the world, is unlikely to be disputed. It is also obvious that one of the central justifications for criminalizing these kinds of conduct is that they harm the victims in a morally problematic way and/or that the state, by criminalizing such types of conduct, will help to prevent or decrease the occurrence of such harmful and morally wrong conduct. However, it is in no way easy to answer the more general question: when the state justifies its position that certain kinds of conduct C ought to be (or remain) a criminal offense, is the relevant kind of harm then a necessary condition of the criminalization of C? In Chap. 2, we critically discussed, among other things, affirmative answers to this question implied by versions of the harm principle. In Chap. 3, we critically discussed a negative answer to the question. We examined versions of the offence principle, according to which reference to harm is not a necessary reason for criminalization decisions, because the prevention of people taking offense can also stand alone as a reason for criminalization. However, as the principles discussed in these chapters, were under serious attack it seems wise to turn our search for a plausible principle of criminalization in another direction.

In this chapter, we shall therefore turn to a class of principles that goes under the umbrella of 'legal moralism'.[1] By its mere name, or at least by using another label, adherents of legal moralism distance themselves from adherents of other principles of criminalization, like the proponents of harm principles and offense principles. This change of label indicates that harm or offense, do not need to figure in justification of the criminalization of a kind of conduct C. Therefore, legal moralists

[1]Hart (1963), p. 6 was the first to use the term 'legal moralism'. Explicit defenders of legal moralism in modern literature on philosophy of law include Stephen (1874), Devlin (1963), Finnis (1980), George (1993), Moore (1997), Dworkin (1999), Kekes (2000) and Duff (2018).

T. Søbirk Petersen, *Why Criminalize?*, Law and Philosophy Library 134,
https://doi.org/10.1007/978-3-030-34690-4_4

will typically answer the above-mentioned normative question in the negative. However, what in more precise terms is legal moralism? What characterizes it, apart from the claim that this class of criminalization principles differ from harm and offense principles in claiming, for example, that harm is not a necessary condition for criminalization? Antony Duff, writes that legal moralism picks out a family of views where 'the justification for criminalizing a given type of conduct depends on the moral wrongfulness of that type of conduct ....'[2] In a similar vein, Victor Tadros writes: 'Very roughly, legal moralism is the view that there is an important connection between moral wrongdoing and criminal wrongdoing.'[3] These initial formulations do not make us much wiser. However, it is obvious, also for scholars like Duff and Tadros that the connection between criminalization and moral wrongfulness, as we shall see in what follows, can be of quite different kinds, and that some of these connections at least make it clear that legal moralism differs from harm and offence principles.

The aim of Sect. 4.2 is to distinguish and analytically discuss some important variations in the ways in which legal moralism is described in the literature. As such, the aim of Sect. 4.2 is not to evaluate the most plausible versions of legal moralism, although some of the most implausible versions of legal moralism will be criticized along the way as we clarify what legal moralists have in common. The normative evaluation of legal moralism is at the centre of Sects. 4.3 and 4.4. However, if we want progress in the normative discussion of principles of criminalization, a vital preliminary task is to identify clearly, what type of principle is under discussion. In Sect. 4.2, I critically examine some of the key understandings that, unfortunately, have not always been carefully distinguished and I propose a specification that I hope will provide more clarity about what characterizes legal moralism.

Section 4.3, begins by reconstructing an argument for legal moralism presented by one of the leading modern figures associated with the position, Patrick Devlin, and gives examples of how it has been critiqued in the literature. I want to demonstrate that Devlin's position is vulnerable to two challenges. In brief the first, which I call '*the challenge from relativism*', alleges: Devlin's position suggests that the state should enforce the shared morality, no matter how evil that morality is. The second, which I call '*the empirical challenge*', alleges: Devlin's position suggests that a legalization of certain aspects of the shared morality of a society (e.g. laws against abortion and euthanasia) will bring about social disintegration. However, I also show that Devlin, contrary to what, for example, Feinberg and Duff argue, can rebut the no difference challenge, which says that there is *no difference* between legal moralism and harm principles such as Mill's harm principle. Section 4.3 does not introduce any significant innovations to the well-known Devlin-Hart debate, apart from the discussion on the no-difference challenge. It does, however, spell out some of the important problems with Devlin's view.

[2]Duff (2018), p. 53.

[3]Tadros (2016), p. 169.

Nevertheless, this critique of Devlin, is important in order to defend the thesis, presented in Sect. 4.4, that a new generation of legal moralists, including some recent and central adherents of legal moralism such as Robert P. George, Michael Moore, John Kekes and Antony Duff are immune to at least some of the criticism of Devlin. Section 4.4 (and its subsections) also points out some new challenges—what I call *the criminological levelling-down challenge* and *the weighing challenge*—that confront this new generation of legal moralists (as well as Devlin).

Although Devlin's version of legal moralism has been scrutinized thoroughly in the literature on criminalization theory, there has been very little systematic, detailed and comparable critique made of each of the proponents of legal moralism.[4] This is surprising for several reasons. Legal moralism is usually mentioned in the literature as one of the principles or class of principles, (together with, for example, versions of the harm principle and the offence principle), that citizens or the state, can adhere to when they are trying to justify what kinds of conduct ought to remain criminal or be criminalized by the state.[5] Further, in practice, the criminalization of specific kinds of conduct is sometimes justified by arguments drawing on legal moralism. Recent instances of this are the ban on the commercial distribution of sex toys in Alabama[6] and the continued refusal to legally permit homosexuality in some countries, such as Saudi Arabia and Iran. If, however, legal moralism can be shown to be challenged, it follows that any laws allegedly justified by it are also subject to challenge. Such laws might, of course, be reasonable. Nevertheless, reasons will exist either to look for justifications other than those given by what is unique to legal moralism (as compared with other competing theories of criminalization), or to force legal moralists to defend their theories in the face of the challenges presented in this chapter and elsewhere.

4.2 What Is Legal Moralism?

However, what is legal moralism? It is impossible within the scope of a book chapter to deal with all the logical possibilities of how principles of criminalization can be connected to moral wrongfulness. Instead, I focus on four descriptions frequently mentioned in the literature. Thereafter, I propose a fifth description that I believe captures the overall structure of the many variants of legal moralism, while also providing more clarity. First, according to Arthur Kuflik, 'legal moralism (at least in its purest or most extreme form) is the view that what is morally required ought to be

[4]The few exemptions are Duff (2018), Chap. 2, Thaysen (2015) and Petersen (2010, 2011).

[5]Compare e.g. Stranton-Ife (2006).

[6]Several arguments in the debate about the limits of the criminal law were in line with legal moralism; for example, the Rev. Dan Ireland stated: 'Dildos and other sex toys are a nuisance and they certainly are conductive for promiscuity and loose morals'; the three-judge panel of the US 11th circuit Court of Appeal declared that 'the crafting and safeguarding of public morality has long been an established part of the States' plenary police power to legislate.' See Kahn (2006).

legally required: law's proper function is to enforce morality as such.'[7] One interpretation of this amounts to the following specification:

(a) If conduct of type C is immoral, then the state *ought to* criminalize C.

It is obvious that this specification makes it too easy to reject legal moralism from a moral point of view. Undoubtedly, it would be immoral to let the state transcribe into the legal code all aspects of what morality requires us to do. First, it would be prohibitively costly, from an economic point of view, to enforce the punishment of every immoral type of conduct, no matter how insignificant the immorality is. It might be so costly that the state could not afford to live up to the responsibility of providing higher-priority goods such as public healthcare, social security, military defence, etc. Second, if (a) in itself is an immoral principle, and people follow the immoral content of (a), the people who act according to (a) should be criminalized! So in one sense (a) is self-defeating—it is a principle about what to criminalize, but those who follow the principle ought to be criminalized as immoral conduct follow from the application of (a). Third, it would obviously be too costly when it comes to personal autonomy and well-being if the state should enforce the illegality of every immorality, no matter how small. However, it comes as no surprise that adherents of legal moralism who accept this specification appear to be non-existent. For example, several of the leading proponents of legal moralism, like Patrick Devlin and Anthony Duff, make the explicit claim that not all types of immoral acts ought to be criminalized.[8] However, since 'legal moralism' is sometimes described as in (a) it seems appropriate to mention and challenge it.

In order to get an initial overview of the many different versions of legal moralism, we can, make a distinction between positive legal moralism and negative legal moralism. Positive legal moralists maintain that the moral wrongfulness of conduct C gives the state a positive reason to favour the criminalization of C—as stated, for example, in specification (a).[9] Negative legal moralists hold that the state must not criminalize conduct unless these are morally wrongful. Let us specify and discuss versions of legal moralism that differ according to this distinction in turn. First, negative legal moralism can be formulated as follows:

(b) If conduct of type C is not immoral, then the state *ought not to* criminalize C.

However, according to Duff, this version of negative legal moralism does not differ from the harm principle or offense principle of modern adherents like Feinberg, Simester and von Hirsch. This is because these adherents acknowledge that if C is not harmful (or involves 'offence'), in a morally wrong way, then the state ought not to prevent C through the criminalization of C.[10] Duff's observation only

[7]Kuflik (2005), p. 185.

[8]See e.g. Devlin (1963), pp. 16–17 and Duff (2018), p. 74.

[9]Specification (a) is a positive version of moral legalism, in the sense that the immorality of C provides a positive reason for the criminalization of C.

[10]Duff (2018), p. 56.

works if we believe that these theories do not differ on a structural level. However, when we give more detailed content to different versions of legal moralism there is, of course, room for the possibility, (to be investigated below from Sect. 4.3 onwards) that versions of legal moralism differ from versions of, for example, harm principles. This happens when adherents of legal moralism and harm principles differ according to which kinds of immoral conduct ought to be criminalized by the state.

Therefore, the problem with (b) is that it does not separate legal moralism as a principle of criminalization that is structurally distinct from central versions of harm and offense principles. However, the same seems, at least at first sight, to be true of a description of the positive legal moralism formulated by Carl Cranor, who writes, 'the immorality of a particular form of conduct provides a reason, but not a sufficient reason for making it illegal.'[11] This view can be stated as follows:

(c) If conduct of type C is immoral, then the state has *a reason* to criminalize C.[12]

However, the problem with this specification is again obvious. Like (b) it lacks distinctiveness from other principles like harm principles and offence principles. To see this, let us begin with the observation that theoretical or practical justifications for making certain kinds of conduct criminal are usually based on the belief that these actions are immoral—either in themselves (*mala in se*) or indirectly (*mala prohibita*). However, if this is true, it is not obvious that we can distinguish legal moralism from other theories of criminalization. For instance, (c) is not necessarily distinguishable from possible versions of harm principles and offense principles.[13] For if immoral harming or 'offense' (to oneself and others) or the prevention thereof are considered to be the only reasons for criminalization, then the difference between legal moralism and most harm principles and offense principles evaporates. However, if one believes in the existence of harmless or offense-free immoralities, and that these immoralities could be used as a reason for criminalization, there is a difference between (c) and for example the harm principle. But then specification (c) should be reformulated to distinguish legal moralism from harm principles (or offense principles) by making it explicit that harm (or taking offense) is not all that matters in criminalization decisions. One could argue, for example, that a kind of conduct C can be immoral, apart from the harm it may do to individuals or that even if C is not harmful at all, there could still be a reason for the criminalization of C.

[11]Cranor (1978), p. 147. For formulations and adherents of legal moralism like the one in (b), see for example Dixon (2007), p. 325.

[12]This specification, like all the others, fits under the umbrella of Duff's and Tadros's initial specification of legal moralism that was presented in the introduction of this chapter. Following Cranor's words, when he claims that the immorality of a conduct does not provide sufficient reason for criminalization, there is also room for the interpretation that immorality provides a necessary reason for criminalization. I will say a little bit about this interpretation in the paragraphs to come.

[13]That (c) is different from Mill's version of the harm principle is obvious, as the harm principle states a necessary reason for criminalization. However, (c) is not different from Feinberg's version of the harm principles as harm is only one reason for criminalization—taking offense is another reason for criminalization according to Feinberg.

Furthermore, (c) seems right in the trivial sense that most theories of criminalization would claim that we only have a reason to criminalize conduct that is immoral, either directly or indirectly. This, however, is clearly distinct from the views of leading legal moralists like Duff, who believe that the state only has reason to criminalize some moral wrongs—namely, public wrongs (like murder and violent attacks) and not private wrongs (like adultery).[14]

However, adherents of (c) and Duff may not differ according to what ends up being criminalized, as it follows from (c) that just because we have a reason to criminalize all types of immoral acts, this does not mean that all these types of acts ought to be criminalized. In the end, both Duff and adherents of (c) believe that the state should only criminalize certain types of immorality. In addition, with this in mind, (c) and Duff's versions of legal moralism are, at least in one sense, trivial in that all theories of criminalization would accept it. Who would argue for the opposite of (c), that we have a reason to criminalize a type of conduct C that, all things considered, is morally right?[15] In sum, specification (c) is not necessarily different from harm principles unless you add to the specification that harmless immoralities can be used as an independent reason for criminalization. Furthermore, (c) is trivial and general in a sense that makes (c) useless in our efforts to clarify what is unique for legal moralism compared to other theories of criminalization.[16]

In the criminal justice literature, however, the label 'legal moralism' is also used in a way that makes clearer the difference between it and, for example, harm principles. For instance, Michael Moore writes that, 'the legal moralist theorist will think that … to prevent behaviour that harms no one but that is nonetheless morally wrong … is proper together with whatever … that morality speaks to prohibit.'[17] Elsewhere he adds, 'the immorality of behaviour, on this theory [legal moralism], will be a sufficient condition with which to justify criminal legislation.'[18] Jeff Murphy relates these descriptions to one another when he writes, 'the legal moralist maintains that criminal sanctions are demanded even when no obvious harm to others occurs. The intrinsic heinousness of sexual deviation, for example, is

[14]Duff (2018), pp. 52–79. A specification of Duff's understanding of a public wrongs will be specified in Sect. 4.4.4.

[15]Remember that (c) only claims that the immorality of C gives the state one reason (among other possible reasons) for criminalization. Furthermore, Tadros (2016) argues that this version of legal moralism is not trivial, and that there are cases where we have good reasons to criminalize morally right acts, e.g. hopping, if preventing hopping would prevent the world from becoming extinct. However, this is not a convincing critique of legal moralism, as it could be argued that hopping, in these conditions, is actually morally wrong even though hopping is not morally wrong if seen in isolation. See Duff (2018), p. 323 for a critique of Tadros in this regard.

[16]In addition, the same kind of critical reasoning can be applied if immorality, according to legal moralists, is not only *a good reason* for criminalization, but instead *a necessary reason* for criminalization.

[17]Moore (1997), pp. 68–69.

[18]Ibid., p. 645.

sufficient to justify its prohibition by statute.'[19] The meaning of these statements can be captured in the following specification of a version of positive legal moralism:

(d) If conduct of type C is immoral, then the state has *sufficient reason* to criminalize C even though C-type conduct does not cause (or risk causing) someone to be harmed.[20]

However, the claim that harmless immoralities are a sufficient reason to place criminal restrictions on conduct seems to have morally wrong implications. For if (d) were right, it would follow that if an act can be described as an instance of a harmless immorality, then it would have to be criminal. However, if one accepts the existence of acts that involve harmless immoralities, one should also accept that some of these acts need not be made criminal.[21] Consider the following example. An American tourist asks me the way to the airport and I reply in Danish with a smile '*Hold kæft og skrid*' which means 'Shut up and get lost.' Assume, further, that I did not know the way to the airport and was not harmed by the action, and that the tourist, who does not understand Danish, was not harmed by my action either.[22]

Nevertheless, some would probably consider this an immoral act—assuming, of course, that I was not mentally disturbed or otherwise out of control. However, although you may consider my answer to the tourist immoral and in this instance harmless, few would claim that such an act should be made criminal.[23] A more plausible description of legal moralism, then, seems to be:

(e) If conduct of type C belongs to a certain class of immoral types of conducts C$*$, then the state has, all things considered, sufficient reason to criminalize C even though C-type conduct does not cause (or risk causing) someone to be harmed.[24]

---

[19]Murphy (1966), p. 51.

[20]See, for example, Feinberg (1988), p. 5, who would also add 'even though it causes neither harm nor offense'. See also Tebbit (2000), p. 122. Feinberg (1988), pp. 4–8, who does not endorse legal moralism, also calls this version '*pure legal moralism*' in contrast to *impure* versions. The former version implies that the immoralities in question are morally wrong in themselves (without any reference to harm or offence) and therefore, all things considered, can be criminalized by law. The latter version relies on a harm principle, in the end, as the so-called 'immoralities' should be made (or remain) criminal because this reduces the amount of harm people in society will experience.

[21]See e.g. Duff (2018), Chap. 2.

[22]This kind of critique, from what not to criminalize, has also been presented in the discussion of specification (a). However, specifications (a) and (d) are different, as e.g. (b) specifies that a kind of conduct C can be morally wrong and ought to be criminalized even if C is not harmful.

[23]As mentioned in the discussion of (a), if we had laws for every immoral act, it would, from both an economic and a moral perspective, be problematic to enforce them. It would be too expensive; the money could probably be better spent elsewhere; almost everybody in a society would be criminalized, and enforcement of the law would usually violate people's privacy and autonomy and therefore also decrease their well-being.

[24]This specification is equivalent to the idea that immorality of a type of harmless conduct C *is pro tanto sufficient* for criminalization. See e.g. Thaysen (2015) for the view that these formulations are closely connected.

With this change of description, it does not follow from legal moralism that my reply to the tourist (or similar types of allegedly immoral conduct) should be criminalized. It does not follow, because although we accept that my conduct is immoral, that conduct does not belong to the class of immoralities that legal moralists want to criminalize. So, whether or not a kind of immoral conduct should be criminalized depends on several details within the machinery of each version of legal moralism; for instance, the kinds of immoralities that the state has sufficient reason to criminalize even if these immoralities do not harm or cause offence to anyone. In addition, this explains the 'all things considered' clause—whether the reason to criminalize the immoralities in question can be outweighed by other reasons. For example, when the immorality of conduct C is compared with the cost of other values like econommic values and the value of privacy, or of any harm that could follow from the criminalization of C, should C then be criminalized? Bear in mind that, as far as I know, no legal moralist would claim that other costs, such as harm to citizens, should *not* matter in the justification of which kinds of conduct should be criminalized or in what kinds of conduct the state should try to prevent through criminalization.

Therefore, we should be aware that specification (e), as is the case with the other four specifications, only indicates something about the plausible *structure* of legal moralism. However, legal moralism does not, as we have seen in this chapter so far, only differ when it comes to structure. When it comes to the *content* of the theory, it is obvious that adherents of legal moralism differ among themselves, as well as differing externally from other classes of criminalization principles. Moreover, what makes them differ from one another depends on what kinds of harmless conduct C are immoral and when C should be criminalized. For example, if you are in favour of a so-called *critical* version of legal moralism, you believe that certain kinds of conduct are immoral independently of what the public believes is morally right or wrong.[25] However, if you are in favour of a *positivist* (not positive!) version of legal moralism, what is morally right or wrong depends on what the public believes on these matters. As Duff writes, 'a positivist legal moralist will ask whether ϕ-ing is thought to be wrong by members of this society—whether the prevailing social morality condemns it as wrongful . . .'[26] Furthermore, the legal moralist can point to any of several reasons, besides those referring to harm, when justifying which acts are immoral and ought to be considered criminal. As we discuss in detail in the next section, one reason is the preservation of social cohesion or conformity to

[25]For the distinction between critical and positivist versions of legal moralism, see Hart (1963) and Duff (2018), pp. 53–55.

[26]Duff (2018), p. 53.

a moral principle like respect for life.[27] Others include the perfection of human nature,[28] or the idea that we should only criminalize so-called public wrongs.[29] However, these reasons may be used to argue for the prohibition of many different acts. The legal moralist usually believes, for example, that regardless of the informed consent or harm of those involved, some conduct (e.g. pornography, cruelty to animals, mutilation of dead corpses or euthanasia) should be criminalized. In short, then, legal moralism can differ according to (i) what *kinds of conduct* are claimed to be immoral and (ii) what *reasons* are appealed to in explaining which immoral acts ought to be criminalized. These more detailed descriptions of versions of legal moralism and a critical discussion of them will be presented in more detail in Sect. 4.4 and its subsections.

Finally, although this is not stated explicitly in (e), adherents of legal moralism accept that the function of the criminal law is broader than, for example adherents of a harm principle. The claim is merely that harm is not a necessary factor in justifying what kinds of conduct ought to be made (or remain) criminal. From a logical point of view, it is possible for legal moralists to accept that harm is not a relevant factor in justifying which acts ought to be criminal. However, I here presuppose that the harm, or the risk of harm, that an action of type C visits on individuals (or the harm that can be prevented or decrease by the criminalization of C) cannot be neglected and must provide a plausible reason for making conduct C criminal. I therefore assume that any plausible version of legal moralism will necessarily entail that harm and harm prevention matter in deciding which acts should be made criminal. In actual fact, I have not seen any work by a legal moralist (or any other normative theorist) that denies this.

Any plausible version of legal moralism will, then, be pluralistic, in the sense of allowing that harm to individuals (i.e. making individuals worse off in terms of well-being) or the prevention of harm to individuals and some other kinds of immorality can justify the criminalization of an act.[30] In the next section and subsections, we shall turn our attention to a critical discussion of versions of legal moralism which apart from some interpretations, fit the structure of our specification (e).

[27] Devlin (1963).

[28] George (1992).

[29] Duff (2018), pp. 75–79.

[30] Without mentioning the word ‘pluralism’, Moore makes the pluralistic nature of legal moralism clear, see e.g. Moore (1997), pp. 69–70. Duff makes such pluralism explicit when he defends his version of legal moralism, see e.g. Duff (2018), p. 272. If this is true, all versions of LM are also theoretical redundant (at least partly, when it comes to harm) to grand moral theory. However, in what follows I will primarily focus on a critique of the non-harm dimension of legal moralism.

4.3 A Critique of Devlin's Legal Moralism

In the following, I begin by briefly describing Devlin's central argument for legal moralism. Next, I describe key aspects of Hart's and others' review of Devlin's argumentation and I attempt to show when this critique is not always fair to Devlin. The Devlin-Hart debate has been described and commented upon many times in the philosophical literature.[31] My purpose in returning to it is to set out a background that makes it clearer whether contemporary legal moralists have been successful in formulating versions of legal moralism that are undamaged by the standard challenges directed at Devlin. A critical discussion of legal moralism beyond the Devlin-Hart debate is provided in Sect. 4.4 and its subsections, where the writings of George, Kekes, Moore and Duff, all of whom have recently defended legal moralism or what they understand to be legal moralism, are discussed in turn.

Developed over many pages, Devlin's argument for legal moralism is not easy to follow.[32] This leaves ample room for interpretative variation concerning both the complexity of the argument and the exact content of its premises. As a result, I begin by trying to make explicit what I believe to be Devlin's central argument. In this presentation, his argument is termed 'the disintegration argument'. The following paragraph summarizes my explication of Devlin's central arguments for legal moralism.

The Disintegration Argument

P1: A society ought, by means of the law, to safeguard itself against disintegration.[33]

P2: The integration of society is based on '*shared ideas* on politics, morals and ethics'.[34] Without these, society will disintegrate.[35]

P3: Certain forms of immoral conduct (e.g. abortion, bigamy, bestiality, euthanasia, fornication, homosexuality, incest between brother and sister, sadism, suicide)[36] pose a threat to the shared ideas of morality and to the cohesion of society.[37]

---

[31]See, for instance, Tebbit (2000), Chap. 7, Häyry (1991), Feinberg (1984), George (1993), Chap. 2, and Kekes (2000).

[32]Devlin (1963), pp. 7–25.

[33]Ibid., pp. 11–13.

[34]Ibid., p. 10.

[35]Ibid., p. 13.

[36]Ibid., p. 7, see also p. 9: "... [monogamy] remains there because it is built into the house in which we live and could not be removed without bringing it down."

[37]Ibid., p. 13.

P4: The enforcement of shared moral ideas via the law is a necessary means of protecting society from disintegration.[38]

Conclusion: Therefore, a society ought, by means of the law, to enforce shared ideas on politics, morals and ethics, by prohibiting conduct (like those mentioned in P3) that poses a threat to the shared moral ideas of that society.

The conclusion is in line with the structure of legal moralism, as presented in specification (e), as the state does not have sufficient reason to criminalize all immoral conduct, but only some kinds of it. Moreover, this line of reasoning is in line with (e), because the state should criminalize the kinds of conduct mentioned by Devlin in P3 even though they are not harmful. Although this latter observation is not made explicit in the disintegration argument, we shall see that in the context of Devlin's overall view and criticism of Mill's harm principle, this is true. Devlin further supports his argument by pointing to the fact that the law as it is, and which we accept, has always regulated people's conduct in order to bolster the stability of society. However, as Hart and several others have made clear, Devlin's argument is not convincing.[39] A systematic evaluation of the above premises demonstrates why. Combined, premise 1 and premise 2 imply that the law ought to enforce *whatever* morality happens to be *shared* in a society.[40] However, it seems obvious that it may be morally good for a society to change its shared morality—and therefore to disintegrate and hopefully rise out of the ashes as something better. A clear example is Nazi Germany of the 1930s and 1940s. Let us accept, for instance, that some of the moral principles of the Nazi regime (e.g. the moral acceptance of anti-Jewish laws and ideas about the superiority of the so-called Arian race) were shared by a prevailing majority of the population, and inflicted monumental harm on minorities like Jews, homosexuals, gypsies and people with physical or mental handicaps. Hence, the shared morality of a society is not always worth defending. The laws used to secure and maintain the shared morality of Nazi Germany, for instance, like those mentioned above, ought to be condemned. We should instead do what we can to

[38]Ibid.

[39]See e.g. Hart (1963), Dworkin (1977), Cranor (1978), Häyry (1991), Murphy (2007) and Duff (2018).

[40]Devlin is not very clear about what it means that some moral principles are shared in a society. It cannot mean that all people in a society should accept (either implicitly or explicitly) these moral principles, as this seems too much to ask for when modern societies usually consists of millions of people, all representing a huge diversity of moral views. However, he seems to mean that if the majority of people accept a certain morality, then it is shared. When Devlin claims that the general morality within a society can be discovered by the reactions from 12 jury members or from the randomly chosen 'man in the Clapham omnibus', see Devlin (1963), p. 15, this points in the direction that what Devlin is talking about, is which moral views a majority (or representations thereof) of the population in a society would accept. However, whether Devil is right about what morality is shared depends on empirical evidence, but unfortunately he does not provides us with such.

disintegrate this kind of a society. Let me term this first challenge '*the challenge from relativism*'.[41]

Furthermore, some critics like Hart believe, with good reason, that premise 3 poses a problem of its own.[42] If Devlin were right about this premise, it would follow that countries like England, Denmark, Sweden, Norway and Finland, where abortion and homosexuality have been decriminalized for about 50 years, would have disintegrated. This is, of course, not true. England, Denmark, Sweden, Norway and Finland still exist as integrated societies, although they differ from the way they were before the legalization of these practices. This is also true for many other Western countries, which have undergone moral upheavals followed by the increased permissibility of, for example, same sex partnership and abortion, and so on. None of these societies has disintegrated, at least in the sense of involving a breakdown of law and order in which people cannot live at peace with each other. Furthermore, as Hart argues, 'though . . . essential universal values must be secured, society cannot only survive individual divergences in other fields from its prevalent morality but profit from them.'[43] Societies that are multicultural, and in which many cultural groups differ when it comes to, for example, sexual or reproductive morality may live peacefully together even though little shared morality exists about these aspects of life.

Devlin needs to offer evidence that these practices present dangers to societies that outweigh the benefits of a more liberal approach to abortion, euthanasia, homosexuality and the like. He does not supply evidence that deviations from a shared morality of sexuality, even by consenting adults in private, disintegrate society in the way, perhaps, that the legalization of treason, rebellion and murder would.

The second challenge is termed *'the empirical challenge'* because the assessment of whether premise 3 is plausible requires us to the gather empirical evidence on disintegration in the light of moral change. Moreover, from an empirical viewpoint Devlin does seem to be wrong when he claims that a society will disintegrate if, for example, abortion, euthanasia and homosexuality are legalized.

In defence of Devlin, one could argue that when, for example, the acceptance of abortion, euthanasia and homosexuality is part of the shared morality of a country, it

---

[41]Devlin could have responded to this kind of criticism by restating P1 as: '*If a society is worth preserving*, then we ought, by means of the law, to safeguard it against disintegration.' However, if this were the case, we would need a political theory telling us what kinds of societies are worth preserving and this is no easy task, and nothing that Devlin developed in any detail. Furthermore, even with this reformulation it seems to me that the challenge from relativism is still there. The challenge is still there, as the preservation of a society that is worth preserving, especially if the comparison is the breakdown of law and order of that society may stand in the way for obvious changes in a society, which could lead to the benefit of all or most citizens. So once again, disintegration may be morally right even for a society S that is worth preserving, if the disintegration of S is necessary for the development of another society that is even more worth preserving than S.

[42]Hart (1971), see also Dworkin (1965).

[43]Hart (1963), p. 71.

will not disintegrate when such acts are made legal. However, the empirical challenge does not disappear because of this possible change in shared values about, for example, homosexuality. In Poland and large parts of Eastern Europe, anti-homosexuality laws are proliferating, and these laws are supported by arguments that are close to the reasoning by Devlin. Arguments proposed by, for example, Jaroslaw Kaczynski, the leader of the Polish party Law and Justice, claim that homosexuality 'is a threat to our civilization, not only to Poland but also to Europe and for the civilization that is based on Christianity'.[44] So, even in countries where the population is divided on the moral issue of homosexuality, it seems difficult to believe that laws supporting homosexual rights, such as same sex partnerships, would destroy the civilization of Poland or Europe. At least, 'destroy' in the sense that law and order will break down, thus making it impossible to live a decent life in peace with each other. This is, of course, an empirical question, but therefore also one that is in need of scientific evidence. It is a question we should not answer through pure speculation and a few selective observations.

As a final critical remark, one can observe that Devlin is unclear about the role that harm plays in his version of legal moralism. So, at the end of the day, would Devlin, as Feinberg and others[45] have proposed, accept that there is *no difference* between Devlin's version of legal moralism and central versions of the harm principle? Remember that, according to one central version of the harm principle, the only plausible reason for the state criminalizing conduct of type C is that the criminalization of C will prevent harm to others (or prevent the risk of harming others). This challenge, which I term the *no difference challenge*, can be sensibly raised, because Devlin, in defending legal moralism, often writes as if his version of legal moralism were entirely based on a concern to prevent harm:

> I do not think that one can ignore disgust if it is deeply felt and not manufactured. Its presence is a good indication that the bounds of toleration are being reached . . . But before a society can put a practice beyond the limits of tolerance there must be a deliberate judgment that the practice is injurious to society.[46]

---

[44]The quote is from the Danish newspaper *Politiken* 10 April 2019.

[45]Feinberg (1988), p. 8, and Häyry (1991), George (1993), pp. 15–19, Husak (2008), p. 196 and Duff (2018), p. 54, who all argue that Devlin's theory is best conceived of as one special or idiosyncratic version of a harm principle.

[46]Devlin (1963), p. 17. This quote indicates that disgust towards a given practice is different from the harm such practices may inflict on society. However, if, as I take for granted, that deeply felt disgust is harmful to individuals, then deeply felt disgust is an instance of harm to society. Further, the words " . . . that the practice is injurious to society" can at first-sight be reduced to the harm each individual in the society is suffering. I mean how can a society be injured if none of its citizens were injured, this at least needs an explanation.

Here, Devlin seems to believe that acts considered immoral by society should only be prohibited by law if they cause harm (thus being injurious) to society.[47] If this is true, he has not replaced the harm principle with an alternative principle of criminalization, but simply argued in favour of a harm principle. The primary intention behind his book, *The Enforcement of Morals*, was to come up with an alternative to the harm principle proposed by Mill.[48] Thus, one interpretation of the quote above is that there is no difference between Devlin's version of legal moralism and Mill's harm principle. Feinberg claims that Devlin advocates *impure* legal moralism on just these grounds.[49] An impure legal moralist accepts, according to Feinberg, that the law should criminalize so-called immoralities in order to prevent harm. This means the legal prevention of immorality, through criminalization, functions as an instrument to prevent harm. *Pure legal moralism*, on the other hand, according to Feinberg, means that some acts are immoral independently of the harm (and offence) they may cause individuals and that such acts provide the state with a reason, sometimes a sufficient reason, in favour of the view that such acts ought to be criminalized.[50]

However, Feinberg's interpretation (and the similar one offered by Duff) is not obviously right. I believe confusion may have been caused by the fact that Devlin is sometimes unclear about whether immoralities should be restricted by the criminal law, because they are bad *in themselves* (or, alternatively, because a majority of citizens find them immoral), or because they *cause* harm, or both. Some of Devlin's lack of clarity in this respect can be illustrated if the remarks quoted above are compared to the parts of his text indicating that some immoralities are wrong in themselves, apart from the harm they cause. One example of this taken from Devlin is: 'Thus, if the criminal law were to be reformed so as to eliminate from it everything that was not designed to preserve order and decency or to protect citizens … it would overturn a fundamental principle.'[51] And that principle is, according to Devlin, *the sanctity of human life*.[52] Devlin does little to specify this principle, which is unfortunate, as it is not obvious how we should understand it, and therefore, how it should be applied to sort kinds of conduct that violate the principle. However, Devlin does present some examples of actions that would overturn the principle; he writes that 'euthanasia or the killing of another at his own request, suicide, abortion, incest

---

[47]Here, I take it for granted that 'harm or injury to society' can, in the final analysis, be reduced to the harm each individual in the society suffers. However, even if this is not true, and we accept that a society can be harmed even if none of its citizens is harmed, Devlin's theory of criminalization could be interpreted as an instance of a harm principle, although different from person-affecting versions of the harm principle such as Mill's.

[48]Ibid., p. 2. Devlin was explicitly questioning Mill's version of the harm principle.

[49]See Feinberg (1988), p. 8, where he specifies the distinction between pure and impure legal moralism.

[50]This specification of legal moralism by Feinberg is very close to definition (e).

[51]Devlin (1963), p. 7.

[52]Ibid., p. 6.

between brother and sister, are all acts which can be done in private and without harm to others and need not involve the corruption or exploitation of others.'[53]

Following Devlin, the immorality of these types of action seems to consist, not in the alleged fact that they can be harmful in themselves or lead to the disintegration of society, but instead in the fact, that they are wrong in themselves because they involve the violation of the sanctity of human life. In addition, they are morally wrong, whether or not that is believed by a majority of the public and whether or not they harm anyone. So, at least when it comes to the morality of the sanctity of human life, Devlin is not what Hart calls a positivist legal moralist, according to which the moral wrongness of a kind of conduct C in society S depends on whether C is considered morally wrong by the majority of members in S. Instead, Devlin accepts that the aforementioned moral principle dictates that the violation of this principle is morally wrong, independently of what members of society believe to be morally wrong or right. According to Hart's distinction between positive and critical legal moralism, Devlin is therefore, at least partly, a critical legal moralist.[54]

This chapter, however, does not delve deeply into the question of whether legal moralism based on the sanctity of human life is a plausible view.[55] First, Devlin's use of the principle is very brief and he does not say anything about the precise formulation and scope of the principle. Second, this principle is usually used to justify *only some of the acts* that legal moralists typically wish to prohibit. Clearly, the principle can be used as a justification for criminalizing kinds of conduct which involve wrongful killing, but it is less clear that it can be so used in connection with kinds of conduct that involves, for example, sex or stealing. For legal moralists and all other scholars, however, killing is not all that matters from a moral and legal viewpoint. Some legal moralists, like Devlin, are also concerned with the prohibition of actions such as bigamy, or reading, writing and selling pornography, or prostitution, and specific sexual acts like homosexual intercourse, premarital sex, masturbation and incest. Thus, at first glance this version of legal moralism, with its acceptance of the principle of the sanctity of human life, mitigates the challenge from relativism, since some acts are morally wrong no matter what morality is shared in society. A second glance reveals, however, that there is still room for this kind of challenge, because the action-guiding principle of the sanctity of human life does not cover all of the relevant actions. For example, although the principle implies that the element of Nazism that involved the killing of Jews was immoral, it does not account for many of the other morally corrupt behaviours that occurred during the Nazi regime (e.g. depriving Jews of their property and other rights like freedom of speech and religion). Here I take it for granted that we should not use (or abuse) the sanctity

[53]Ibid., p. 7. Here Devlin also writes that actions that violate the moral principle of the sanctity of human life 'can be brought within it [the law] only as a matter of moral principle'. This quote also indicates the idea that some actions are wrong in themselves.

[54]For Hart's distinction between critical and positivist legal moralism, see Hart (1963). For adherents of the same distinction, see also e.g. Duff (2018), p. 52.

[55]The literature on the specification and value of the sanctity of human life is vast; see e.g. Dworkin (1994) and Kuhse (1987).

of human life principle to cover every immoral act, whether it is done by the Nazis or other unscrupulous people.

If the no difference challenge to Devlin is unsound, as I have argued, we are left with a version of legal moralism that entails a moral principle of respect for the sanctity of human life. However, Devlin's justification for the proposition that harmless immoralities are relevant as reasons for criminalizing acts is not convincing. This is because, as has been demonstrated, either a moral principle is stipulated, and this does not cover all the acts that Devlin wishes to categorize as criminal, or a rationale is provided, but one that is connected to the argument from disintegration. Moreover, as shown, the latter appears unsound, because Devlin's version is damaged by the following two challenges: (i) *The challenge from relativism.* It is problematic that Devlin's position suggests that the state should enforce the shared morality, no matter how evil that morality is—apart, of course, from evils that violate the sanctity of human life principle. This is obviously morally wrong. (ii) *The empirical challenge.* Devlin's position suggests that legalization of certain aspects of the shared morality, or what is believed to be morally wrong in a society (e.g. abortion, euthanasia and homosexuality) will bring about social disintegration in the sense of the breakdown of law and order. This is obviously an empirical falsehood.

The next focus is on the second generation of legal moralists, all of whom (except Duff, as will be explained in Sect. 4.4.4) have formulated versions of legal moralism immune to both of the above-mentioned challenges to Devlin's legal moralism.

4.4 Legal Moralism Beyond Devlin: George, Moore, Kekes and Duff

In recent books and articles, Robert P. George, Michael Moore, John Kekes and Antony Duff have, along with others, defended distinctive varieties of legal moralism. In the next four subsections, the positions of this quartet of post-Devlin legal moralists are examined. In each case the examination begins with a brief description of the version of legal moralism in question, and then proceeds to ask whether this version of legal moralism is subject to the no-difference view and how it handles the two challenges to which we have seen Devlin's position is vulnerable. Furthermore, I want to introduce some new challenges for legal moralism, challenges that can be made to both Devlin and his successors. These new challenges, which I call *the criminological levelling-down challenge* (CLDC) and *the weighing challenge* (WEC), will be presented and discussed in detail in the subsection immediately below, where the focus is on George's legal moralism. In the remaining three subsections, the question to be asked will be whether all these challenges pose a threat to the theories of Moore, Kekes and Duff versions.

4.4.1 A Critical Discussion of George's Legal Moralism

George defends a version of legal moralism that, at least when it comes to the challenges discussed in Sect. 4.3, is more plausible than Devlin's, although some challenges do exist regarding George's version. First, one of the reasons George's version is more persuasive is that he accepts that Devlin is liable to what I termed 'the challenge from relativism' and ensures that his own position supplies an answer to this kind of challenge.[56] He argues that a concern for social cohesion *per se* is not sufficient grounds for enforcing morality by means of the criminal law.[57] On the other hand, a concern for social cohesion around a shared morality can justify the enforcement of morals, but *only* if that morality is *true*. Thus, according to George, only the disintegration of truly morally valuable practices is bad in itself. In that sense, George is an adherent of a version of critical legal moralism, and therefore not subject to the challenge from relativism.[58] What, then, is the right or true morality according to George? As a perfectionist, George believes that true morality (or truly moral behaviour) promotes or perfects basic human goods.[59] The following quotation explains what George believes these goods are:

> What are the basic human goods, that is, the ends or purposes that provide basic reasons for choice and action? John Finnis has usefully classified them as follows: life (in a broad sense that includes health and vitality); knowledge; play; aesthetic experiences; sociability (i.e. friendship broadly conceived); practical reasonableness; and religion... Thus, the complete human good—integral human well-being and fulfilment—is intrinsically variegated.[60]

According to George, these goods are most effectively promoted by virtuous people; I take it for granted that virtuous people would not promote a life according to the values of Nazism, for instance.

Concerning the *empirical challenge*, George's idea is that Hart's critique of premise 2 of Devlin's argument, which refers to social disintegration, is based on a misinterpretation of the word 'disintegration'. According to George, the misinterpretation occurs because people like Hart identify disintegration with the collapse or breakdown of society.[61] George states: 'I, however, take Devlin to be claiming that the price of toleration is the loss of a distinctive form of interpersonal integration in community understood as something worthwhile for its own sake ... regardless of

---

[56]George (1993), pp. 73–74.

[57]See e.g. ibid. pp. 71, 78.

[58]Bear in mind the distinction between critical and positivist versions of legal moralism in Sect. 4.2.

[59]Whether George's version of legal moralism is plausible depends, of course, also on the plausibility of his views that e.g., morality has truth-value and that moral perfectionism is the best normative moral theory. However, due to the confines of the relative shortness of this chapter, these meta-ethical and normative theoretical matters are not examined.

[60]Ibid., p. 13.

[61]Ibid., p. 65.

whether this loss is accompanied by the breakdown of order.'[62] George's interpretation of legal moralism is therefore different from that of critics of Devlin like Hart and Feinberg, in at least two respects. First, he believes that the decriminalization of kinds of conduct not in accord with the 'shared morality' will not necessarily bring about the breakdown of social order and society. Instead, such acts will entail loss of social cohesion—or, in other words, the curtailment of a distinctive form of interpersonal interaction in a community. Second, George believes that disintegration, so defined, is bad (and integration good) in itself.[63]

Based on the first of these differences, it follows that premise 3, in the argument about disintegration, is not refuted by showing that people can continue to live in peace together in countries where (say) abortion, euthanasia, prostitution, marihuana and homosexuality are not criminalized. George uses marriage as an analogy to make his position clear. The idea is that social disintegration does not have to involve the breakdown of a society, just as the drifting apart of spouses in a marriage need not imply the breakdown of the marriage. Spouses can live together, though they have ceased to integrate their lives around common interests or concerns. However, according to George, something intrinsically valuable has thereby been lost. As George puts it: 'Their relationship has been instrumentalized.'[64] Thus, George's interpretation of Devlin rules out the empirical challenge raised against Devlin, since, for George, disintegration can and does happen without the breakdown of societies.

George's position, like Devlin's, is apparently also immune to the *no difference challenge*. Whether George's version of legal moralism collapses into a version of the harm principle, however, is not always easy to detect. At first glance, this appears to be the case. Following George's argumentation, immorality can be used as a reason for making acts criminal only when it harms or benefits people.[65] By the word harm, George means the corrupting of their characters (their virtues).[66] This is, of course, a moralistic notion of harm, and it is different from the notion of harm typically used by adherents of a harm principle. Nevertheless, it is still a kind of harm (that is, harm to individuals). This interpretation is supported by the following passage, in which George states what he believes ought to be the function of criminal law:

> [The law] should prohibit at least 'the grosser forms of evils', to encourage people to achieve, and help them to maintain, the good of a morally upright character. Such a character is ... a benefit primarily to the individual who possesses it.[67]

---

[62]Ibid., p. 66.

[63]Remember that e.g. Feinberg interprets Devlin as an instrumentalist concerning the negative value of disintegration; disintegration has negative value only because it leads to harm.

[64]Ibid., p. 68.

[65]Ibid., pp. 45, 72.

[66]Ibid., p. 80.

[67]Ibid., p. 72.

Further thought, however, suggests that it is a mistake to claim that George's version cannot meet the no difference challenge, because there is an important difference between George's notion of harm and the notion usually used by advocates of a harm principle. The type of harm George refers to can be referred to as 'moral harm'.[68] A moral harm (caused, say, by using pornography or engaging in sodomy) changes your character for the worse, so that you become more inclined to do bad or evil things. If you have been harmed morally, your rating as a moral agent declines regardless of how that affects your well-being. However, moral harm is not the notion of harm that adherents of the harm principle generally have in mind. Advocates of a harm principle in its many versions usually give a *welfarist* account of harm *where the welfare or well-being of the person* whose life it is, and not the *moral value of that person*, is what matters when it comes to the harm that is relevant to criminalization decisions.[69]

Despite George's improvement of legal moralism, I will argue that his position is problematic for at least two reasons when I describe what I term *the criminological levelling-down challenge* (CLDC) and *the weighing challenge* (WEC). Let me discuss these two challenges in turn.

The first challenge is inspired by ideas developed by moral philosophers like Joseph Raz and Derek Parfit in their challenge to certain versions of egalitarianism.[70] According to Raz, Parfit and many other philosophers, it is a challenge that can be raised against egalitarians, who hold that equality has intrinsic value or value in itself, and therefore that an increase in equality must always, at least, in isolation, be a change for the better. To make the challenge more vivid, imagine the following levelling down of equality of well-being in a society. The population in society S is divided between the 90% who are well off in their well-being, and 10% who have lives that are barely worth living. Then a natural disaster occurs which implies that they are all very badly off in S, and all are worse off than before the disaster. But after the disaster they are all equally worse off. However, according to egalitarians of the aforementioned kind, this implication of the disaster is, at least in one regard, a change for the better—namely, in terms of equality. However, this sounds wrong. How can such a levelling down be in any sense better, if everybody is worse off compared to the situation where there is no levelling down? I believe that we can translate this kind of reasoning against egalitarianism into a challenge for legal moralism as mentioned before, we can call this challenge the criminological levelling-down challenge (CLDC). Let me try to make this challenge clear with the following example.

[68] See e.g. Sumner (2004), pp. 35–36.

[69] There is, of course, often a causal link between moral harm and harm as reduction of well-being, in the sense that if you are morally harmed, your well-being is reduced. Nevertheless, there is no necessary connection between the two.

[70] See e.g. Parfit (1998). For an egalitarian defence of the Levelling-Down Objection, see e.g. Persson (2001).

Imagine two populations, A and B, each consisting of one billion people. All the people in A are extremely well off in terms of well-being. However, and everything else being equal, in A one allegedly non-harmful but allegedly immoral kind of conduct X (such as homosexual sex, marriage between homosexuals, etc.) is legal. By contrast, all the people in B have lives that are not worth living, their level of well-being is constantly below the level of a life worth living. However, and everything else being equal, in B conduct X is part of the criminal law. Imagine, now, that you can choose which population should continue to exist. The obvious conclusion to draw is that it should be population A, because everybody in A is much better off than everybody in population B. However, it follows from George's version of legal moralism that population B *could* be claimed to be better than A even though *everybody* in B is worse off than all the people in A. The reason for this is that George could argue for B being a better world than A, because B, compared to A, criminalizes a non-harmful kind of immorality X. I do not mean to imply that George, all things considered (remember that legal moralists are usually pluralists), would claim that B is better than A, but he must at least claim that B, is in one sense, better than A, because B criminalizes a kind of immorality X that A does not. But how can population B be, *in any sense*, better than A, if everyone in B is worse off than all the people in A? As we shall see in the next few sections, CLDC is a challenge to all legal moralists who believe that non-harmful immoralities can be a sufficient reason for criminalization.

The issue of concern up until this point is not whether non-harmful immoralities exist, but rather why if they do, they should be relevant at all to our normative endeavour to justify which type of conduct ought to be criminalized. In other words, if these kinds of conduct (say X), for example, only bring benefits to individuals without harming anyone, they ought not to be candidates for criminalization. To take one of George's own examples, it is not at all clear that the drifting apart of a married couple is always a moral loss in itself, as George indicates. It might benefit all involved. For instance, the fact that, almost 30 years ago, I drifted away from my alcoholic girlfriend was not, at least in the long run, a morally relevant loss. It left me single and gave me the energy to meet another woman with whom I now have two wonderful children and a good family life. Following the breakdown of the earlier relationship, my ex-girlfriend realized that she had a problem and went into a rehabilitation programme that helped her combat her alcoholism. Consequently, drifting apart, although often sad for a while, can result in more valuable interpersonal relationships. In short, and all else being equal, if no-one regrets or is harmed by drifting apart from their spouses (in the long run), and if there are some benefits for the affected parties, it is difficult to see why drifting apart should be legally or even morally problematic. Note that Devlin is also vulnerable to this challenge: why should a type of act that would violate respect for the sanctity of human life be criminal if committing such acts would nevertheless affect some for the better and harm no one? Before turning to the second challenge, I believe it is fair to briefly consider how George and companions might answer CLDC.

A potential objection to my presentation of CLDC is that I am just begging the question. In other words, George and other legal moralists could claim that by merely stipulating that non-harmful immoralities ought to be excluded from the criminal law, I am prejudiced in favour of some version of the harm principle. Prejudiced, because harm principles would not imply that population B is better than A, in one sense. This is a comment I have received a few times when I have presented this chapter of the book at seminars. So let me try to describe my answer. My response to this counterargument is threefold. First, my challenge is not a mere *stipulation* in the problematic sense of the word. CLDC makes it clear that legal moralism brings up at least one theoretical issue. A good argument is necessary if one wants to accept that legal moralism implies CLDC, and neither George nor any other legal moralist has even touched upon the issue.

Second, it is incorrect to claim that, in proposing CLDC, I am prejudiced in favour of some version of the harm principle. Incorrect for at least two reasons: to begin with, there is room for versions of harm principles that could be subject to CLDC. Imagine deontological harm principles, which claim that there is a restriction to the criminalization of certain types of harmful conduct C (e.g. the production and consumption of alcohol, or drug use by pregnant women) even if the decriminalization of C would minimize the total amount of harm in society. George could claim that I am prejudiced in favour of a consequentialist version of a harm principle. But, as should be clear from the criticism of harm principles set out in Chap. 2, it is not right to claim that I am prejudiced in favour of a harm principle, it is more correct to claim that I may be prejudiced in favour of a consequentialist principle of criminalization. However, the question whether or not I am prejudiced, in the problematic sense, because I simply state that consequentialism is right will be the subject of Chap. 6. In that chapter, I defend a utilitarian theory of criminalization which—contrary to, for example, harm principles and versions of legal moralism—delivers both a necessary and a sufficient condition for how the state should justify what kind of conduct ought to be criminalized.

Thirdly, I believe that the one begging the question is George. He not only stipulates (1) the existence of non-harmful immoralities, (2) the idea that we should accept criminalizing kinds of conduct C even though no victim is harmed, and (3) that there exists a reason to criminalize kinds of conduct C in society S, even if everyone in S is harmed by the criminalization of C, but who also declares (4) that a person can enjoy well-being by perfecting his or her human nature even though this perfection does not lead to a fulfilling life for the person themselves.[71] In a relatively short book like this one, it is not possible to deal with every issue in detail, so the aim is simply to promote an awareness of their existence to challenge George and legal moralists like him.[72]

---

[71]For a critique of a perfectionist view of well-being like George's, and thereby dealing in more detail with stipulation (4), see the Appendix.

[72]For a discussion of (1), see e.g. Feinberg (1988), and for a critical discussion of (2), see Murphy (1966), who argues that the idea of victimless crimes is conceptually wrong.

The second objection, which I have termed the *weighing challenge* (WEC), concerns how the weighing of values should be executed when we are determining whether a certain type of conduct C is immoral, and when it is, should be criminalized. While CLDC has something to do with the problematic implications of George's legal moralism, WEC has more to do with how we can best understand and apply George's legal moralism. The WEC, which Devlin is also exposed to because, as we have seen, he too is a value-pluralist,[73] gives rise to at least two questions or challenges: (a) how should basic human goods (also called *basic values* by George[74] and *shared values* by Devlin) be weighed against other goods (e.g. George's instrumental values or values which, according to Devlin, comply with the sanctity of human life doctrine) when we are deciding what to criminalize? In addition (b) how should basic values be weighed against each other when they come into conflict with one another (e.g. the goods/values of *life* and *play*)? This is how I understand the challenge, then: if a theory of criminalization cannot deliver a plausible answer to these two questions, it is subject to WEC.

What the response to the first question would be, based on George's version of legal moralism, is obvious. Imagine, for instance, that some politicians and judges are jointly considering criminalizing types of actions like C. However, if C, in isolation is regarded as immoral (e.g. anabolic steroids or narcotic drugs or alcohol), because it undermines a human good, like health, but nevertheless will (everything else being equal) bring a huge and sustainable profit to seven billion people annually, then C should be criminalized. Thus, C should be criminalized because, although it provides numerous people with the instrumental good, money, it violates a basic value. According to George, basic values always outweigh instrumental values.

On George's view, what would be the best response to the second question? When we have to choose between two human goods, what should we do then? The choice could be, for example, between helping someone stay alive by making a phone call, or continuing to play golf. According to George, basic values cannot be weighed and measured,[75] which means that his theory does not, at least initially, provide an answer to this question. Therefore, when we have two basic values ('life' and 'play'), and these goods are incommensurable, the choice between them, e.g. the choice between saving a life and continuing to play golf, is arbitrary. This cannot be right!

Well aware of this problem, George believes that of course one should save the person's life instead of playing golf. His idea is that when 'choosing between options

[73]As far as adherents of harm or offense principles do also believe in value or principle pluralism they are also subject to the WEC. Adherents of harm principles like e.g. Feinberg do also believe that we should accept an offense principle, and Mill by claiming the harm is only a necessary reason for criminalization will also have to accept that there are other reasons or values that we should take into account when deciding whether we have a sufficient reason in favour of criminalizing a certain kind of conduct.

[74]George (1992), p. 187.

[75]Ibid.

in which competing basic values are involved ... the situation is controlled by a moral norm, albeit one that does not require the weighing and comparison of values that is ruled out by the incommensurability thesis'.[76] George refers to two moral norms that ought to be applied when choosing between actions that involve, no matter what, the failure to live according to at least one of two basic values.[77] The two moral norms are:

(1) The Pauline Principle: never do evil that good might come of it
(2) The Golden Rule: do unto others, as you would have them do unto you

From George's perspective, application of the Golden Rule leads to the correct answer in the case of the golfer. This seems obvious, as we can assume that the golfer would rather save a life, at least if the cost to him or her of saving the life is low. However, if moral norms exist that tell one what to do in a situation where the choice is between conflicting basic values, then it seems obvious that the value of life, as compared with the value of play in a situation like the one above has the most weight. To argue, like George, that the justification for saving a life instead of playing golf has to do with a general rule like the Golden Rule, and not with the importance of life over play in that particular case, seems to be unnecessarily abstract and far away from common-sense moral thinking.

Furthermore, this manoeuvre makes it appear that George has simply moved the weighing challenge to another plateau. Instead of having a conflict between basic values, the conflict can now be between different moral rules, and the question is then how this should be resolved. The Pauline Principle and the Golden Rule can easily be in conflict with one another. Imagine a situation in which the choice involves wanting others to do evil that good might come of it (e.g. intentionally harming one person slightly to prevent one billion people from being harmed severely) because doing evil is preferable (and therefore in accordance with the Golden Rule) under these circumstances. George's position does not offer a solution to this type of dilemma. Note that he, as a non-consequentialist, cannot declare that harm or evil should be committed when it would maximise the total sum of well-being.

In sum, although George's version of legal moralism is not threatened by the challenge from relativism, the empirical challenge or the no difference challenge, it remains vulnerable to the two newly introduced challenges, CLDC and WEC. Using some of the new challenges applied here, the next subsection discuss the position of legal moralist Michael Moore.

[76] Ibid., p. 190.
[77] Ibid., p. 193.

4.4.2 A Critical Discussion of Moore's Legal Moralism

Before investigating whether Moore is exposed to the two new challenges to legal moralism presented in the previous sections, let me briefly present the main elements of his theory and explain why he is untroubled by the three objections discussed in the section on Devlin's legal moralism.

Moore believes that there are certain acts, such as cruel treatment of animals, the mutilation of dead bodies and the extinction of certain species, which ought to have criminal laws prohibiting them, even if the following three assumptions are true: first, that a large number of citizens do not know about, and therefore could not be harmed or offended by, these acts; second, that animals, corpses and species are not the sorts of individuals that can be harmed; and, finally, that these acts may not be bad for the person executing them.[78] Moore, then, sees himself as a true, or pure, legal moralist. In his view, there are actions (such as the mutilation of corpses) which, even if they do not involve any harm or offence, ought to be given criminal status. That it follows from legal moralism that these kinds of conduct ought to be criminalized even though no-one is harmed or offended when they are performed speaks in favour of the plausibility of legal moralism, according to Moore. He adds to the justification for this view: 'I suspect that most of us would feel that there ought to be laws against these kinds of behaviours anyway.'[79] This kind of justification, however, does not seem convincing, as it appeals to what we feel might be morally wrong and history has shown us that the majority of people can be morally wrong. In what follows, I will discuss whether Moore is also subject to the challenges to legal moralism, which is the focus of this chapter.

First, the above-mentioned paragraph makes it obvious that Moore need not worry about the no difference challenge, as we have reasons to criminalize certain kinds of conduct even though this will not prevent harm. Second, Moore's version of legal moralism cannot be said to be vulnerable to the challenge from relativism, as he explicitly defends democracy, liberty and equality[80] and declares that some acts are morally wrong even if a government dictates the opposite.[81] Finally, it seems fair to say that Moore is not troubled by the empirical challenge, as nowhere does he state that a change in the shared morality of a society concerning abortion or euthanasia, for instance, will bring about social disintegration. He could, of course, claim something weaker, namely, that if society were to fail to respect the values that he mentions (e.g. by way of mutilation of dead bodies), it would partly disintegrate. But, he does not make this weaker kind of claim. He believes that such acts are wrong in themselves.

Is Moore's version of legal moralism subject to the criminological levelling-down challenge (CLDC) and the weighing challenge (WEC)? Before dealing with this

[78] Moore (1997), p. 646 and Moore (2009).

[79] Moore (1997), pp. 646–647.

[80] Ibid 661.

[81] See e.g. Moore (2009), p. 31.

question, i would like to critically discuss the plausibility of the three assumptions Moore accepts and mentioned at the beginning of this subsection. This will allow me to illustrate why harm principles are unattractive, and show that only legal moralism avoids this unattractiveness. From these assumptions, Moore believes that it will follow from harm principles that cruelty to animals, the mutilation of dead bodies and the extinction of certain species should not be made (or remain) criminal. Is it right, however, to think that it will not follow from harm principles that these acts ought to be criminalized in practice? Perhaps not.

First, normally the three types of acts Moore uses as examples will be detected by others and they would therefore cause some harm.[82] For instance, if the parents of a dead daughter were to discover that her corpse had been mutilated, it would certainly harm them. Moreover, the risk of this occurring should be enough to criminalize the mutilation of dead bodies. Of course, the criminalization decision depends on the way in which mutilation is defined. Some people would probably claim that organ transplantations from dead donor bodies are a form of mutilation. But from this it does not follow that it is morally wrong to use organs from the dead, even if one would describe it as mutilation. If my daughter died and her organs could be used to save another person's life, I would judge it to be morally right to donate them to help others, especially if this was what she had wanted. If my daughter died, she would no longer benefit from the organs, and other people might well benefit and extend their lives by receiving them, even if her body were mutilated in the process.

Second, the extinction of certain species S can also be considered harmful to members of the species S and another species O that is dependent on species S for its food or habitat. If we accept that early death is harmful for an individual, as it would deprive the individual from living extra (good) years, one could say it would inflict harm on a large number of tigers if all tigers were killed in a worldwide hunt. Furthermore, when Moore insinuates that cruelty to animals can be inflicted without causing harm to animals, he seems to employ an anthropocentric concept of harm that most adherents of harm principles simply would not accept. Since animals are clearly harmed by cruelty, what else do we mean by cruelty to animals? It follows that defenders of a harm principle have a reason to forbid cruelty to animals, even if no humans are harmed by that cruelty. Third, it may well be true that those who inflict cruelty on animals, mutilate dead bodies or participate in the extinction of certain species can be harmed before, during and after their participation in these kinds of acts.

Well aware of this, Moore argues that his legal moralism is one that liberals, like proponents of harm principles, should accept. He believes that his position is a 'quite liberal-in-outcome ... if not liberal-in-form theory of legislation'.[83] Moore's argument in support of the view that legal moralism and harm principles are quite equal in outcome—i.e. equivalent, as far as the question of what type of acts to criminalize is concerned—follows roughly these lines. First, Mill's harm principle is a suitable

---

[82]See also Husak (2008) and Petersen (2010).

[83]Ibid., p. 661 (italics added).

rule of thumb, as Moore believes that the most stringent moral obligation is not to cause harm to others.[84] Second, the cost of illegalization should make the legal moralist settle on liberal outcomes concerning what acts should be criminalized. Moore believes that the costs will 'impose certain limits on the sorts of things that might be legislated, because such hidden costs are so heavy that the gains to be achieved (in retributive justice) simply cannot outweigh the cost'.[85] The direct costs are, for example, resources spent on police time, on court personnel, and on harm to criminals and relatives. There are also the costs of loss of privacy created by efforts to enforce the laws backed by many legal moralists. Take, for instance, the surveillance of people's sex lives in their homes; the apparatus required to enforce laws of this nature might cause greater harm than it prevents. Finally, Moore mentions that the prohibition of behaviour in which people would engage in any case could 'increase the profits of supplying such services [e.g. prostitution] or products [e.g. alcohol or cigarettes], which in turn sustains organized criminal activities'.[86]

However, if Moore really believes that legal moralism and adherents of a liberal harm principle like Mill's are quite equal in outcome, why operate with two different theories? As stated earlier, I adopt the following interpretation: Moore's version of legal moralism is theoretically different because he accepts that it can be right to argue that an act of type A ought to be criminalized, even when no one is harmed by instances of A. From a practical point of view, cases may never arise where someone is not harmed by acts like A, but they could arise and if they do it will matter from a practical point of view. From the above-mentioned paragraphs, it is clear that Moore's position is vulnerable to CLDC, because it would follow from his legal moralism that it would be, in one sense, wrong to make the malaria mosquito, for instance, extinct, even if this extinction causes no harm and only benefits individuals (humans as well as other sentient animals).

So, once again, even if legal moralists such as Moore can handle the challenge from relativism, the empirical challenge and the no difference challenge, they are confronted with the problem of providing a plausible rationale for the claim that certain acts should be criminal even though the criminalization of such acts may benefit some individuals and harm nobody. In short, Moore's position, like Devlin's and George's, is damaged by CLDC. Again, why should we not mutilate a dead body in order to harvest the organs to save and benefit the lives of others, if no one is harmed by such an arrangement and some benefit? However, even if we accept that some acts are wrong in themselves and therefore should be criminalized independently of whether they will benefit or harm individuals, Moore is also seriously threatened by WEC. This is because nowhere in Moore's writing does he make clear how the weighing between acts which are morally wrong in themselves—especially when they are in conflict—should proceed within criminalization decisions. Should it still be criminal, for instance, to mutilate a dead body if that would save the lives of

[84]Ibid., p. 649.

[85]Ibid., p. 663.

[86]Ibid., p. 664.

three children? What if mutilating a dead body would save the human race from becoming extinct? What about medical research on animals that is in some quantifiable way cruel but can save the lives of thousands of humans?[87] We need the answers to such questions about criminalization to be as clear as possible, and Moore has not provided us with answers of that detailed kind.

The next section presents an analysis of the next of the four modern legal moralists studied in this chapter.

4.4.3 A Critical Discussion of Kekes's Legal Moralism

Like George and Moore, Kekes has recently tried to formulate what he believes is an improved version of legal moralism. The point of departure for Kekes is his clarification of a distinction between two kinds of values that are required in good lives. Primary values relate to the minimum requirements of all good lives and include 'adequate nutrition, health, shelter, rest and protection against murder, torture, enslavement'.[88] Secondary values, which vary between and within societies according to tradition and conceptions of a good life, include 'aesthetic appreciation, religious faith, a prestigious job, carefree love affairs, raising children, and peak physical condition'.[89] According to Kekes, a good society protects these values by means of conventions.[90] Kekes calls the conventions that protect primary values *'required conventions'* and those that protect secondary values *'variable conventions'*.[91] Examples of required conventions include those prohibiting murder, rape, torture and stealing.

If a society does not promulgate and enforce required conventions (mainly through moral education and the legal system), it will disintegrate into a barbarian society in which the minimum requirements of a good life would be lost and people would live lives full of fear and danger.[92] Kekes agrees with George's stance that critics of Devlin, like Hart, have misunderstood the disintegration argument, i.e. they are missing the point when they claim that that argument has been falsified by the existence of changes in our morality without the breakdown of this society.[93] According to Kekes, legal moralists should be more precise about what kinds of conduct would entail the relevant disintegration. Kekes believes that the basic intuition in Devlin's viewpoint is right, but that this is so if, and only if:

[87] For a critical discussion of Moore's legal moralism that, by and large, is different from my criticism, see Husak (2008), pp. 196–206.

[88] Kekes (2000), p. 23.

[89] Ibid., p. 24.

[90] Ibid., p. 23.

[91] Ibid., p. 24.

[92] Ibid., p. 23.

[93] Ibid., pp. 27–28.

(1) decision-makers in a society observe the distinction between required and variable conventions in selecting the kinds of conduct that the law ought to prohibit; and (2) it is recognized that a good society need only enforce the required conventions.[94] To quote Kekes:

> A society [a state] cannot be good if it fails to enforce its morality. Its enforcement does not require control of the minute particulars of the lives of people who live in it [thus protecting the secondary values]. It requires only the enforcement of required conventions protecting the primary values, which is the minimum necessary for civilized existence.[95]

If Devlin had explicitly stated that he only accepts lawful intervention when it is directed against violations of required conventions, the dispute between him and his liberal critics would, according to Kekes, cool off.[96] Based on my position, it would settle down because the challenge from relativism and the empirical challenge would cease to apply. This would be the case because Kekes's position does not oblige him to (1) accept a Nazi society that, for instance, would promote the extinction of Jews, or (2) approve of whatever change in the shared morality of a society would lead to the breakdown of society, although it would oblige him to agree that the legalization of, for example, murder would result in the breakdown of society. Finally, Kekes's reformulation of legal moralism is very close to the liberal perspective many adherents of a harm principle accept. Liberals typically believe that there are basic rights (e.g. to life, to property, to privacy, or to freedom of expression) that the law should protect, and sometimes also promote, and that the law should not interfere with private matters such as a person's voluntary choice of religion, clothes, sexuality, and so on (unless, of course, these choices wrongfully harm other people).

Legal moralism seems improved by Kekes's suggestion that the focus of Devlin's argument based on disintegration (abortion, bigamy, euthanasia and so on) is best replaced by a focus on murder, torture and enslavement. A society that does *not* respect required conventions protecting primary values would undoubtedly be worse for most individuals than a society in which the opposite is the case. However, in addressing liberals like advocates of harm principles and offence principles, Kekes is perhaps too optimistic when he claims that his version of moral legalism 'is one that reason recommends to everyone, liberals included'.[97]

---

[94]Ibid., pp. 25, 27.

[95]Ibid., pp. 25, 27.

[96]See ibid., p. 26 and especially p. 28, where Kekes writes, 'If Devlin had made it clear that he favours these responses only when they are directed against the violations of required conventions [e.g. disgust as a response against murder, torture or enslavement], and if his liberal critics had made it clear that what they find morally objectionable is when these responses have the violation of variable conventions [e.g. disgust against homosexuality] as their target, then their heated dispute would have cooled off.'

[97]Ibid., p. 26.

Kekes's version of legal moralism looks initially very much like a species of the harm principle. His reasons for maintaining that required conventions should not be violated are not very different from those the defenders of a harm principle would typically offer. That is, defenders of harm principles (at least, if they are consequentialists) and Kekes can agree that the required conventions should only be violated in cases where it would avoid greater evil or lead to greater good.[98] In a similar tone, Kekes states the reasons for protecting the required conventions as (1) the immediate danger a violation of these conventions would put people in, and (2) the fact that it would become impossible to live a good life.[99] Thus, although Kekes claims that these reasons are not only embraced by the notion of harm, when he states that 'What is feared is not that one will suffer, but that life will become barbaric because morality loses its foothold in it,'[100] it seems that one can straightforwardly claim that in a barbaric society, many people are harmed or will be at risk of being harmed. Although it might not be the whole story, it seems obvious that what is morally wrong with murder, torture and enslavement is that such acts harm people. Moreover, they are harmed in the sense that there is little prospect of a good life for the people who live in a society where murder, for example, is not criminalized by the state.

In his efforts to revitalize moral legalism, Kekes evidently has constructed a version that is threatened by the no difference challenge. Admittedly, Kekes's position does not collapse into the sort of harm principle accepted by liberals like Mill or Hart, but as I will show in what follows, it collapses into another, narrower sort. He therefore fails to achieve a version of legal moralism at all.

Let me explain why Kekes's theory is a version of a harm principle, albeit one that differs from the harm principles that are usually discussed in the literature (e.g. Mill's harm principle). The criminalization principles of Mill and Kekes differ in respect of the kinds of conduct they imply should be enforced by the criminal law. If so-called legal moralists like Kekes and Devlin and advocates of a harm principle like Mill's are placed on a scale according to how many different kinds of conduct should be criminal, Kekes would appear to represent one end of the scale. Remember Kekes's assertion that 'A good society ... requires only the enforcement of required conventions protecting the primary values, which is the minimum necessary for civilized existence.'[101] On the basis of this statement, it seems fair to categorize Kekes as a legal minimalist. At the other end of the scale is Devlin's form of legal moralism, where the category of acts that typically can be criminalized is expanded to include the sorts of acts mentioned by Devlin in premise 3 of the disintegration argument (abortion, bigamy, certain kinds of sexual behaviour, and so on). Devlin and some other legal moralists, like George, can be labelled 'legal maximists'. Liberal defenders of a harm principle, like Mill, Hart and Feinberg, tend to favour

[98]Ibid., p. 25.

[99]Ibid., p. 32.

[100]Id.

[101]Ibid., p. 25, see also p. 27 (italics added).

the criminalization of fewer types of acts than do Devlin and George and yet more kinds of conduct than do supporters of a minimalist approach like Kekes's. In the following, I would like to present an example that illustrates the latter difference and that also indicates a further reason for why I believe Kekes's minimalism is problematic.

Following Kekes, women and Muslims subjected to discrimination on the labour market, in the sense that several big companies will not hire women or Muslims in prestigious jobs, cannot claim that a required convention has been broken. For according to Kekes's view, this kind of discrimination should not necessarily be criminalized. And it should not be so, as having a prestigious job is only a secondary value, and because secondary values are only protected by variables conventions, discrimination of the type mentioned before need not be criminalized.[102] Kekes's approach implies that the state could criminalize this type of discrimination if it violated secondary values. The problem is that states *could* do that—when they instead *ought* to do it. From Kekes's perspective, for example, the reasons for criminalizing the discrimination of women and Muslims would differ from country to country, which would mean the existence of the possibility that in some countries there would be no reason at all to criminalize such discrimination. However, if it is true that job discrimination is morally wrong because it is harmful to people, for example (in the sense of making those discriminated against worse off, in respect of well-being, than they would be, were they not discriminated against), there would be good reason to make such discrimination a crime.[103]

More generally, Kekes' claim that it is only harmful kinds of conduct that violate required conventions that should be prohibited by law is not convincing. There always seems to be at least *a reason* to prohibit wrongful harms, no matter what type of convention is being violated. In other words, we should *not* be morally concerned merely with harms or injustices occurring in connection with primary values. Harm is a morally relevant factor (and remember that all plausible forms of legal moralism would imply that it is, because they are pluralist in character and agree that harm also matters in criminalization decisions), we should be concerned about it regardless of whether it is caused by the violation of a primary *or* a secondary value.

To summarize, Kekes's alleged version of legal moralism is, similar to George's and Moore's, not hurt by the challenge from relativism and the empirical challenge. However, unlike Devlin, George's and Moore's positions, Kekes seems to be vulnerable to the no difference challenge. First, he should not identify himself as a legal moralist; and second, if my suppositions are correct, he defends an extreme and problematically narrow variety of a harm principle. Finally, however, comparing Kekes with George and Moore, Kekes does not seem to be vulnerable to CLDC and WEC, as George and Moore are. First, Kekes stands unscathed by CLDC as, if I interpret him correctly, he does not believe that non-harmful immoralities ought to

[102] Ibid., p. 25.

[103] For a critical and detailed presentation of the ways in which discrimination can be morally wrong, see e.g. Lippert-Rasmussen (2014).

be enforced by the state. Remember that for a society to be a good society for individuals, the state, according to Kekes, should *only* enforce the conventions that secure the primary values, i.e. adequate nutrition, health, shelter, rest and protection against murder, torture and enslavement. Hence, non-harmful immoralities are not part of the package.

Second, concerning WEC, Kekes's distinctions between primary and secondary values and between required and variable conventions make it clear that if an act is in accordance with a variable convention but contrary to a required convention, the latter carries more weight. This mirrors George's theory, in which his distinction between instrumental values and basic values makes it clear that the latter carry more weight. When it comes to weighing up different primary values, or within a single value, Kekes' answer is, as shown, that required conventions could be violated where greater evil is avoided or it leads to greater good. However, according to this element of WEC, Kekes fair better than all the other legal moralists that we have been discussing so far.

4.4.4 A Critical Discussion of Duff's Legal Moralism

One of the most recent defences of a version of legal moralism is presented in the writings of Antony Duff.[104] Duff's version of legal moralism is centred on what he calls 'a "civil order" or "public wrongs" principle'.[105] This principle can, according to Duff, be divided into the following two claims, making it clear that it is not all kinds of moral wrongs that we or the state, in principle, have reason to criminalize:

A. We have reason to criminalize a type of conduct if, and only if, it constitutes a public wrong.
B. A type of conduct constitutes a public wrong if, and only if, it violates the polity's civil order.[106]

However, in order to apply Duff's principle in criminalization decisions, we need to clarify three things. First, when is a type of conduct *public* and not merely private? Secondly, when is a public conduct *morally* wrong, or in other words, when does a type of conduct C violate the polity's civil order? And last, but not least, when should a public wrong be criminalized?

Let me first present what I take to be Duff's answers to these three questions. Hereafter, when we know more about his version of legal moralism, we can investigate to what extent his theory stands up to the five challenges used in testing the various versions of legal moralism in this chapter.

---

[104]See e.g. Duff (2014, 2018) and Duff and Marshall (2019).

[105]Duff (2018), pp. 277 and 296.

[106]Id.

According to Duff, an act is part of the public realm if it is 'of proper interest to all citizens in virtue of their participation in the civic enterprise'.[107] Although this do not provide us with a clear distinction between 'the private' and 'the public' realm—when is an act of 'proper interest to all citizens in virtue of their participation in that enterprise'?—I believe that we at least have an idea of when this distinction makes sense.[108] To put it bluntly, while committing a terrorist attack, murder or rape, for example, or building a huge bridge that connect two countries or running for president, is of proper public interest, your choice of underwear or partner is not. But what, then, is a public wrong according to Duff, and when should it be criminalized? Acts that harm others, for example murder, rape and violent terrorist attacks, are, according to Duff, public wrongs that the state need to criminalize if it wants to protect its civil order.[109] On the other hand, private wrongs like lying to your mother or a friend about your job situation should not be the law's business. And the same goes with what literally we could call public wrongs, for example queue-jumping (which often take place in public), as they can be dealt with in other more effective ways than criminalization and because they do not threaten the civil order of a liberal society which, generally speaking, is the society Duff adheres to.[110]

Therefore, not all public wrongs must be criminalized. Duff accepts that the cost or collateral consequences of criminalizing a certain kind of public wrong can be so high that sometimes these wrongs should not be criminalized.[111] As mentioned before, queue-jumping, although a public wrong, does not usually threaten the civil order. In addition, enforcing it may, in many different ways, be very costly and it may more efficiently be prevented through social codes or norms.

Being a legal moralist, however, Duff also believes that certain public wrongs should be criminalized even though they are not harmful kinds of conduct (or kinds of conduct that risk harm to individuals) or even though the criminalization of such acts would not prevent harm. Some acts are public wrongs because they seriously violate *the respect* we owe each other. As an example of this, Duff mentions '"extreme" pornography that graphically depicts the humiliation or torture of one sex or group as a source of sexual gratification for readers or viewers; and of certain kinds of racist or otherwise discriminatory insult'.[112] Furthermore, Duff mentions conduct that 'might not be straightforwardly harmful, but that seriously violates the dignity of those subjected to it (or taking part in it) . . . this is true, I think, of "dwarf-throwing".' Dwarf-throwing or also called midget-tossing is a bar attraction, in which people with dwarfism is thrown onto mattresses or at Velcro-coated

[107] Duff (2018), p. 234.

[108] For a critique of Duff's distinction between private and public, see Moore (2009); for a defence, see Duff and Marshall (2019).

[109] Duff (2018), p. 300.

[110] Duff (2018), p. 186.

[111] Duff (2018), p. 95.

[112] Duff (2014), p. 233.

walls.[113] Participants competes to toss a midget the farthest. Duff also believes that certain kinds of public 'offence' that involve inconvenience like, for example, noise and minor vandalism of public spaces are proper grounds for criminalization. However, before we shall evaluate in what way Duff's version of legal moralism can handle the different kind of challenges for versions of legal moralism that we have discussed in this chapter, I would like to draw attention to two initial challenges for Duff's theory.

First, there seems to be some kind of tension between Duff's central claim that it is only public wrongs violating the civil order that we have reason to criminalize, and then that we have reason to criminalize 'dwarf-throwing' and 'minor vandalism'. Maybe I am ignorant, but it is difficult for me to understand that it should be true that these kinds of conduct violate the civil order of our society. If it does mean, that the civil order of a society is destroyed if voluntary dwarf-throwing/tossing is legal, this does not seem right. Second, as was shown in Chap. 3, on the most plausible theories of well-being, the examples of 'offense' that Duff mentions here can all be categorized as instances of harm (understood as a reduction in well-being). In addition, the same kind of reasoning can be applied when it comes to an understanding of his examples concerning the violation of respect. Torture and discriminatory insult, as examples of violating respect for people, will typically involve serious harm, either directly or indirectly.

However, when it comes to the challenges for legal moralism that we have discussed throughout this chapter, we can begin by observing that it is obvious that Duff is not subject to the no-difference view, as he clearly believes that harm is not all that matters in criminalization decisions. For instance, Duff believes that we have a reason to criminalize dwarf-throwing not because it might involve harm, but because it violates dignity.

However, if we take the public wrong principle literally, I believe there is good reason to say that Duff's version of legal moralism is subject to the challenge from relativism. For it follows from his principle that what seems morally right, for example, to hide Jews during the times of Nazi Germany in order to prevent them from being executed, could be considered a public wrong that would violate the civil order of a Nazi polity. In addition, it would then follow from Duff's principle of criminalization that hiding Jews in order to prevent them from being executed should be considered a criminal offence. However, Duff is aware that his principle of public wrongs seems to favour a problematic kind of relativism.[114] In addition, he defends his version of legal moralism by claiming that external critique is always possible if, for instance, a state commits horrible and morally wrong acts.[115] However, this kind of defence of his public wrong principle is not very convincing. It is unclear what kind of work is left for the 'public wrong principle' if the plausibility of substantial

[113]Ibid. For a more detailed description of what dwarf throwing is, see e.g. https://en.wikipedia.org/wiki/Dwarf-tossing.

[114]See Duff (2018), p. 232.

[115]Duff and Marshall (2019), p. 38.

different public wrongs depends on external moral criticism. This being said, however, it is fair to mention that in several places in Duff's writing, it is of course very clear that he does not favour anything close to the polity of totalitarian societies. By advocating a democratic liberal society and by accepting that harm to others, like murder and rape, or the violation of people's dignity or respect, plays a central part in his legal moralism,[116] it would not, all things considered, be fair to criticize Duff's overall political philosophy by means of the challenge from relativism. Although problematic relativism does seem to follow from his public wrong principle of criminalization.

Furthermore, unlike Devlin, Duff is not subject to the empirical challenge that was raised against Devlin. Although Duff wants to criminalize kinds of conduct that it is necessary to criminalize in order to protect the civil order of a society, he would not, like Devlin, criminalize first-trimester abortion, for instance.[117] It seems empirically more right to claim that law and order will break down if the proper public wrongs like murder and rape were not criminalized. In addition, this is much more plausible than, say, Devlin claiming that the legalization of abortion and homosexuality will make a society disintegrate. However, as hinted at earlier, he is subject to another empirical challenge: namely, to show that the legalization of dwarf-throwing violates the public order of a society.

Duff is also subject to CLDC, as he believes that we at least have a reason to criminalize kinds of conduct C, even if everybody affected by a specific kind of conduct C is better off because of C. Say, for example, that dwarf-throwing made everybody affected better off in terms of well-being than if dwarf-throwing did not happen. In that case, it would follow from Duff's viewpoint that we would still have reason to criminalize dwarf-throwing even though nobody would be better off because of its criminalization. Furthermore, there is no doubt that Duff is subject to WEC. First, as Duff accepts that there are reasons other than public wrongs that should play a part when we make criminalization decisions, e.g. cost of enforcement, his theory is challenged by how we should weigh these different values in order to determine when a kind of conduct should be criminal. Second, Duff is also challenged when two kinds of public wrongs are in conflict. Say that, by violating people's dignity through criminalization, you can prevent them from being harmed. This could happen, as we will see in Chap. 6, if you help strangers in need by donating them money that would save their lives, but where you only use these strangers as a mere means to make you look morally superior in the eyes of others. However, Duff is well aware of these challenges and believes that we should 'not … specify the kinds of substantive considerations that can give us reasons to criminalize rather than responding in some other way, but to indicate the kinds of question that we must ask in deciding whether we should, in principle, criminalize, rather than responding in another way'.[118]

---

[116]Duff (2018), p. 186.

[117]Ibid., pp. 169–170.

[118]Ibid., pp. 296–297.

In addition, the questions he wants us to ask are some of the following: is it important to respond to the wrong as a wrong, and how important is it? Is it important that the response is collective in the sense that both offender and victim should have control of the case? Is it important that the proper response is state punishment? However, although it seems right to raise these questions when making criminalization decisions, I believe that, when working within the field of criminalization theory, we should try to formulate a principled answer to these questions that can guide us in criminalization decisions. In Chap. 6, I will defend a consequentialist criminalization theory that will, as Duff says " . . .specify the kinds of substantive considerations that can give us reason to criminalize."

So, the interim conclusion concerning Duff's theory of legal moralism is that, compared to George, Moore and Kekes, Duff's theory is not an improvement on Devlin's legal moralism. Duff's legal moralism is subject to the challenge from relativism, an empirical challenge (although different from the empirical challenge that Devlin's theory is subject to), CLDC and WEC.

4.5 Conclusion

In Sect. 4.2, I hope I have shown the importance of holding an analytical discussion about how to specify or understand the more precise structure of 'legal moralism', with only specification (e) of the five versions discussed standing out as a plausible version. In order for dialogue among politicians, legislators, the public and scholars to be constructive, the reasons behind different proposals regarding which acts the state should criminalize should be as clear and as plausible as possible. My intention in the rest of the chapter has been to argue that legal moralism, in the versions presented by its most prominent defenders, is problematic.

Since the days of Devlin, the theory has doubtlessly been improved by three of the four legal moralists that we have critically discussed under Sect. 4.4 and its subsections. Apart from Duff, recent advocates of legal moralism are not vulnerable to the challenge from relativism and none of the four is subject to the empirical challenge that has been raised against Devlin. As we have seen, however, each of the legal moralists discussed in this chapter (whether that be Devlin or any philosopher from the new generation of legal moralists) faces the following objections: either they are reproved by the CLDC and the WEC, or their rationale for claiming that certain kinds of conduct ought to be criminalized involves a version of the harm principle, in which case the no difference challenge arises. George, Moore and Duff are only subject to the first two objections; Kekes only to the latter.

References

Cranor CF (1978) Legal moralism reconsidered. Ethics 89(2):147–164
Devlin P (1963) The enforcement of morals. Oxford University Press, Oxford
Dixon N (2007) Boxing, paternalism, and legal moralism. In: Ethics in Sport, 2nd edn, pp 389–405
Duff A (2014) Towards a modest legal moralism. Crim Law Philos 8(1):217–235
Duff A (2018) The realm of criminal law. Oxford University Press, Oxford
Duff RA, Marshall SE (2019) Crimes, public wrongs, and civil order. Crim Law Philos 13(1):27–48
Dworkin RM (1965) Lord Devlin and the enforcement of morals. Yale Law J 75:986
Dworkin RM (1977) The philosophy of law. Oxford University Press, Oxford
Dworkin RM (1994) Life's dominion. Vintage Press, New York
Dworkin G (1999) Devlin was right: law and the enforcement of morality. William Mary Law Rev 40:927
Feinberg J (1984) Harm to others. Oxford University Press, Oxford
Feinberg J (1988) Harmless wrongdoing. Oxford University Press, Oxford
Finnis J (1980) Natural law and natural rights. Oxford University Press, Oxford
George RP (1992) Does the 'incommensurability thesis' imperil common sense moral judgments? Am J Jurisprud 37:185–195
George RP (1993) Making men moral, civil liberties and public morality. Clarendon Press, Oxford
Hart HLA (1963) Law liberty and morality. Oxford University Press, Oxford
Hart HLA (1971) Immorality and treason. In: Wasserstrom RA (ed) Morality and the law. Wadsworth, Belmont, pp 49–54
Häyry H (1991) Liberalism and legal moralism: the Hart—Devlin debate and beyond. Ratio Juris 4 (2):202–218
Husak D (2008) Overcriminalization: the limits of the criminal law. Oxford University Press, Oxford
Kahn T (2006) United States Court of Appeals, Eleventh Circuit. No. 06-11892
Kekes J (2000) The enforcement of morality. Am Philos Q 37(1):23–35
Kuflik A (2005) Liberalism, legal moralism and moral disagreement. J Appl Philos 22(2):185–198
Kuhse H (1987) The sanctity of life doctrine in medicine: a critique. Clarendon Press, Oxford
Lippert-Rasmussen K (2014) Born free and equal. Oxford University Press, Oxford
Moore M (1997) Placing blame: a general theory of the criminal law. Clarendon Press, Oxford
Moore M (2009) A tale of two theories. Crim Justice Ethics 28(1):27–48
Murphy J (1966) Another look at legal moralism. Ethics 77(1):50–56
Murphy MC (2007) Philosophy of law. Blackwell Publishing, New Jersey
Parfit D (1998) Equality or priority. Ratio 10(3):202–221
Persson I (2001) Equality, priority and person-affecting value. Ethical Theory Moral Pract 4 (1):23–39
Petersen TS (2010) New legal moralism: some strengths and challenges. Crim Law Philos 4 (2):215–232
Petersen TS (2011) What is legal moralism? SATS: North Eur J Philos 12(1):80–88
Stephen JF (1874, 1967) Liberty, equality and fraternity, 2nd edn. Cambridge University Press, Cambridge
Stranton-Ife J (2006) The limits of law. Stanford Encyclopaedia of Philosophy
Sumner W (2004) The hateful and the obscene. University of Toronto Press, Toronto
Tadros V (2016) Wrongs and crimes. Oxford University Press, Oxford
Tebbit M (2000) Philosophy of law: an introduction. Routledge, Abingdon
Thaysen JD (2015) Defining legal moralism. Sats 6(2):179–201

Chapter 5
On Dignity Principles of Criminalization: A Critical Discussion

5.1 Introduction

The research question that has guided this book is by what moral principle(s) should criminalization decisions be guided? Versions of, the harm principle, the offence principle and legal moralism have been elaborated and criticized in Chaps. 2, 3 and 4.[1] Dissatisfied with these rationales of criminalization, some theorists have proposed an alternative approach based on the notion of human dignity and its violation.[2]

This chapter critically discusses this approach. The relevant dignity principle of criminalization is captured by the general idea that the violation of human dignity by conduct C is a reason to criminalize C (whether such violation should be considered

[1]See e.g. Feinberg (1984, 1985, 1986, 1988), Duff et al. (2010), Duff (2018) and Tadros (2016).

[2]See e.g. Dan-Cohen (2002), Hörnle (2012) and Buchhandler-Raphael (2013). If you adhere to the view that legal moralism consists of a class of criminalization principles according to which the criminalization of a kind of conduct C depends on the moral wrongness (e.g. harm or non-harmful immoralities) of C, it seems fair to categorize dignity principles as versions of legal moralism. So, as different versions of legal moralism—for instance, those defended by Moore (1997) and Duff (2018), for whom dignity does only play a small part in their writings (as one value of several others)—dignity principles can be categorized as formulations of legal moralism that offer alternatives to those defended by some of the most famous defenders of legal moralism like Devlin, George, Kekes, Moore and Duff that were the subject of Chap. 4. However, as will be clarified in what follows (Sect. 5.3), Dan-Cohen's dignity theory of criminalization can be interpreted as special in the sense that for him, contrary to all other legal moralists discussed in this book, harm does not matter as an independent factor in criminalization decisions. According to Dan-Cohen, all that matters, in criminalization decisions, from a moral point of view, is the idea—based on Kant—of defending the unique value of every individual. Dan-Cohen is thus defending a monistic type of legal moralism, whereas the above-mentioned legal moralists all defend a pluralistic type of legal moralism, according to which not only harmless immoralities but also morally wrongful harm matters.

T. Søbirk Petersen, *Why Criminalize?*, Law and Philosophy Library 134,
https://doi.org/10.1007/978-3-030-34690-4_5

a necessary or a sufficient reason or just *a* reason will be discussed in Sect. 5.3). While several theorists within criminal justice ethics have invoked the violation of human dignity in justifying what type and amount of *punishment* are immoral,[3] few have argued in detail in favour of *criminalizing* conduct that violates human dignity. Although it is easy to sympathize with this latter idea, the primary aim of the chapter is to argue that recent attempts to justify it can be challenged. As will become clear, my criticism will be different from, and critical of, the only explicit and detailed critique of a dignity rationale for criminalization.[4]

Section 5.2 clarifies the concept of dignity. I detail the distinction between common-sense interpretations of dignity and a Kantian interpretation. In Sect. 5.3, I present some recent Kantian interpretations of the dignity principle of criminalization and argue that we should understand such principles as providing a necessary justification for criminalization. By doing so, I show why a certain critique by Dennis Baker of *a Kantian dignity principle of criminalization* (KDPC) is off-target. In Sect. 5.4, I make it clear that the supposed attraction of such a principle is, that, unlike prominent versions of the harm principle, KDPC provides us with the right answers in certain test cases. KDPC can, for example, be invoked to legitimize the criminalization of certain kinds of conduct, such as the enslavement of happy slaves, a legitimation of which adherents of KDPC believe harm principles cannot deliver. In this sense, harm principles are criticized for their under-inclusiveness, or in other words, for not being able to justify what ought to be criminalized, namely, all types of slavery whether or not the slaves are happy. However, in Sect. 5.5, I will argue why KDPC, at least in certain situations, suffers from the very same kind of under-inclusiveness that advocates of KDPC take to be problematic for harm principles.

In Sect. 5.6, I will briefly consider non-Kantian interpretations of the dignity principle. One such interpretation implies that 'references to human dignity can justify the existence of penal prohibitions which aim to prevent conduct which is severely humiliating.'[5] I criticize this rationale for criminalization, arguing that it seems to be redundant given the availability of the familiar principle of criminalization, such as versions of the harm principle and the offence principle, and especially that it is difficult to make a relevant distinction between Hörnle's dignity principle of criminalization and the criminalization principle generally referred to as the offence principle. Section 5.7 sums up the chapter's findings.

---

[3]E.g. Dan-Cohen (2016), Kleinig (1998) and Gerstein (1974). For a critique of the last two authors, see Petersen (2010).

[4]Which is Baker's (2011).

[5]Hörnle (2012).

5.2 What Is Dignity?

What are we talking about when we use the word 'dignity'? It is beyond doubt that ascriptions of dignity *to a person* or *acts of a person* represent (psychologically, aesthetically or morally) positive appraisals.[6] However, within this general observation, the word dignity can be used in a variety of ways. In the common-sense use of the word we can, for example, say that a person *has* dignity, meaning something like: this person has poise and a sense of self-worth. Or we can say that a person who occupies an important position in society (e.g. a Supreme Court judge or a general) enjoys dignity by virtue of their position; such a person can, of course, lose their dignity if they do not do the job well or are sacked. The word dignity also has a variety of common-sense usages in which we say that people *act* in a dignified way; thus, a person can 'speak with dignity'. We can also 'grow old with dignity'.[7] However, in the identification of reasons for criminalization it is clear that these interpretations of the word dignity are not relevant. Advocates of the dignity rationale for criminalization take dignity to mean something else. Quite what this is will be discussed in the remainder of this section.

In the philosophical literature, since at least Kant's time, there seems to be a consensus that all persons have dignity in the sense that each has *unconditional* and *incomparable* worth.[8] This notion of dignity clearly differs from all of the common-sense interpretations mentioned above. For, according to many of these interpretations, dignity is *not* something everybody has; and when dignity is identified with certain types of actions, these are not types of acts that everybody do. The idea that personal dignity is *unconditional* surely means that dignity is something everybody has, no matter what condition they are in or how they act. Furthermore, I and other philosophers take the assertion that dignity is of *incomparable worth* to mean that the dignity of a person cannot be sold or gained in exchange for something else, such as money, gold or human organs.[9] Again, the idea is that dignity is something every human being possesses.

In this chapter, my point of departure is this interpretation of the concept of dignity, that is, what I shall call the *Kantian interpretation of dignity*. Embedded in this interpretation of the concept of dignity is also the idea that dignity is more than a description of what characterizes humans; it is also a moral concept. According to Kant's well-known second version of the categorical imperative, 'man should always treat a person as an end in itself and never merely as a means.' According to this imperative, acts violating the dignity principle are morally wrong.

However, what it means to *value* the dignity of a human being is far from obvious. In one interpretation, I value such dignity if I bring it about that a greater

---

[6] Waldron (2012).

[7] See Waldron (2012) for other, related understandings of the term 'dignity'. See also Schroeder and Bani-Sadr (2017).

[8] Kant (1785/2002).

[9] Kamm (2013).

number of people are treated with dignity. This we could call the *consequentialist interpretation*. For instance, I might minimize the violation of several people's dignity by violating the dignity of one person: it may be that by enslaving one person I prevent two others from being enslaved. In the consequentialist interpretation, I should (everything else being equal) enslave that one person. According to another interpretation, I value the dignity of people by *respecting* their dignity. This might involve refusing to violate the dignity of one person even for the sake of achieving fewer such violations of the dignity of e.g. 10 other people. This we could call the *deontological interpretation*.[10] In what follows, I will stick to the deontological interpretation, as this seems more in accordance with adherents of a dignity principle.

Whatever we wish to say about these categorizations, there is no doubt that dignity is an important and often-used moral concept. It is at the centre of one of the main branches within ethical theory, namely, deontological ethics. Moreover, beyond research in pure ethical theory, it plays a central role in applied ethics, in connection with such topics as abortion,[11] euthanasia,[12] cloning[13] and human enhancement.[14] So far so good, but specifying dignity, and identifying it as a central moral concept, is only a preliminary, though necessary, step in our investigation. What we should now be concerned with is whether—and if so, how—respect for a person's dignity can give precise and plausible guidance in decisions about the criminalization of certain kinds of conduct. In what follows, I will present and critically discuss two attempts to use guidance of this kind. First, a few Kantian versions, followed by a non-Kantian version.

[10]In defining 'deontology', I follow several philosophers who categorise deontology as a moral theory which puts restrictions on certain kinds of conduct (e.g. lying or treating persons as mere means) even where such conduct promote the good. It is standard practice to divide deontology into *absolutist* and *moderate* versions. In absolutist versions we are never allowed to violate a moral constraint, M, no matter how good the consequences would be. This would be in line with a standard reading of Kant. In moderate versions, we are allowed to violate M, but only if the consequences are significantly good. See e.g. Kagan (1998), p. 79; Lippert-Rasmussen (2005), pp. 17–18 for this distinction. So, as a moderate you may, all else being equal, accept violating the dignity of one person in order to prevent e.g. 100 people from having their dignity violated. However, a moderate deontologist will not accept that the dignity of one person is violated in order to prevent two people from having their dignity violated. If they accepted the latter scenario, their position would collapse into consequentialism.

[11]Kamm (2013).

[12]Kass (2002).

[13]Kamm (2013).

[14]Bostrom (2009).

5.3 Kantian Versions of the Dignity Principle of Criminalization

Several philosophers have argued that we should abandon traditional and well-known foundations of criminalization like versions of the harm principle and develop a Kantian 'dignity principle of criminalization'.[15] Dan-Cohen, for example, sets out such a principle in the following way:

> **Dan-Cohen's Dignity Principle of Criminalization**
> [The dignity principle is] the view that the main goal of the criminal law is to defend the unique moral worth of every human being.[16]

Dan-Cohen accepts that his principle is vague, but he also insists that when it is elaborated, it can 'provide a more adequate criterion for criminality than the harm principle'.[17] According to Dan-Cohen, we can specify the action-guiding feature of the dignity principle, as he understands it, by returning to Kant's second formulation of the categorical imperative—also called the 'dignity principle'[18]:

> **Kant's Dignity Principle**
> Act in such a way that you treat humanity, whether in your own person or in any other person, never merely as a means to an end, but always at the same time as an end.[19]

When, for example, you deceive another person in order to gain an economic advantage for yourself, you do not treat the other person as an end in themselves. Instead, you use them merely as a means to your end. In addition, the same can be said with conduct like murder and rape. For Dan-Cohen, this principle is not just one moral principle among other plausible moral principles. He believes that all immorality, in the final analysis, consists in violations of this version of the categorical imperative: 'all morality derives from a single master principle—the categorical imperative—which by enjoining the treatment of persons merely as means rather than as ends, spells out the meaning or the implication of according dignity to people.'[20] Therefore, at least in one sense, Dan-Cohen's theory of criminalization is more plausible than, for instance, harm principles. Contrary to any of the former mentioned theorists, who believe that harm matters in criminalization decisions, Dan-Cohen's theory is not redundant to a moral theory independent of the principle

---

[15]See e.g. Dan-Cohen (2002) and Buchhandler-Raphael (2013).

[16]Dan-Cohen (2002), p. 150.

[17]Ibid.

[18]Compare Kant (1785/2002) and Hill and Zweig (2002).

[19]Kant (1785/2002), p. 230.

[20]Dan-Cohen (2002), p. 160.

of criminalization at hand. This is because, according to Dan-Cohen, the categorical imperative is itself a grand moral theory that can guide all our moral actions and, as we shall see, also our criminalization decisions. However, to explain why Dan-Cohen believes we should replace harm principles with a Kantian dignity principle of criminalization, we need to spell out the latter principle in a little more detail. I suggest the following formulation of this principle.

> **The Kantian Dignity Principle of Criminalization (KDPC)**
> The main goal of the criminal law is to defend the dignity (or unique moral worth) of every human being by criminalizing acts that treat people, whether yourself or others, as mere means and not as ends in themselves.

The moral worth of every human being could, of course, be protected by strategies other than *criminalization*. We could create and support a non-punitive culture where people never treat each other as mere means but always as ends—e.g. through education and by teaching ourselves and our children about the moral worth of every human being, and how we respect that value by living in accordance with Kant's second rendering of the categorical imperative.[21] However, our purpose here is to discuss a specific principle of criminalization. In doing that, it seems fair, at least as a starting point, to specify KDPC as a combination of Dan-Cohen's view that defending the unique moral worth of every human being is the main goal of the criminal law and Kant's dignity principle, as I have done above.

Although KDPC can easily be used to argue in favour of criminalizing kinds of conduct (like murder, rape and violent attacks) that any principle of criminalization should be able to do, this specification of KDPC remains imprecise. First of all, what is meant by the words 'the main goal of the criminal law'? The phrase seems to indicate that there are goals for the criminal law other than defending the dignity of human beings. I mean, why refer to *the main goal* if the only goal is to defend the dignity of people? However, if there are other goals besides defending the dignity of every human being, what are they, and can they sometimes outweigh the main goal? Unfortunately, Dan-Cohen does not answer these important questions.[22] Therefore,

[21] See e.g. Duff (2018), Chap. 7, Section 2 for a fine discussion of reactions to moral wrongdoing that do not involve criminalization of wrongdoing.

[22] When we are considering what kinds of conduct the state should criminalize, goals other than defending dignity that we could obviously contemplate include those having to do with the economic costs of enforcing the criminal law. One could argue, for example, that the money spent on criminalizing conduct C would be better spent on criminalizing conduct A and B, in the sense that more crime or more severe crime would be prevented at the same monetary cost. Another goal of the criminal law would be to ensure that, from a democratic point of view, a majority of the public favour the existing criminal law. For if, the vast majority of the population is against the criminal law, the law could be categorized as undemocratic. However, if protecting dignity is not the only goal of the criminal law, these other goals must be categorized as non-moral goals—at least if, like Dan-Cohen, we believe that all immorality consists, in the end, in violation of Kant's dignity principle. I will not enter the debate over the sense in which we can understand these other goals as non-moral goals. However, I believe we can easily categorize the other goals I have mentioned as

because of this interpretation we can say that KDPC is also subject to the weighing challenge that was presented in Chap. 4. However, if the state can and should pursue goals other than defending dignity in its criminalization of certain kinds of conduct, it can be argued that this rules out the interpretative idea that the dignity principle is a sufficient condition for criminalization.

Actually, there are good reasons to interpret KDPC, as set out above, as providing a necessary condition for criminalization and not a sufficient condition. I base this interpretation on two observations. First, if we accept that all immorality consists of the violation of Kant's second categorical imperative,[23] and we combine this view with the claim that only immoralities ought to be criminalized,[24] it follows that any act that ought to be criminalized must violate human dignity. This is really just another way of saying that a necessary condition for criminalizing conduct C is that C violates the second categorical imperative. So far, so good, when it comes to an initial understanding of the version of KDPC set out above.

Second, there are good moral reasons to deny that the violation of dignity by C *per se* is a sufficient condition for C's criminalization. There are kinds of conduct, which we believe to be immoral because they involve treating another person as a mere means, but which we would hesitate to say should therefore be criminalized. Consider a lie treating another person as mere means and not as an end. For example, I falsely promise my friend that I will clean her car tomorrow if she visits my father in hospital today. It is far from obvious that such conduct ought to be treated as a criminal offence. Prohibiting, and especially enforcing laws against, what we can call small false promises, besides its huge economic cost, would probably have an immensely negative impact on the liberty and well-being of the state's citizens.[25] So, when Dennis Baker argues that we should not accept a dignity rationale for criminalization because it would support the criminalization of such activities as even the smallest kind of promise-breaking, his criticism does not undermine a charitable interpretation of the above version of KDPC.

That said we should be aware of two things. First, to argue that KDPC does not give a sufficient condition for criminalization is not to show that, on a proper understanding of it, the KDPC provides a necessary such condition. It may provide just one (perhaps important) reason among others for criminalizing conduct. This interpretation, however, would not fit well with Dan-Cohen's understanding of the KDPC since, as we have seen, for him all immorality is grounded in Kant's dignity principle. But it is, of course, a possible position. In Sect. 6.5, I will discuss a

moral goals; e.g. that we ought (morally) to take into account how much crime prevention we get from the money spent, within the criminal system, and the criminal law ought (morally) to be accepted by the majority. These observations make it less obvious how we should understand the content of these other so-called non-morals goals of the KDPC.

[23]Dan-Cohen (2002), p. 160.

[24]Something very close to this roughly described view is defended by Duff (2018), p. 53; Tadros (2016), p. 2. Simester and von Hirsch (2011), p. 22; Husak (2008), p. 83 are other advocates of this view.

[25]See e.g. Baker (2011), p. 157.

(non-Kantian) version of the dignity rationale for criminalization according to which respect for dignity is one moral reason among others for criminalizing conduct (and therefore neither a necessary nor a sufficient condition for criminalization). Secondly, we should be aware that, although we shall take KDPC to provide a necessary condition for criminalization, there could be conduct, such as cases of torture, where respect for dignity also delivers a sufficient reason for criminalization. It might be argued, for example, that torture ought to be criminalized even though there are other moral (and perhaps non-moral) reasons for making it legal in certain circumstances. This observation, however, does not mean that KDPC offers, or entails, a sufficient reason *tout court* for criminalization.

Let us now look at a reason Kantians often give for holding that a KDPC is more attractive than other principles of criminalization, especially if compared with harm principles.

5.4 A Dignity-Based Critique of Harm-Based Principles of Criminalization

The primary complaint those sympathetic to KDPC make about harm principles is that (unlike the version of KDPC we have discussed) they deliver the alleged wrong answers about criminalization in certain test cases.[26] Specifically, it leaves certain kinds of conduct, which clearly ought to be criminalized, legal. We can call this objection *the objection from under-inclusiveness*.[27] Let me briefly examine a famous case discussed by Dan-Cohen: the case of the happy slave.[28] Dan-Cohen says that adherents of a harm principle would not allow us to argue for a total ban on slavery, because we can imagine a situation where a person voluntarily agrees to be sold to another person as a slave and is happy about his situation. As the slave is happy, let us accept that no harm is done, and therefore, allegedly, harm principles cannot be used to show why such slavery should be criminalized. This is a problem, according to Dan-Cohen, because 'slavery is the paradigm case of injustice because it denies people's equal moral worth and thus treats them with disrespect.'[29] This verdict depends, of course, on how we specify the term 'harm'. However, if we accept the following standard account of what is involved when one person is harmed by

[26]The most famous exposition of a harm principle is Mill's: 'the only purpose for which power can be rightfully exercised over any member of a civilised community, against his will, is to prevent harm to others. His own good, either physical or moral, is not a sufficient warrant' Mill (1859/2003). However, harm principles of criminalization come, as was described in Chap. 2, in many different versions.

[27]This is a well-known type of objection raised against principles of criminalization: see e.g. Duff et al. (2010), pp. 49–51.

[28]Dan-Cohen (2002, 2016).

[29]Dan-Cohen (2002), p. 157. From a reading of Dan-Cohen, it is clear that this quotation is just another way of saying that slavery violates dignity.

another, it is clear that the happy slave is not harmed by being enslaved by a slave owner.

Being Harmed by Another Person

A person P1 is harmed by another person P2 doing C, if and only if P1 is made worse off in terms of well-being because of C.[30]

Before a presentation of three problems with this line of attack from under-inclusiveness, I would like to make a few comments on the use of the happy slave case. First, to evaluate principles of criminalization (like harm principles or dignity principles of criminalization) by showing what they imply in a case like the happy slave seems a little bit off-target. A bit off-target, because happy enslavement is a very unusual phenomenon that is not playing any significant role in real life criminalization decisions, compared to criminalization discussions about, say, prostitution or cannabis. Furthermore, the case of the happy slave is probably a case where we have tenuous intuitions. However, when philosophers try to find examples of conduct that are morally wrong but do not involve harm, they tend to focus on kinds of conduct that, like happy enslavement and dwarf-throwing, are not very common.[31]

Nevertheless, in order to take seriously the defenders of KDPC, I will discuss a type of case (the happy slave case) that they themselves present in arguing for the use of a dignity principle for criminalization. Furthermore, I believe that the critique of KDPC that I offer in Sect. 6.5 will apply not only to the unusual cases like that of the happy slave, but also to other cases of dignity violation, whether they are usual or unusual. Now to the three problems.

First, although it is possible for a person to volunteer to become a slave and then be happy as a slave, it seems fair to assume that this would be the exception rather than the rule. Adherents of a harm principle could therefore argue that we should criminalize slavery, as the risk that a person (as well as his relatives) would be harmed by enslavement is very high.[32] By analogy, someone driving at 100 km/h through an urban area where the speed limit is 40 km/h and by pure luck happen to benefit one in the process is not a good argument for legalizing such risky driving. The probability of harming a person seriously is extremely high with such driving, compared to driving at only 40 km/h, even though in one instance it did no harm. However, this empirical defence of harm principles will probably not satisfy adherents of KDPC. They will typically argue, because they are deontologists, that a person's dignity is still

[30]For this understanding of harming, see e.g. Holtug (2002), p. 364; Kagan (1998), p. 84; Feldman (2010), p. 165; Tadros (2016), p. 177. See also Chap. 2 for a more detailed specification of this view.

[31]When Duff (2014), p. 231 gives an example of an act that 'might not be straightforwardly harmful, but that seriously violates the dignity of those subjected to it . . . even if they freely consent to it . . . I think of "dwarf-throwing".' See also Chap. 4 Sect. 4.4.4 for a critical discussion of Duff's illustration.

[32]See e.g. Gardner (2007).

violated, even if the risk of harming people by slavery is low and sometimes non-existent. In KDPC perspective, harm or risk of harm does not matter in criminalization decisions, unless it involves treating a person as a mere means.

Furthermore, as I want to show in the next section, there are two additional problems with KDPC. So second, I want to argue, like some other philosophers, that the moral foundation of KDPC is problematic, as it may not always be morally wrong to treat a person as a mere means. Third, it is not obvious that adherents of the KDPC can deliver what is, for them, the right answer in the happy slave case, namely, that enslaving a happy slave is wrong and should be criminalized. However, if they cannot, one can criticize KDPC for being inconsistent. However, in order to determine whether it is always morally wrong to treat a person as a mere means and what KDPC implies when it is applied to the case of the happy slave, or indeed other more realistic cases, we need to specify in more detail how KDPC is to be interpreted. I take up this question in the next section, together with an elaboration of the above-mentioned critique of KDPC.

5.5 A Critique of the Kantian Dignity Principle of Criminalization

I would like to begin with the observation that two distinct moral values are at stake in KDPC, namely:

(i) Always treat a person as an end in themselves
(ii) Never treat a person merely as a means[33]

One could object that it does not make sense to divide the central part of KDPC in this way, because the two values are equivalent formulations of one and the same principle: you cannot have one without the other. The reasoning here is: (A) if I treat a person P as an end in herself, thus satisfying (i), it follows that I am not treating P merely as a means, and therefore that I satisfy (ii); and (B) by not treating a person P as merely a means, thus satisfying (ii), I thereby treat P as an end in herself, and thus satisfy (i).

While (A) seems perfectly right, e.g. if my aim by doing X is to help you achieve what you want, thereby treating you as an end in yourself, then I do not treat you merely as a means. On the other hand, it seems that you can satisfy (ii) without satisfying (i), thus refuting (B). Imagine that I am indifferent to a stranger in need,

---

[33] Apart from writing ‘a person’ instead of ‘humanity’, I here follow Hill and Zweig (2002), p. 76 in their interpretation of the principle as a formula that ‘expresses two closely related [moral] requirements: (a) we must always treat humanity as an end in itself, and (b) we must never treat humanity merely as a means’. See also Kamm (2007), p. 13 for this division of the categorical imperative into two components. Since, in his second version of the categorical imperative, Kant writes ‘Act in such a way that you treat humanity, whether in your own person or in any other person,’ it seems plausible to replace ‘humanity’ with ‘person’.

S. In that case, it seems fair to say that while I have not used S as a means at all, I have, by ignoring S's needs, failed to treat S as an end in herself.[34] Therefore, the two values are not necessarily connected in such a way that, if an act satisfies one of the two values, it satisfies the other. However, to make the case as strong as possible for KDPC, let us accept that if you violate one of these two values, you violate dignity. Therefore, an agent violates the dignity principle if and only if his act violates *at least one* of the values (i.e. either (i) or (ii)).[35]

With these two values in place, we can apply KDPC to the happy slave case. It is easy to see how dignity is violated in the happy slave case—at least, as long as the slave is treated either as a mere means of serving the interests of the slave owner, or is not being treated as an end in himself. Let us accept that the decisive factor in determining whether a person, R, has treated another person, P, as a mere means is R's *intention*.[36] Given this, if R intends to treat P as a slave only for his (R's) own sake, we can consistently claim that P is treated as a mere means.

However, it speaks against the claim that KDPC can deliver the allegedly right answer in the happy slave case (that slavery, including happy slavery, should be criminalized) that there could be happy slave cases where both value (i) and value (ii) are satisfied. Imagine that R is the slave owner, and that his only *intention* is to help P to become a slave for altruistic reasons. Assume, further, that P is a rational person and that P voluntarily wishes to become a slave. In this scenario, the enslavement of P is not a case of R treating P as a mere means to his (R's) own ends and P is treated as an end in himself as this is how he wants to be treated. The main problem with this scenario is that it makes KDPC vulnerable to objections from under-inclusiveness similar to those which Kantians, like Dan-Cohen, typically marshal against a harm-based approach to criminalization. Vulnerable, because there exist scenarios where the enslavement of happy slaves will not violate dignity, quite the contrary.

A further problem, at least for the moral foundation of KDPC, is that it does not always seem morally wrong to treat a person as a mere means. For example, imagine that I donate 100 euros to a stranger in need, S, and that I know the donation saves S's life. However, my donation is purely self-interested—e.g. I want to feel the warm

---

[34]For a similar case and argument, see Hill and Zweig (2002), p. 76.

[35]Kant has something stronger in mind. Remember the part of his principle which combines the two values with the words 'but always at the same time', a phrase which indicates that both values ought to be satisfied if one ought to act in accordance with this moral principle.

[36]Although it is possible for you to treat a person as a mere means without intending to do so—e.g. by saving yourself from drowning by standing on another person you take to be a stone lying under the water—I stick with the standard interpretation. The standard interpretation of treating a person as a mere means dictates that it is the *intention* of the actor that determines whether an act can be described as treating another person as merely a means. Kant himself focused on intention in this way: 'he who intends a deceitful promise to others sees immediately that he intends to use another man merely as a means, without the latter at the same time containing the end in himself' (Kant 1785/2002, p. 230).

glow of helping S, or to feel morally superior to other people.[37] It will follow from the Kantian dignity principle that it is morally wrong to save the life of the stranger S in the case we have been examining.[38] This does not seem right, and therefore we have a good reason to question the moral foundation of KDPC. Kantians, of course, could argue that I saved the life of the stranger for the wrong reasons, and that it would have been better to save him for the right reasons. I believe most would agree with this, but to claim that my act of saving S's life is, all things considered,[39] morally wrong seems implausible, at least if my alternative was not to donate anything to anyone. Parfit has argued that Kantians, faced with examples like those that I have just mentioned, could rephrase value (ii) with the following wording: 'that it is wrong to treat anyone merely as a means . . . if our act will also be likely to harm [or has harmed] this person'.[40] This solution would give the so-called right answer in our case with the stranger S. However, making the morality of a dignity-based principle of criminalization depend on harm seems to undermine the very idea behind KDPC, namely, that violating dignity (and thereby morality) is different from harming people. Furthermore, if we accept this plausible rewriting of the dignity principle by Parfit, KDPC cannot give the so-called right answer in the happy slave case, as it is not morally wrong to enslave happy slaves. And it is not morally wrong because happy slaves are not harmed by the enslavement, even though they are treated as mere means for the slave owner. If rational people have voluntarily agreed to be slaves, and further, are happy as slaves, it seems plausible to claim that they are not harmed. So even though the slave owner's only intention is that of using the happy slave for the slave owner's own good, slavery in this situation is not morally wrong because the happy slave is not harmed by being enslaved. We can here note that KDPC is also subject to the criminological levelling-down challenge presented in Chap. 4, as it can be difficult to see what is wrong with happy enslavement if everybody is better off (which is, of course, very unlikely) due to the enslavement.

So, we have observations suggesting that in some scenarios, KDPC fails to deliver what appears to be a right position (especially for adherents of KDPC such as Dan-Cohen) on happy enslavement. On the one hand, a person's dignity may not be violated by such enslavement, if the intention of the slave owner is to help the slave. Adherents of KDPC are therefore also subject to their own objection of under-inclusiveness. On the other hand, if dignity is violated, for example, if the intention of the slave owner is only to help himself, but the slave is happy for his enslavement, then it is far from convincing to claim that such a violation should be considered

---

[37]For a critique of Kantian moral philosophy like this, see Parfit (2011), p. 216; Guerrero (2016).

[38]However, we should be aware that although adherents of KDPC could argue that it is morally wrong to donate to strangers for egoistic reasons, it does not follow from KDPC that such conduct should be criminalized, since, as was argued in Sect. 5.3, KDPC only implies a necessary condition of criminalization.

[39]Remember that Dan-Cohen, for example, believes that the dignity principle is the only moral principle or that other moral principles, if there are any, can be derived from it.

[40]Parfit (2011), p. 217.

morally wrong. So the moral foundation for KDPC can be challenged, but when reformulated, as plausibly suggested by Parfit, for instance, in order to meet that challenge, KDPC runs again into the problem of under-inclusiveness, as happy slavery is not morally wrong then. Defenders of KDPC are therefore inconsistent when they reject harm principles because such principles do not give the so-called right answer in the case of the happy slave, and at the same time are in favour of KDPC, which does not give the right answer in the happy slave case either.

In the next section, we shall discuss a non-Kantian conception of the way in which a concern for human dignity can be given a place within a theory of criminalization.

5.6 A Critique of a Non-Kantian Interpretation of the Dignity Principle of Criminalization

Tatjana Hörnle has recently presented a non-Kantian dignity-based principle of criminalization.[41] In two important respects, Hörnle's principle differs from KDPC. First, she does not argue that a dignity principle should be the main principle (or provide a necessary condition for criminalization) that guides us in our attempt to identify the kinds of conduct that the state ought to criminalize. Instead, she argues for the more modest position that respect for dignity is a moral right '*alongside* the multitude of individuals' other rights'.[42] Therefore, respect for dignity is a right that should be taken into account in discussions of the kinds of conduct we are entitled to criminalize. Unfortunately, Hörnle does not spend much time specifying the other rights, although she does refer to, and apply, 'the right to autonomy' and 'the right to freedom of speech' in a few examples. This is unfortunate if we want to use the multitude of rights to justify what kinds of conduct the state has reason to criminalize, and if we wish to show how the various rights (among them, the right to dignity) should be weighed against each other when they are in conflict. Hörnle is therefore also subject to the weighing challenge that we discussed in detail in Chap. 4.

Second, Hörnle argues that the use of Kant's second formulation of the categorical imperative as guidance in criminalization decisions is problematic because 'the "merely as means" formula is too broad and too vague, but at the same time also too narrow for our purpose.'[43] In addition, the aim of criminalization theory is, according to Hörnle, to obtain principles which can guide us with some clear boundaries 'rather than some vague master formula'.[44] Without explaining in more detail why Hörnle believes that the incorporation of this Kantian principle in

---

[41]Hörnle (2012).

[42]Hörnle (2012), p. 308.

[43]Ibid., p. 311.

[44]Ibid., p. 312.

a principle of criminalization is problematic, I would like to highlight one of the problems lying at the centre of Hörnle's critique. The problem has to do with the alleged under-inclusiveness, or narrowness, of Kant's second formulation of the categorical imperative.

According to Hörnle, an act of torture conducted out of pure contempt for the victim, and therefore without any intention of achieving any further goals like making a suspect confess or retrieving important information, is obviously morally wrong. However, Hörnle says that such an act does not treat the victim as a means to anything and therefore cannot be defined as morally wrong using Kant's second formulation of the categorical imperative.[45] I disagree. I believe that torture performed out of pure contempt for the victim can readily be interpreted as a violation of Kant's principle. Remember that two values are at stake in Kant's principle: always treat people as ends in themselves *and* never treat people merely as means. It is obvious that the kind of torture Hörnle has in mind violates the first value. By torturing a person out of pure contempt for them, you do not treat them as an end in themselves, as you ignore or give little weight to their well-being. Moreover, it seems just as plausible to claim that the torturer treats the tortured individual merely as a means of, or instrument to be used in, expressing his contempt of the victim. Contrary to what Hörnle claims, this kind of torture is therefore a violation of Kant's famous principle.[46]

Whether or not this criticism of Hörnle is correct, we must attend to the fact that Hörnle rejects Kant's principle as a plausible principle of criminalization. Instead of relying on Kant's second formulation of the categorical imperative, as Dan-Cohen does, she argues for the following principle:

> **Hörnle's Non-Kantian Dignity Principle of Criminalization**
> References to human dignity can justify the existence of penal prohibitions which aim to prevent conduct which is severely humiliating.[47]

In what follows, and in the context of principles of criminalization, I take this to mean that one effective way, among others, of preventing conduct that severely humiliates people is by prohibiting such conduct. According to Hörnle, all human beings share an interest in not being severely humiliated. However, what does she take severe humiliation to involve? First, she accepts that the term 'humiliation' is fuzzy.[48] But she explains that 'humiliation' in the relevant sense—a sense linked to a

---

[45]Ibid.

[46]This is true as both values (i) and (ii) have been violated.

[47]Ibid., p. 308. One way to understand why this interpretation of dignity is different from Kant's dignity principle is this: imagine a case where a person is being humiliated, but where the intention is not to use the person being humiliated as a mere means to another person's end, and where the person being humiliated is a rational person who voluntarily approves of the humiliation. In this case, Hörnle's principle of dignity can be used to argue in favour of the prohibition of such conduct even though the conduct does not in any straightforward sense violate Kant's dignity principle.

[48]Ibid., p. 315.

wider discussion of the criminalization of conduct—does not depend on feelings of humiliation caused by, say, racist or sexist remarks. Instead, Hörnle believes that humiliation is a matter of objective meaning.[49] You may not feel humiliated by a person who says that you should be killed because you are Jewish or Afro-American, but I believe most of us would regard this kind of remark as a clear case of not just humiliation, but severe humiliation. Although you will often feel humiliated by such a remark, in some cases you may not. That may happen, for example, because you are convinced that the person making the comment is psychologically unhinged and does not deserve serious attention. However, you still have *good reason* to feel severely humiliated, and that alone is enough, for Hörnle, to justify criminalization of the conduct in question.

Second, it is important for Hörnle that it is only *severe* humiliation that the state has reason to criminalize. The criminalization of humiliation generally, including minor insults and mildly offensive jokes, would, according to Hörnle, erode the value of free speech. The value of free speech trumps concerns about less than severe humiliation.[50]

To explain the role that human dignity—understood as freedom from severe humiliation—plays in decisions about criminalization, Hörnle presents examples of conduct which she judges to be severely humiliating and therefore suitable for criminalization. I will briefly present some of these examples before assessing Hörnle's view. Speech offences which, for example, declare that a person or group of people ought to be killed or deported are severely humiliating because, according to Hörnle, they 'negate the quality of a human being in principle'.[51] To negate, in this sense, is to 'negate the person's right to be accepted as co-citizens in principle'.[52] In cases of severe humiliation, freedom of speech is trumped by respect for human dignity. However, if a person is insulted by a negative comment about, for example, his weight, this is not an episode of severe humiliation and should not be treated as a criminal offence. Hörnle also mentions some kinds of conduct that should be criminalized because they are severely humiliating, including involuntary slavery, torture and sexual offences like rape and the production of pornography with people who have not consented to be involved in the sexual acts.[53]

I turn now to criticism of Hörnle's non-Kantian principle of criminalization.[54] We need to ask, first, whether her principle, like KDPC, invites the objection of under-inclusiveness. What verdict would the theory deliver, for example, in the case of the happy slave? It would appear that Hörnle is not committed to the wrong answer in the happy slave case—i.e. her theory is consistent with the view that such slavery

[49]Ibid., p. 316.

[50]Ibid., p. 318.

[51]Ibid.

[52]Ibid.

[53]Ibid., pp. 317–323.

[54]Apart, of course, from the objection that her critique of Kant's categorical imperative, discussed in a later paragraph, is on the wrong track.

merits criminalization. First, it would be entirely in keeping with her views to claim that enslaving an individual is severely humiliating to the slave even if he or she is happy and does not feel the humiliation. Hörnle can point out that the slave has objective reasons to feel humiliated. Second, even if we deny that the happy slave has objectives reason to feel humiliated because they are content and happy, we should bear in mind that, for Hörnle, respect for human dignity, understood as freedom from severe humiliation, is just one right among others informing criminalization. With a variety of rights principles in place, there is still room to argue that conduct which does not involve severe humiliation—if that is what the enslavement of people who are happy when enslaved is to be understood as—should be criminalized.[55]

However, I believe that Hörnle's theory is problematic for at least one important reason. The theory seems to be *redundant* in two ways, compared to some current theories of criminalization. First, it is difficult to specify the job that Hörnle's principle of dignity does, compared to the jobs done by harm principles, or the offence principles, or versions of legal moralism. If the state can just as well argue that acts which expose people to severe humiliation ought to be criminalized because this will help to prevent instances of wrongful harm, wrongful offence or some other moral wrong from being committed, the job of her dignity rationale becomes unclear. It no longer seems necessary to refer, as Hörnle does, to human dignity in explaining why offensive speech, slavery, torture and rape ought to be criminalized. Instead, we can simply say that these kinds of conduct ought to be criminalized because they e.g. are instances of wrongful harm-doing or because criminalization will prevent conduct that is morally harmful (in line with harm principles), or which some people take serious offence at (in line with offence principles), or because they are morally wrong for other reasons (legal moralism).

Second, and more specifically, it is difficult to see how respect for dignity in the form of protection from 'severe humiliation' differs from an offence principle like Feinberg's: 'It is always a good reason in support of a proposed criminal prohibition that it would probably be an effective way of preventing *serious offense* (as opposed to injury or harm) to persons . . . .'[56] An intuitive interpretation of what is involved in being severely humiliated by conduct C is that such humiliation involves being seriously offended by C. To flesh out what it would be to take serious offense at conduct C, Joel Feinberg has famously tried to describe in detail various kinds of offense, and these seem to be close to, if not identical with, what Hörnle means by 'humiliation'. Feinberg says that the taking of serious offense involves both a subjective element (a mental state like shame, anxiety or feeling insulted) and the

[55]So this implication of being able to deliver the so-called right answer in the happy slave case makes it clear that Hörnle is also subject to the criminological levelling-down challenge, as we at least have a reason to criminalize kinds of conduct that cause severe humiliation even though everyone (which is, of course, very unlikely) is better off because of these kinds of humiliations.

[56]Feinberg (1985), p. 1.

objective element that the action causing these states is morally wrong.[57] It is regrettable that Hörnle does not explain how her understanding of the dignity principle of criminalization differs from the offense principle.

Therefore, Hörnle's argument that the discourse on criminalization would benefit from references to human dignity does not get off the ground. In support of her conclusion, she says 'human dignity arguments can simply . . . give a fuller picture of wrongdoing (in addition to arguments relating to other rights),'[58] and that this is something we should value. However, why is it important, or valuable, to operate with this fuller picture of wrongdoing, if references to wrongful harm, or wrongful offence, or other kinds of wrong (e.g. violations of rights other than the right to human dignity) provide *sufficient* grounds to criminalize practices and kinds of conduct such as slavery, torture and rape? Hörnle's dignity principle appears, then, to be redundant, at least when it comes to the implications that can be drawn from hers and other well-known principles of criminalization. In addition, we have reason to prefer simpler theorizing: for reasons of thought-economy, we should opt for fewer principles rather than more.

As a theory of criminalization should guide our choices, Hörnle could, of course, claim that we have a stronger reason to criminalize conduct that violates several rights (among them, the right to be treated with dignity) than we do to criminalize conduct that violates fewer rights. She could also argue that the right to be treated with dignity can be used to argue for the criminalization of a type of conduct C, where C is conduct that clearly ought to be criminalized. But a kind of conduct that at the same time cannot be shown to merit criminalization using other principles, such as the traditional ones (the harm principle, the offence principle, etc.) or some of the rights principles she favours in her own theory of criminalization. She could, in other words, argue that other principles of criminalization are *under-inclusive* compared to her theory. Again, Hörnle could argue that her theory of criminalization, unlike harm principles, for instance, cannot be used to justify the criminalization of acts that ought not to be criminalized. Thus she could argue that alternative principles of criminalization are *over-inclusive*, compared to her theory. However, these arguments do need to be made and specified in order for us to make a proper evaluation of them. Unfortunately, however, Hörnle or others have not yet made and specified these suggestions in any plausible way.

5.7 Conclusion

I hope to have shown that the view that the concept of human dignity should play at least some role, if not the main part in a principle of criminalization is problematic for several reasons. First, I have tried to spell out in detail how we should understand

[57]Feinberg (1985), pp. 1 and 10–13. See Chap. 3 for a more detailed presentation and critique of Feinberg's offence principle.

[58]Ibid., p. 308.

the vague concept of dignity and the Kantian-inspired dignity principle of criminalization. Second, I have argued that adherents of KDPC are inconsistent as KDPC (at least, in some scenarios) suffers from the very same kind of under-inclusiveness that its advocates locate in standard versions of the harm principle. Third, I have shown that although KDPC do not seem to be redundant to moral theory (as it is a moral theory in itself), KDPC seems to be subject to the weighing challenge as respect of dignity is not all the matters in criminalization decisions. Furthermore, KDPC does have morally problematic implications, as it is obvious that it is not always wrong to violate the dignity of others. Fourth, I have tried to show that two recent criticisms of KDPC, advanced by Hörnle and Baker, can be successfully challenged. By interpreting KDPC as a sufficient reason for criminalization, Baker misses the target with his allegation of over-inclusiveness; and Hörnle presents an excessively narrow interpretation of Kant's second formulation of the categorical imperative. Finally, I have argued that Hörnle's dignity rationale is redundant for two reasons: the kinds of conduct she believes can be shown to merit criminalization by referring to human dignity, understood as severe humiliation, can just as easily be shown to merit criminalization by referring to other principles such as standard versions of the harm principle. Furthermore, and more specifically, her understanding of dignity seems to be identical with moral concerns that are entailed in Feinberg's version of the offense principle.

References

Baker DJ (2011) The right not to be criminalized: demarcating criminal law's authority. Ashgate Publishing Limited, Farnham

Bostrom N (2009) Dignity and enhancement. Contemp Read Law Soc Justice 1(2):84–115

Buchhandler-Raphael M (2013) Drugs, dignity, and danger. Human dignity as a constitutional constraint to limit overcriminalization. Tenn Law Rev 80:291–345

Dan-Cohen M (2002) Defending dignity. UC Berkeley Shool Law Public Law Leg. Theory Reserach Pap. No. 92, 2002

Dan-Cohen M (2016) Normative subjects: self and collectivity in morality and law, Chapter 7. Oxford University Press, Oxford

Duff RA (2014) Towards a modest legal moralism. Crim Law Philos 8(1):217–235

Duff RA (2018) The realm of criminal law. Oxford University Press, Oxford

Duff RA et al (2010) The boundaries of the criminals law. Oxford University Press, Oxford

Feinberg J (1984) Harm to others. Oxford University Press, Oxford

Feinberg J (1985) Offense to others. Oxford University Press, Oxford

Feinberg J (1986) Harm to self. Oxford University Press, Oxford

Feinberg J (1988) Harmless wrongdoing. Oxford University Press, Oxford

Feldman F (2010) Pleasure and the good life. Oxford University Press, Oxford

Gardner J (2007) Offences and defences: selected essays in the philosophy of criminal law. Oxford University Press, Oxford

Gerstein RS (1974) Capital punishment – "cruel and unusual?"A retributivist response. Ethics 85 (1):75–79

Guerrero A (2016) Appropriately using people merely as a means. Crim Law Philos 10(4):777–794

Hill TE, Zweig A (2002) Kant: groundwork for the metaphysics of morals. Oxford University Press, Oxford

Holtug N (2002) The harm principle. Ethical Theory Moral Pract 5(4):357–389
Hörnle T (2012) Criminalizing behaviour to protect human dignity. Crim Law Philos 6(3):307–325
Husak D (2008) Overcriminalization. Oxford University Press, Oxford
Kagan S (1998) Normative ethics. Westview Press, Boulder
Kamm FM (2007) Intricate ethics: rights, responsibilities, and permissible harm. Oxford University Press, Oxford
Kamm FM (2013) Bioethical prescriptions. Oxford University Press, Oxford
Kant I (1785) Groundwork for the metaphysics of morals. 2002. Oxford University Press, Oxford
Kass L (2002) Life, liberty, and defence of dignity: a challenge for bioethics. Encounter Books, New York
Kleinig J (1998) The hardness of harsh treatment. In: Ashworth A, Wasik M (eds) Fundamentals of sentencing theory. Clarendon Press, Oxford
Lippert-Rasmussen K (2005) Deontology, responsibility, and equality. University of Copenhagen Press, Copenhagen
Mill JS (1859/2015) On liberty, utilitarianism, and other essays. Oxford University, Oxford
Moore M (1997) Placing blame. Oxford University Press, Oxford
Parfit D (2011) On what matters, volume one. Oxford University Press, Oxford
Petersen TS (2010) Punishment and dignity. In: Ryberg J, Corlett JA (eds) Punishment and ethics. Palgrave Macmillan, London
Schroeder D, Bani-Sadr A (2017) Dignity in the twenty-first century: Middle east and west. Springer Publishing, Basingstoke
Simester AP, Von Hirsch A (2011) Crimes, harms, and wrongs: on the principles of criminalization. Bloomsbury Publishing, Oxford
Tadros V (2016) Wrongs and crimes. Oxford University Press, Oxford
Waldron J (2012) Dignity, rank, and rights. Oxford University Press, Oxford

Chapter 6
A Soft Defence of a Utilitarian Principle of Criminalization

6.1 Introduction

When the state criminalizes certain kinds of conduct, like murder, rape and assault, consequences for the autonomy, opportunities, rights and well-being of its citizens follow. The punishment that often follows the detection of a crime can have positive consequences. For example, it may deter both the offender and others and thereby prevent further crimes from being committed in the future. However, criminalization does not only have positive effects. Usually, it also has negative consequences for those offenders who transgress the criminal law and receive punishment, and for the relatives of such offenders. Moreover, the enforcement of the criminal justice system—the process of detecting criminal offenders through policing, putting offenders to trial and punishing them—comes with serious economic costs, and in that sense, criminalization places a burden on the citizens who, through their taxes, pay for the system. These facts inform the guiding research question of this chapter, namely: to what extent should the consequences of criminalization matter morally in a theory of criminalization?[1]

The chapter proceeds as follows. In Sect. 6.2, I present three possible answers to the question just stated and explain why I shall discuss only two of these answers at length. Section 6.3 presents a specification of *the utilitarian principle of criminalization* (UPC) and provides some reasons in favour of spending ink on a critical discussion of UPC. In Sects. 6.4 and 6.5, I explain why central critics of UPC (or a consequentialist theory of criminalization), like Douglas Husak and Victor Tadros, have not given UPC a fair trial in their recent work. In Sect. 6.6, the central aim is to present a positive reason for thinking that UPC is attractive as a principle of criminalization. The reason is as follows: UPC is consistent with what I call *the*

[1]Bear in mind that by 'a theory of criminalization' I mean a theory that gives us a justified answer to the following normative question: by what moral principle(s) should criminalization decisions be guided?

T. Søbirk Petersen, *Why Criminalize?*, Law and Philosophy Library 134,
https://doi.org/10.1007/978-3-030-34690-4_6

counterproductive criminalization principle (CCP), while non-consequentialist theories of criminalization (like legal moralism the dignity principle of criminalization) usually are not.[2] In a first and very rough approximation, CCP says that, where everything else is equal, if the consequences of criminalizing a morally wrong kind of conduct C in society S will result in C becoming more widespread in S, the criminalization of C is morally wrong. In Sect. 6.6, I will furthermore spell out this principle in detail and examining some examples of counterproductive criminalization *en route*. Finally, I will suggest how non-consequentialist theories of criminalization have difficulty complying with CCP, and I will critically discuss one possible objection to CCP. Section 6.7 sums up the findings.

It should be clear from the outset that the overall aim of the chapter is not to present a so-called *hard* defence of UPC. I shall not argue that UPC is the best of the existing theories of criminalization. Given the vast literature on criminalization theory and the many different theories and principles that have been proposed and defended, it would be arrogant to think that I can show in a book chapter that UPC is the best of all theories or principles on criminalization. Instead, the aim is to present a *soft* defence of UPC, the purpose of which is to show that UPC has not been given what I consider to be a fair trial and therefore should not be dismissed by default. UPC is better than its poor reputation suggests and, as a principle of criminalization, it is preferable to the other principles of criminalization that have been critically investigated in this book.

6.2 Setting the Stage

To what extent should the consequences of criminalization matter morally in a theory of criminalization? In this section, I present three possible answers and explain why I shall discuss only two of these answers. First, I will outline the difference among anti-consequentialists, non-consequentialists and consequentialists.

Anti-consequentialists believe that the consequences of criminalizing a type of conduct C do not matter at all, and should therefore always be omitted from moral evaluation of whether or not the state ought to criminalize C.[3] For non-consequentialists, by contrast, consequences do usually matter in moral evaluation of whether the state ought to criminalize C, but they are not all that matters. Thus, we are not allowed to violate certain moral constraints (e.g. killing an innocent person or violating a person's autonomy or treating a person merely as a means) even if the violation of one or more of these constraints by criminalizing C would promote the

[2]As we shall discuss in Sect. 6.3 moderate versions of a non-consequentialism can in some instances comply with CCP.

[3]Bare in mind when I write 'C' for conduct in what follows, I mean *type of conduct C*. Criminal laws apply to types of conduct, not tokens. See also Chap. 2, footnote 3.

best consequences.[4] A third position is occupied by consequentialism. This position claims that consequences are all that matter in the justification of criminalization. We can frame a principle of criminalization within consequentialism as follows:

A Consequentialist Principle of Criminalization
Criminalizing conduct C in manner X (e.g. by imprisonment for 2 years) is morally right if and only if, among all possible kinds of conduct, that criminalization will promote the best consequences.

There are, of course, many versions of consequentialism, for example, depending on what counts as 'the best consequences'. The most famous version of consequentialism is utilitarianism, where the best consequences are brought about with the maximization of well-being.

Which of these three positions, if any, is a plausible candidate for a theory of criminalization? We can begin by ruling out anti-consequentialism. If criminalizing C would *imply* disastrous consequences like a civil war or a bloody riot, such consequences should matter in the normative evaluation of whether the state should criminalize C.[5] However, as anti-consequentialism rules out taking into account such consequences, we should reject anti-consequentialism. Therefore, the search for a plausible theory of criminalization should be conducted among theories of a non-consequentialist or consequentialist kind. However, for the last 40 years or so consequentialism, and especially utilitarianism, have received little support from philosophers developing normative theories or principles of criminalization and punishment.[6] Nevertheless, I believe the time has come for a rethink concerning support for a utilitarian principle of criminalization.

---

[4]It is standard practice to divide non-consequentialism into absolutist or moderate (or-non-absolutists) versions. In absolutist versions, we are never allowed to violate a moral constraint M, no matter how good the consequences would be. In moderate versions we are allowed to violate M, but only if the consequences are significantly good. See, for example, Kagan (1998), p. 79; Lippert-Rasmussen (2005), p. 17 for this division.

[5]If the criminalization of C in the latter examples amounts to a violation of a moral constraint, M, absolutist versions of non-consequentialism could in this case reach the same implausible verdict as anti-consequentialism, namely, that the consequences of criminalizing C ought not to matter in our evaluation of whether C ought to be criminalized. However, these two moral theories are different, and they can therefore be used to evaluate certain situations differently. The reason for this is that absolutists, unlike anti-consequentialists, are usually taken to adopt a theory according to which we have a *pro tanto* reason to promote the best consequences (see e.g. Kagan 1998), pp. 16–17. Therefore, if the criminalization of C will lead to a civil war, and criminalizing C does *not* violate a moral constraint M, then an absolutist non-consequentialist would accept that the consequences of criminalizing C ought to matter in a normative evaluation of whether C ought to be criminalized.

[6]See e.g. Feinberg (1986), Moore (1997), Husak (2008) and Tadros (2013, 2016) for a critique of consequentialism used as a theory of criminalization. However, there are some recent publications speaking in favour of consequentialist theories of tort law and criminalization (criminal law): they include Chiao (2016), Fried (2012) and Priel (2018). In an effort to shift the discussion beyond these three very valuable articles, this chapter deals explicitly and primarily with UPC and, more importantly, seeks to defend UPC against recent criticism not touched upon by the three scholars just mentioned.

6.3 Specifying UPC and the Importance of Defending UPC

Before turning to critical discussions of UPC, we first need to specify UPC in a little more detail. Furthermore, in what follows, I would also like to present a few reasons why it is a worthwhile project to defend UPC. So first things first, one of the most extensively developed criticisms of UPC is down to Douglas Husak. Husak begins his critique with the following specification of UPC: 'that the state is justified in enacting whatever set of proscriptions maximize utility'. However, this specification of UPC is very sketchy and I prefer the following formulation:

> **The Utilitarian Principle of Criminalization (UPC)**
> Criminalizing conduct C in manner X (e.g. by imprisonment for 2 years) is morally right if and only if, among all possible kinds of conduct, that criminalization will promote the greatest total amount of well-being.

In other words, if everything else is equal, and the total amount of well-being created by criminalizing C in manner X outweighs the total amount of well-being that could be created by any other kind of conduct, then it is morally right to criminalize conduct C in manner X.[7] The 'in manner X' description, is added to make it clear that estimating whether or not criminalization of a conduct C will maximize well-being, will also depend on how and how hard a person committing C is punished.[8]

[7]By 'morally right to criminalize conduct C' I mean here that it is morally obligatory for the state to criminalize C. Furthermore, in what follows, I will, for stylistic reasons, leave out the words 'in manner X'.

[8]Some philosophers, like Douglas Husak and Michael Moore, have argued in favour of what Edwards (2017) has called *the punishment thesis,* which is a thesis about the relationship between criminalization and punishment. The punishment thesis roughly claims that: when we want to identify the conditions under which it is permissible to criminalize, we must first identify the conditions under which it is permissible for the state to punish. For a critique of the punishment thesis, see Edwards (2017). In a consequentialist/utilitarian theory of criminalization, it is not obvious that the temporal or logical order in which the different consequences of criminalizing conduct C are calculated does matter. According to a utilitarian principle of criminalization, what matters is that the state should take into account all consequences when deciding which conduct the state ought to criminalize. Furthermore, one could here claim (thanks to Jesper Ryberg for this observation) that theories of criminalization are redundant to theories of punishment, as the latter would imply which kind of conduct should be criminalized: just criminalize those acts that we believe are permissible to punish. Nevertheless, there are reasons to be sceptical of this view. First, there could be, at least from a logical perspective, utilitarian reasons in favour of criminalizing a kind of conduct C even though doing C ought not to be punishable. Second, as already hinted at, there may also be consequences of criminalization that are not entailed by the consequences of punishment. For instance, the criminalization of a conduct C might not only send a signal about the punishment of C, but also a signal of what the state believes is morally right or wrong, like a kind of moral censure of certain kinds of conduct that is not only entailed in the mere punishment of doing conduct C. See Duff (2018), p. 8 for this latter claim. However, even if Ryberg is right, the defence

In what follows, I will not present a systematic discussion of the many variants of UPC. This alone would merit a book-length study. For present purposes, I hope it will suffice to make the points I wish to make with reference to the rough-and-ready version of UPC presented above. I would add that I believe that the objections to UPC or consequentialist theories of criminalization which have been presented in the literature, and which are to be discussed in what follows, apply to the version of UPC described above.

However, why is it a worthwhile project to defend UPC? I believe there are several reasons for spending ink on defending a utilitarian principle of criminalization. First, although some philosophers, like Bentham,[9] Hart,[10] and Simester and Sullivan,[11] have accepted something like UPC, none, to my knowledge, has devoted much time to the defence of UPC. Either, like Bentham, they have focused primarily on describing UPC and its applications in justifying the content of the criminal law, or they flag their adherence to something like UPC without discussing possible objections to it. The latter happens, for example, in the work of Simester and Sullivan when they write: 'it is retributivism which resolves who will be punished and how much punishment will be meted ... to be sure, utilitarianism is given the task of determining which conduct should be punished.'[12]

Second, and very importantly, as I want to show in the next two sections there are good reasons to think that the objections to UPC presented in the literature are not knockdown arguments. Finally, as I want to show in Sect. 6.6, it is an attractive feature that only consequentialist theories like UPC are always consistent with CCP.

Before presenting and critically discussing some objections to UPC, I will somewhat briefly explain why we might consider it an attractive principle of criminalization. First, I think we can safely assume that UPC can justify the criminalization of core cases of criminal conduct such as murder, rape and assault. Empirical studies show us that murder, rape and assault flourish where they are not criminalized and punished by the state, or where the detection and conviction rate is very low because, for example, there is a police strike or war.[13]

of UPC in what follows can easily be translated into a defence of a utilitarian theory of punishment, so the arguments would still be philosophically valuable.

[9]Bentham (1781).

[10]Hart (1968). According to the prevailing interpretation of Hart's philosophy of law, he may also approve of a view in which we accept one theory for the justification of punishment (retributivism) and another theory for the justification of criminalization (utilitarianism). For this interpretation, see e.g. Husak (2008), p. 192. However, this may be incorrect, as nothing I have seen in Hart's writing rules out the idea that his retributivist justification for state punishment can be combined with the idea that punishment is an instrument to maximize the total amount of well-being. Rachels (2007) is an example of a philosopher who, without mentioning Hart, favours using the known principles of retributivism (e.g. not punishing innocents, proportionality between crime and punishment, same punishment for same crime) as instruments to maximize the total amount of well-being in society.

[11]Simester and Sullivan (2000).

[12]Ibid., p. 22.

[13]Andenaes (1966).

Second, UPC can, compared to well-known principles of criminalization such as versions of the harm principle, legal moralism or dignity principles that we have discussed in this book, deliver a necessary and sufficient condition for criminalization. Remember that, in their most plausible version, these other principles only deliver either a necessary condition or just one condition (sometimes a sufficient one) among others for when the state ought to criminalize a type of conduct. I believe this feature of delivering both necessary and sufficient conditions for criminalization, although very ambitious, speaks in favour of UPC. And we need that, instead of having to add additional, usually consequentialist considerations concerning economic costs or respect for other values (than e.g. harm or offense)—as is the case with all the other criminalization principles that have been the subject of this book—in order to point out why we ought to criminalize certain kinds of conduct C.

Third, unlike harm principles and offence principles, UPC will not be redundant to grand moral theory (compare Chaps. 2 and 3) in order to specify what we shall understand as morally wrongful harms or offences. This is true because UPC is already embedded in a utilitarian theory that makes it clear not only when a type of conduct C is morally wrongful, but also when C ought to be criminalized. Fourth, UPC fares better than central versions of legal moralism (compare Chap. 4), as it is obvious that UPC is not subject to, for example, the challenge from relativism or the criminological levelling-down challenge.[14] According to UPC, it is morally right to criminalize a kind of conduct C if it will maximize well-being, no matter how that verdict relates to, for instance, what the leaders (and/or a majority) in a totalitarian society believe is morally right. Furthermore, it will never follow from UPC that an outcome of criminalizing a type of conduct C would be better in any sense, if everyone became worse off in terms of well-being, if C were criminalized. Finally, UPC fares better than the dignity principles of criminalization that were discussed in Chap. 5, either because UPC would not, like a KDPC, run into problems of inconsistency when applied to specific cases of criminalization like the happy slave case, or because it is obvious that UPC would not, like Hörnle's dignity principle, be redundant to Feinberg's offense principle.

6.4 A Critical Discussion of Husak's Objection to UPC

In this section, I will respond to Husak's critique of UPC. In Sect. 6.5, I will discuss some of Tadros's objections to consequentialist versions of harm principles, as these, with little translation, can be used to challenge UPC.

Husak presents an argument against UPC based on the premise that it is morally wrong to criminalize a kind of conduct in which one person is sacrificed in order to promote the greatest total of well-being. Husak's argument here builds on a famous case in which H. J. McCloskey attempted to argue that a utilitarian *justification of*

[14]UPC is also not subject to WEC, as it is a non-pluralistic principle of criminalization.

punishment should be rejected.[15] A version of the case runs roughly like this: a sheriff convicts and punishes an innocent man called Bob in order to prevent a mob from lynching six innocent men in revenge for a murder. No one, besides the sheriff and Bob, will ever know that Bob is innocent. Let us call this case 'Mob'.

According to McCloskey and Husak, Mob is enough to refute a utilitarian justification for punishment. And, because it follows from utilitarianism that the morally right thing to do in Mob is to punish an innocent person, a utilitarian justification for punishment cannot be right. In itself, the Mob case is not directed at UPC, as it only says something about the morality of punishing innocents, and little about the morality of criminalization. However, Husak translates Mob, which is designed to show that a utilitarian *justification of punishment* is wrong, into a new counterexample designed to refute a utilitarian *justification of criminalization* (i.e. UPC) in the following way:

> Suppose a theorist purported to remedy this injustice [punishing an innocent person in a case like Mob] by amending the penal code so that... [Bob] no longer was innocent of a criminal offense. The content of the new crime of which [he] would be guilty would be (roughly) to be a person whose punishment would produce the greatest utility. Clearly, this imaginary crime would violate nearly every constraint on criminalization ever defended. No commentator would be taken seriously if he suggested that the enactment of this new crime would remedy the injustice to... [Bob].[16]

So, although in this suggested translation of Mob (let us call it 'Mob∗') Bob is guilty, it is still incorrect, according to Husak, to claim that Bob has done something (being a person in a certain situation) that ought to be criminalized and therefore should be punished. Let us call the type of crime that Bob is legally guilty of in Mob∗ for X. One way to capture the general idea of such a crime could be the following:

> **Crime X**
> A person P is guilty of committing crime X if P happens to be in a situation S or to engage in a conduct C, where the punishment of P would produce the greatest total amount of well-being.

Crime X can entail many different kinds of situations or conducts. To take an example of a crime X other than that in Mob∗, imagine that it will produce the greatest amount of well-being to criminalize people who do not exercise for 30 min at least four times per week. Following Husak, however, crime X ought not to be treated as an offence by the criminal law, as that would be contrary to "nearly every constraint on criminalization ever defended".[17] So let us grant that the criminalization of people who do not do the proper amount of exercise would violate constraints

---

[15] McCloskey (1957).

[16] Husak (2008), pp. 192–193.

[17] Ibid. I take it for granted that criminalizing a person who does not exercise for 30 min at least four times per week would, according to Husak, violate constraints like 'respect for autonomy', 'not treating a person as a mere means' or 'treat people as they deserve'.

imposed by, for example, respect for autonomy or dignity. I believe, however, that there are good reasons to insist that Mob∗ should not force us to reject UPC.

To begin with, several empirical observations suggest that making it a criminal offence to be involved in e.g. doing less than four times 30 min exercise per week, would probably fail to maximize total well-being. First, if the criminalization of doing less than four times 30 min exercise per week were a reality, we might all end up living in constant fear (especially if the enforcement were omnipresent and the punishment harsh). Either that, or at least we might be worried (even if the enforcement were lax and the punishment lenient) about constantly finding ourselves in situations where the state could criminalize our conduct. These fears and worries may decrease well-being in the society in which we live more than any increase to be gained through criminalizing types of situations or conduct that one could worry would fall under the description of crime X.

However, in contrast with Mob, where Bob is legally innocent, there is a stronger reason to believe that the criminalization of Bob in Mob∗, where Bob commits a crime of the type X and therefore is legally guilty, will not maximize well-being. To see why, let us agree that every criminal law must be public, and that people should be informed about the content of crimes that fall under the criminal law and therefore also crimes of type X.[18] Because of this difference, the original counterexample levelled at utilitarian reasoning works better in Mob than in Mob∗. It works better because something has been lost in the translation from Mob to Mob∗, namely, that in Mob it is more likely that it can be kept secret that an innocent person, Bob, has been punished. It seems obvious that in Mob∗, where Bob has committed a so-called crime X, it is going to be difficult to keep his criminal conduct secret. This is true given the way the criminal justice system ought to function: it should be known by the public which types of conduct are criminal and it should be public, at least to a certain extent (to e.g. the police and judges) who has transgressed the criminal law. And this should of course also be the case with crimes categorized as examples of crime X. Therefore, empirical observations about secrecy and the way the criminal law ought to be administered suggest that Husak's critique of utilitarianism using Mob is severely weakened when it is translated into Mob∗ as a way of criticizing UPC.

Second, as it seems extremely difficult to specify, identify and administer a law prohibiting crimes of type X, it seems exceedingly likely that introducing a law criminalizing crimes of type X would not produce the greatest total amount of well-being.

[18]Utilitarians and retributivists could easily be in favour of making the criminal law public. Utilitarians could do so because secret laws would not deter people from committing crimes, and retributivists could argue that in order for a responsible offender to be punished, the offender should know or ought to know that he had done something morally wrong and one effective way to convey that would be by means of a publicly known criminal law.

However, it is very plausible and obvious to say that these defensive moves on behalf of UPC are contingent on empirical assumptions, and that criminalizing Bob in Mob∗ and punishing him for committing a crime like crime X is not, according to UPC, wrong in principle. In what follows, I will therefore focus on another, and non-empirical, defence of utilitarianism and UPC.

Let us accept that moral factors such as just deserts, respect for autonomy, and being treated as an end and not merely as a means drive the arguments against utilitarianism and UPC. The basic idea is that these factors work as constraints, in the sense that they should not be violated even when that would lead to the greatest amount of well-being. The strategy that is used to convince us that these constraints should not be violated is to show us that violations of such constraints lead to acts that, from a moral point of view, are counterintuitive.

A second type of defence can be mounted on the basis of methodological considerations concerning the use of moral intuitions in attempts to debunk utilitarianism and UPC. I am uncertain how much weight moral intuitions should have in our deliberation over what we ought to do, and over what moral theories and principles we ought to accept. Should moral intuitions not matter at all? Should they have some weight? Alternatively, should they be decisive in the sense that, if a theory is inconsistent with some of them, the theory is incorrect? Husak and other critics of UPC seem to accept the last of these views. They are convinced that if what happens in Mob∗ is counterintuitive, that alone is enough to warrant rejection of UPC. I believe that there are good reasons to be sceptical about this attitude.[19] However, this is not the place to enter into complex meta-ethical discussion of the proper use of intuitions in the evaluation of moral theories. For now let us nevertheless accept that it does at least speak in favour of a moral theory that it is consistent with one or more of our core moral intuitions (e.g. intuitions that 'if life is worth living, it is morally better to be alive than to be dead' or 'all else being equal, it is morally better that one person dies than two'). However, accepting this modest claim, we can just as well construct scenarios in which non-consequentialism would imply moral conclusions that would see counterintuitive, at least to some people. Consider the following two scenarios:

World 1: Everything else is equal; at time T1, an innocent person A is killed by person P and a moral constraint M is therefore violated. This killing of A, however, will prevent the innocent persons B and C from being

[19]I am sceptical because our moral intuitions may differ according to the many different possible circumstances, depending on, for example, culture, nationality, gender, information level, and, well, smell and hand wash. See e.g. Doris and Plakias (2008), Haidt and Bjorklund (2008) and Zamzow and Nichols (2009) for how these different factors may influence our moral intuitions. These observations raise the question of whose intuitions we should trust, and when we should accept them as support for a moral view. History has shown us that many of our intuitions about, for example, women and people of color proved to be immoral. Furthermore, I and some of my colleagues, for instance, do not believe that it is counterintuitive, as we have seen in the original Mob case, to punish an innocent man (for, let us say, 1 year in prison), in order to save the lives of six other innocent individuals.

killed by P∗ at T2. P's killing of A will therefore prevent two violations of M. Therefore, A is killed but B and C are saved.

World 2: Everything else is equal; at time T1, an innocent person A is not killed, because a moral constraint M is respected by P. This non-killing of A, however, implies that the innocent persons B and C will be killed by P∗ at T2. P's non-killing of A will therefore imply two violations of M. Therefore, A is saved but B and C are killed.

The moral constraint M in question could be that we are not permitted to violate a person's autonomy[20] or that we are not allowed to kill an innocent person even if this would maximize well-being. It is obvious that it follows from the utilitarian reasoning behind UPC that World 1 is a better world than World 2. In World 1, two people will live and one person will die. In World 2, one person will live and two people will die. According to non-consequentialism, however (whether absolute or moderate), World 2 must be the morally better of these two worlds. It must be the morally best, because in World 1, P violates the moral constraint M, whereas in World 2 P does not violate constraint M. Translating these answers into answers given by principles of criminalization, let us accept that UPC would not criminalize P in World 1 but would criminalize P in World 2, and that the opposite would be the case for a non-consequentialist theory of criminalization. However, non-consequentialist theories of criminalization must accommodate two principles to reach their conclusion.

(I) It is morally more important to criminalize the violation of a moral constraint M at T 1, rather than saving an extra life at T 2 (as in World 1).

(II) It is morally more important to prevent the violation of one moral constraint than it is to prevent the violation of two moral constraints (as in World 2). Let me briefly discuss why I believe there are strong reasons to reject these two principles.

First, concerning (I), why is it better, morally speaking, that a constraint M is not violated, than saving an extra life (P killing A minus, P∗ not killing B and C)? This seems to be an implausible view, at least, if we accept the intuition that each life is equally valuable and that it doesn't matter whether it is P or P∗ who kills a person. In other words, it does not seem right to sacrifice two people, B and C, in order to save one person, A. Why should saving the life of A be worth more, morally, than saving the lives of B and C, if all lives matters equally? The answer that it is morally more important not to violate a moral constraint than to save a life, as in World 2, is therefore far from convincing.

Second, concerning (II), why is it better, morally speaking, to only prevent the violation of one moral constraint (P not killing A), than to prevent two similar moral constraints (P∗ not killing B and C), as in World 2? One could also argue for the very plausible claim that it is morally better that one violation of M occurs, than it is that two occur. This claim fits well with what I believe is a strong moral intuition,

[20] Ripstein (2006) and Tadros (2011).

namely, that if what we do leads to more of the very thing that we ought not to do, then we should not do it. Moreover, with this kind of reasoning it would follow that World 1 is the preferable world. However, if this is the case, we are back to a theory that looks like consequentialism: a version of consequentialism according to which you ought to promote the non-violation (or minimize the number of M-violations) of constraints like M.[21]

Non-consequentialists may say that I am just begging the question, since I just assume or beg the question that not violating moral constraints M, in a case like World1/World 2, when violating M costs extra lives or when violating M does maximize violations of M, are morally wrong. I am not convinced, however, that this is a fair criticism. First, non-consequentialists seem to use the same tactic when they assume, as e.g. in the 'Mob' case, that punishing an innocent person is morally wrong, even if doing so could save the lives of six innocent people. Therefore, either we should accept the critical reasoning used in both 'Mob' and 'World 1/World 2' by both critiques of consequentialism and non-consequentialism, or we should not accept this kind of critical reasoning. Second, besides (or instead of) appealing to intuition when evaluating the cases we have discussed so far, we can instead draw on what seems to be a rational decision procedure for finding out what is morally plausible.[22] Imagine that you are behind a veil of ignorance. Furthermore, accept that behind such a veil, you do not know your income, your sex, and whether or not you have a handicap. But you are a rational person who prefers more well-being to less. Now imagine that you can choose whether you want to live in World 1 or World 2, but you do not know whether you will be killed or saved. For the sake of the argument, accept furthermore that these two worlds are the only ones available to you, and that the only person you could be in the two worlds are A, B or C mentioned in the descriptions of World 1 and World 2. If you choose World 1, there is an approximately 33% chance of your being killed. On the other hand, if you choose to live in World 2, you have an approximately 66% chance of being killed. You would choose World 1, would you not?[23]

---

[21]For an excellent elaboration and critical discussion of deontological arguments in favour of the view that deontologists should not always permit the number of violations of moral constraints M to be minimized through the act of one violation of M, see Lippert-Rasmussen (1999). This also holds for threshold deontologists, as they would not morally accept that it is right to violate a moral constraint M in order to decrease the number of M-violations with two. Therefore, threshold deontologists can argue that if the violation of M can decrease the number of M-violations with three, they could accept the first M-violation, but not if the decrease in M-violations amounts to two—otherwise, their theory would collapse into consequentialism.

[22]A procedure employed by, for example, John Rawls (1999). Rawls used the procedure to justify which principles should be satisfied in a just society. See also Harsanyi (1975), who has argued that the rational thing to do, contrary to Rawls's idea that rights-based principles are what rational people would choose, would be to choose utilitarianism as your guiding principle for the construction of a just society.

[23]The same kind of reasoning could also be used in favour of defending utilitarianism against the objection raised by the Mob case.

I have argued that Husak's objections to UPC are less than decisive, and that UPC does have some morally intuitive and rationally appealing implications, compared to some of the implications of non-consequentialist theories concerning the evaluation of worlds like World 1 and World 2.[24] Remember that my purpose in this chapter is only a soft defence of UPC. Therefore, I am not trying to show that UPC is the best principle of criminalization, but only that we should hesitate to reject it, in light of the fact that the objections against UPC dealt with in the chapter do not seem convincing. In what follows, we shall discuss two objections recently made by Victor Tadros, which can be raised against UPC.

6.5 A Critical Discussion of Two of Tadros's Objections to UPC

(a) **On small benefits to the many, compared to significant harm to the few**

The first objection is based on the familiar worry that consequentialism does not give proper weight to the serious harming of a few persons, compared to very small benefits bestowed on each of very many other people. The problem is that it follows from consequentialism, and more specifically utilitarianism, "... that any suffering no matter how great, to some people can be justified by making sufficiently many other people only slightly better off".[25] In discussing a consequentialist version of the harm principle,[26] Victor Tadros formulates a similar worry:

> Most people ... do not think that it is always permissible to act in a way that prevents the greatest amount of harm on aggregate. It also matters how the harm is distributed. For example, it would be wrong to act in a way that prevents very many people being harmed to a very small degree if, as a side effect, one person is harmed a great deal. ... [a consequentialist version of the harm principle] appears to rule out prohibition of such action and for this reason it is implausible.[27]

[24]In discussing what I take to be counterintuitive implications of non-consequentialism, I have designed the case with World 1 and World 2 as favourably as possible for adherents of non-consequentialism (or deontology). Instead, I believe it would have been even more counterintuitive for more people if I had used other cases. For example, where it would be wrong, according to non-consequentialists, to punish an innocent person for 10 s in order to prevent six innocent persons from being killed, or where it would be wrong to kill one person in order to save all the lives of all children in the world.

[25]Bykvist (2010), p. 81.

[26]The version of the harm principle that Tadros here takes under discussion is the following: 'It is wrong to criminalize some conduct *v* if criminalizing *v* does not prevent harm on aggregate.' (Tadros 2011), p. 51. Furthermore, Tadros argues that this version of the harm principle can only be plausible if consequentialism is true.

[27]Tadros (2011), p. 52. When Tadros writes 'prohibition', I take him to mean 'criminalization', as the whole subject of his article is on principles of criminalization.

I believe Tadros's reasoning can be harnessed as an argument against UPC, because a central focus of his remarks is the consequentialist component of the type of harm principle that he is criticizing. A fair reconstruction of the argument seems to be this:

The argument from small benefits to the many vs significant harm to the few

P1:	It is morally wrong to engage in a type of conduct C if, as an unintended side-effect, doing so causes one person a great deal of harm, even if C benefits very many people each to a very small degree and even if engaging in C will therefore cause more benefit than harm.
P2:	UPC appears to rule out the criminalization of C because criminalizing C would not maximize well-being.
P3:	It is not only morally wrong to engage in C, but morally wrong to appear to rule out the criminalization of C.
Conclusion:	UPC is morally wrong.

Conduct C, for example, could be the production and selling of small children's toys which usually benefits a lot of children, but unfortunately, in very rare circumstances, do result in the death of a child. As hopefully will be clarified in what follows, I believe there are good reasons why we should not be convinced by this argument. Concerning P1, it can be argued that we should not trust our intuition in cases where many people, or large numbers, are involved. While we might understand what it is to harm one person significantly, we do not find it easy to understand the significance of a vast number of tiny benefits of the kind that would be needed to outweigh severe harm done to one person.[28] However, even if you do not accept this kind of criticism, there are problem with premises P2 and P3.

Whether P2 is true depends on circumstances which would need to be investigated empirically. It may very well be true that criminalization of the kinds of conduct C mentioned in P1 would, all things considered, maximize well-being, People might, for example, lose faith in the criminal justice system if a conduct C like that in P1 is not criminalized. They could lose faith to such a degree that it would maximize well-being to criminalize conduct C in P1. So there is room for scenarios where UPC could be used as a justification for the criminalization of conduct C. It is not convincing to claim, as Tadros does in the passage quoted, that consequentialism is implausible because it *appears* to rule out criminalization of conduct C. The important thing is whether it *actually* follows from consequentialism that the state should rule out criminalization of C. However, this is an empirical question. We should not jump unreflectively from premise P1, P2 and P3 to the conclusion that the consequentialist account of criminalization is morally wrong or implausible, especially when premise P2 relies on empirical speculation.

[28]Broome (2004), p. 58.

Turning to P3, I believe there are good reasons to hold that it is *sometimes* plausible to rule out the criminalization of a type of conduct C when C will benefit very many people each with small amounts of well-being, but also seriously harm a small number of people. In many actual cases, as with the production and selling of children's toy we accept that it is right to benefit very many people slightly even though we know that some people will also bear some enormous costs as a result.[29] As another example, take, for instance, the fact that millions of people drive a car, even though this causes death and injury (directly in accidents, and indirectly through pollution and climate change) to a comparatively small number of people every day. Few would say we should ban cars, and the reason for this could be that by doing so, we prevent every one of a large number of people a small amount of well-being. I am not sure if this example provides a satisfactory answer to Tadros's objection. One could say that many people benefit a lot from driving cars, not just to a small degree, because that enables them to take up job opportunities. Furthermore, some driving, such as ambulance driving, literally saves lives. However, if you believe that driving cars should not be criminalized, you might be in favour of something like the following:

Lives for Driving
There is some finite amount of car driving, such that it ought to be legally permissible to allow thousands of people to die as a side-effect of the legalization of driving cars in order to benefit very many people by allowing them to drive cars.

But if Lives for Driving is accepted, it could be argued that we should replace P1 with a new premise stating that it is legally acceptable to harm, as a side-effect, comparatively few people in order to benefit every one of a large number of people a small amount. Suppose that, as a side-effect of helping to relieve the headaches of very many people, we harm one person seriously (e.g. he is killed). Let us call this case 'A Life for Headaches'.

A Life for Headaches
There is some finite number of headaches such that it is legally permissible to act in a way that will, as a side-effect, kill one person, but prevent these headaches.

If we accept A Life for Headaches because we accept Lives for Driving, and if premise P1 is replaced by the reasoning entailed in A Life for Headaches, it follows

[29]I take it for granted that we accept the production and selling of children's toys even though we know that we can expect that a few children will be choked while sucking on these toys. Moreover, one reason why we accept this will probably have to do with the observation that many children will benefit from playing with these toys.

that we should deny P3, because it would then be plausible to rule out the criminalization of the kinds of conduct C mentioned in P1. Nevertheless, perhaps there is a moral distinction between the two cases, and this distinction means that we cannot infer A Life for Headaches from Lives for Driving.

I do not have space here to discuss the many different suggestions about whether there is a morally relevant difference between Lives for Driving and A Life for Headaches, and whether this difference supports the claim that the former is morally acceptable while the latter is not.[30] But let me briefly discuss three possibilities discussed by Alistair Norcross.

An obvious suggestion is that A Life for Headaches is morally worse because a person is *killed*. But in Lives for Driving, people are merely *allowed* to die. Although there is no consensus over how we should understand the distinction between killing and letting die, and its moral significance, let us assume that we have a clear idea of what the distinction amounts to and agree that it has moral significance. We can still ask: how much worse is it, morally speaking, to kill a person than it is to allow a person to die? Is it, for example, morally worse to kill one person than it is to allow 100 people to die, but morally better to kill one person than it is to allow 200 people to die? Where the line is drawn will have an impact on whether you believe that A Life for Headaches is worse than Lives for Driving. If, for example, you accept that the laws permitting people to drive a vehicle in Canada are morally acceptable even though, say, 1000 people die every year as a result of them, you will be in favour of Lives for Driving. Furthermore, if you accept that it is morally better that one person is killed, as a side effect, than it is that 1000 people are allowed to die, it will follow that you should also accept A Life for Headaches. It will follow because you accept two things: (1) that we allow 1000 people to die for the sake of some gains in the convenience of driving, and (2) that it is morally better to kill one person, as a side effect, than it is to allow 1000 people die. More generally, we can say that if you believe we can successfully justify allowing 1000 people to die by pointing to the resulting gains in the convenience of car-driving in Canada for millions of people, you must also have reason to accept that we can justify killing one person, as a side effect, if the resulting gains in convenience are just as good as or higher than the gains to be had from allowing people to die in Lives for Driving.

Another way to support the idea that there is a moral distinction between Lives for Driving and A Life for Headaches is to argue that the harm done to one person in order to prevent a small amount of harm to very many people in A Life for Headaches is morally wrong, whereas the harm done in Lives for Driving by driving a car is not morally wrong but morally right. Again, I believe that there are good reasons against this strategy.

[30] Philosophers who try to defend utilitarianism from the objection here posed by Tadros (and others, e.g. Scanlon 1998, p. 235) include e.g. Bykvist (2010) and Schönherr (2018). Norcross (1997) presents a critical discussion of eight contenders for the morally relevant difference between Lives for Driving and A Life for Headaches and. He concludes that none of these can justify the conclusion that the former is right and the latter wrong.

To begin with, it is not obvious that driving a car is morally right. That assessment depends on lot of things. If alternative forms of transport are available to you (say, train or bicycle), and if these are both safer and more climate-friendly, it is arguably morally wrong to drive a car. But even if car-driving is morally wrong, it does not follow that it should then be criminalized, since (to give just one reason) the transaction and enforcement cost may be enormous. Therefore, we could accept Lives for Driving even if car-driving is morally wrong. Furthermore, another explanation of the alleged moral distinction based on a difference concerning harm is to point out that, whereas driving a car is a low-risk harm as it only causes significant harm in rare cases, the harm caused in A Life for Headaches is high-risk in the sense that the harm will certainly happen. However, whether there is a moral difference between the two cases should not simply depend on whether there is a difference in the risk of the harm being done in each. It also depends on *how much harm* is involved in the two situations. Imagine that a state only has the resources to criminalize and enforce one of two types of conduct; (a) Criminalize conduct C, that immorally expropriates land from one person to the state, where it is certain that this person will be significantly harmed; or (b) criminalize conduct D, motorcycling, and thereby preventing 100 people from dying in motorcycling accidents. Confronted with such a choice, I think there are good reasons for the state to criminalize motorcycling, even though there is a low risk that a single motorcycle trip will result in someone being killed. Even so, if we add up all of these single motorcycle rides they will, in sum, inflict a lot of harm.

The cases above show that there is not necessarily a morally relevant difference between Lives for Driving and A Life for Headaches. A difference, that is, which speaks in favour of the claim that A Life for Headaches is morally worse than Lives for Driving. So again, if we are not in favour of criminalizing driving cars, we ought to accept A Life for Headaches; but then again, P1 is wrong and the conclusion will not follow. The conclusion that UPC is wrong.

(b) **Preventing the lesser good**

Tadros's second challenge—which was, again, originally deployed against certain versions of the harm principle but can be used as an argument against UPC—is based on reasoning about a case involving self-sacrifice:

> [I]t is sometimes permissible to sacrifice oneself for a lesser good. Suppose that I could sacrifice my life to prevent my child from being tortured. The torture of my child might be less weighty than the loss of my life. But there is nothing wrong with my sacrificing my life for this lesser good. It would be wrong to prevent me from doing this. Were another person to prevent me from giving up my life for the sake of my child, resulting in the torture of my child, it would be permissible to punish that person.[31]

Before I critically discuss this view, I need to clarify a few things. First, when Tadros mentions that punishment is permissible, we should take him to mean *state* punishment, as this is the topic of the paper from which the above quotation has been

[31] Tadros (2011), p. 57.

taken. Second, according to Tadros, it is clear from the quotation that it should be permissible to punish the person P who prevents the self-sacrifice of the parent who wants to prevent his child from being tortured. And the reason for this is that we "... ought to prevent interference with self-sacrificial acts because each person is entitled to give up her life for the ends that she chooses for herself."[32]

However, I believe we should be reluctant to reject UPC because one, as Tadros, believes that UPC would imply that we ought not to punish a person like P when he prevents self-sacrifices (done by other than P) that imply lesser good. First, whether the conduct of preventing others from sacrificing themselves for the lesser good should be criminalized according to UPC is an empirical question. It might turn out that criminalizing those who prevent other people from sacrificing themselves for the lesser good, might maximise well-being. In addition, if this is true, Tadros's claim and UPC could reach the same verdict in a case like the one quoted above. But it might also be the case that criminalizing those who prevent other people from sacrificing themselves for the lesser good, might not maximise well-being. And it might not do so, because limiting people's autonomy when they want to help others (by preventing them from sacrificing them for the lesser good) might lead to less well-being for the agent as well as others. Second, it will probably be extremely expensive to enforce such criminal law, and the public may come to have less faith in the criminal justice system, which again might deplete total societal well-being. These observations about the possible loss of well-being caused by criminalization of such types of conduct do, from the point of view of UPC, speak against the criminalization of such types of conduct.

In principle, however, UPC cannot accommodate the criminalization of a type of conduct C in which, all else being equal, one person prevents another person from sacrificing himself for the lesser good. And that alone is enough, for Tadros, to show that UPC must be rejected. So, third, in order to make a strong case for this type of objection, let us grant that the torture a father could prevent his son S from experiencing is not just a very light form of torture (e.g. five seconds of Chinese water torture[33]), but a substantial form of torture that will diminish the overall well-being of S. Imagine, for example that the torture is extremely painful, and that S will suffer from severe post-traumatic stress disorder (PTSD) afterwards.

In what follows, I would like to raise three challenges to the critique that UPC is morally wrong because it implies that it is impermissible to criminalize and punish a person who prevents, for example, a father from sacrificing his own life in order to prevent a lesser evil, such as torture, to his son.

The first challenge is where to draw the line between interfering to prevent forms of self-sacrifice that should be criminalized and interfering to prevent self-sacrifice that should not be criminalized. In other words, in what situations should the state criminalize a person P who prevents a father F from sacrificing himself for the lesser good of his son S? Let us call such scenarios 'one-on-one scenarios', as they concern

[32]Tadros (2016), p. 56.

[33]Chinese water torture involves slowly dripping water onto a person's forehead.

relations between one person sacrificing himself for the sake of another person. I take it as read that if a sane, healthy, 30-year-old father, F, wants to sacrifice his life because he wants to ensure that his son receives an ice cream, it is morally unobjectionable for a bystander to intervene and prevent F from making the sacrifice. However, in these kinds of cases, at what precise point is paternalistic intervention morally right or wrong (and if wrong, when is it a subject for criminalization) is not very clear in Tadros's writings. This, however, is at least a theoretical problem to which UPC has an answer (namely, maximize well-being). And the right answer is, that it is morally right for a bystander to prevent F from sacrificing his life to ensure his son receives an ice-cream, and that preventing such self-sacrificing acts should not be criminalized.

Things are even more complicated for Tadros's view if, instead of considering a one-to-one scenario, we consider a 'one-to-others' scenario. What if F sacrifices his life in order to benefit 1000 people slightly? Imagine that F sacrifices his life so that 1000 people each get an ice-cream. Suppose that F loses more well-being by his sacrifice than the other 1000 people will gain collectively by eating ice-creams. According to utilitarianism, F does something that is morally wrong, because he fails to maximize total well-being. According to Tadros's reasoning, F's action seems to be morally right as F is entitled to give up his life for the ends that he chooses for himself. And if this were correct, according to Tadros's reasoning it could be permissible to punish someone who prevents F from sacrificing himself because he wants to benefit 1000 people slightly by giving them each an ice-cream. However, if you believe that A Life for Headaches is counterintuitive, you should think that this implication of Tadros's is even more counterintuitive. For in the ice-cream case, unlike the case of A Life for Headaches, you are not even maximizing well-being. Again, however, in these other kinds of cases, it is not very clear what follows from Tadros's view, whereas UPC also has an answer to the 'one-to-others' scenario (namely, maximize well-being). Again UPC gives the right answer, as it is morally right for a bystander to prevent F from sacrificing his life in order to give 1000 people an ice-cream each, and that preventing such self-sacrificing acts should not be criminalized.

The second challenge revolves around what we should think where self-sacrifice like that involving the parent and child described by Tadros is in conflict with another deontological constraint. Such conflict emerges when Tadros says that he is in favour of a principle like the following: 'It is wrong . . . to harm a person as a means to the greater good of others.'[34] To see this conflict, we should be aware that in the case of self-sacrifice involving the parent and child, the parent harms himself as a means of ensuring the greater good of his child. This, however, seems to be a violation of Tadros's means principle just quoted. A possible reply for Tadros would be to say that, because the parent has consented to self-sacrifice, it is morally unproblematic. Again, I suspect that if the parent has consented to sacrifice his own life to give his child an ice cream, his sacrifice should not be respected even

[34] Tadros (2011), pp. 52, 56.

though he has consented. So, where should we draw the line between consent we ought to accept and consent we should not? Furthermore, what about the constraint (to which Tadros also subscribes) that we should respect people's autonomy?[35] What if the child does not want his father to sacrifice himself for him? How much weight should be accorded to respect for the child's autonomy in this case, and should that respect outweigh respect for the autonomy of the father? Unfortunately, Tadros does not specify how these theoretical problems should be solved. The two challenges above may not overturn our feeling that UPC is counterintuitive, but they show us that Tadros's theory is not developed to handle the different 'ice cream cases' that we have discussed so far. Nor is his theory developed to handle conflicts between moral constraints in a way that makes the theory applicable to delivering answers in certain cases. Again, UPC do not have any of these problems.

The third challenge has to do with the problems that arise in cases that imply what we can call 'second-order self-sacrifice'. The problem here is that it is unclear what follows from Tadros's theory if the person who prevents the self-sacrifice of F also, because of the prevention, makes a self-sacrifice. Remember that Tadros's view is that it would be permissible to punish a person who prevents a self-sacrificing father, F, from doing less overall good by preventing his son S from being tortured. However, imagine a grandfather, G, who sacrifices his life to prevent his son F from sacrificing his life to prevent G's grandson (and F's son), S, from being tortured. I am not sure what Tadros would say here, given his view on the permissibility of punishing people who prevent others from making sacrifices that would lead to lesser goods. Would it be permissible to punish G—thereby violating G's entitlement to give up his life for the ends he chooses—when G's intervention in itself is an instance of self-sacrifice?

Tadros could answer that, in such cases, we have a real moral dilemma. In addition, he could say that it should only be permissible to punish a person X who is preventing a grandfather, G, or his son, F, from their self-sacrificing acts, given that X would not sacrifice himself in doing that. This answer, however, is not sound, as preventing a person from doing something that may be very important to them may always involve some kind of self-sacrifice when it comes to time and resources spent on persuasion, manipulation or coercion. Alternatively, Tadros could say that it is permissible to punish G because, although we would thereby violate his autonomy, we would also respect the autonomy of F. However, everything else being equal, we would then need an argument for holding that it is more important to respect the father's autonomy than it is to respect the grandfather's. Tadros does not do that, and it is difficult to see how this can be done in any consistent manner without embracing some kind of consequentialism. Moreover, Tadros could and does say that respect for autonomy is not the only moral factor that we should take into account when considering which types of act the state ought to criminalize. Well-being matters too. But again, whether, according to Tadros's way of reasoning, it should be permissible to punish G in the second-order self-sacrifice case is not clear, whereas UPC also has an answer to this case (namely, maximize well-being).

[35] Tadros (2016), p. 103.

I have argued that Tadros's two objections against consequentialism and UPC are not persuasive. First, there are good reasons in favour of the claim that the premises in Tadros's argument from small benefits to the many vs significant harm to the few are either resting on empirical uncertainties or are morally implausible. Second, that Tadros's reasoning about the permissibility of criminalizing a person who prevents another person from sacrificing himself for the lesser good is not very well developed (compared to UPC). For in Tadros's writing it is unclear what the answers would be in different versions of the ice cream case; in cases where moral constraints are in conflict with other moral constraints and in second-order self-sacrificing cases.

6.6 The Counterproductive Criminalization Principle and UPC

Before concluding, I would like to present a new and strong reason in favour of UPC. The reason is that UPC, unlike non-consequentialist principles of criminalization, is consistent with a very plausible principle, which I call *the counterproductive criminalization principle* (CCP).[36] In what follows, I will briefly describe what I take to be the most plausible version of CCP. Thereafter, I will explain why consequentialist theories of criminalization like UPC are consistent with CCP, and why non-consequentialist theories of criminalization easily can inconsistent with it. CCP can be formulated like this:

> **The counterproductive criminalization principle (CCP)**
> Everything else being equal, if the criminalization of conduct C in society S (where C is clearly morally wrong and a plausible candidate for criminalization) will result in C being more common, then the criminalization of C in S is morally wrong.

The exact meaning of the notion 'clearly morally wrong' is, of course, vague. However, to make my point in what follows, it is enough to hold that, for example, excessive drinking, organized crime, murder, rape, and drug use by pregnant women are usually morally wrong. If you still think this is too vague, let C be whatever conduct you believe is morally wrong.

So it follows from CCP that if the criminalization of, say, drug use by pregnant women, all else being equal, would result in more pregnant women using drugs (and

[36]UPC will always be consistent with CCP if 'morally wrong' in the specification of C is defined by the maximization of well-being. If the criminalization of conduct C (which is morally wrong because C does not maximize well-being) results in C being more common, this will clearly not maximize well-being.

therefore more fetuses being harmed by maternal drug use), compared to non-criminalization, then drug use by pregnant women should not be criminalized.[37]

It is easy to see that CCP is consistent with a consequentialist principle of criminalization like UPC.[38] Imagine a state that wishes to criminalize conduct C—say, drug use by pregnant women—because it expects that, this will maximize well-being. Imagine, furthermore, that it turns out that the criminalization of C will increase the number of fetuses being harmed, by illegal drug use by pregnant women, or cause other, clearly harmful conduct such as harm to drug using pregnant women. In such a case, UPC will agree with CCP: in this case, drug use by pregnant women should not be criminalized.

By contrast, non-consequentialist theories of criminalization (e.g. dignity principles of criminalization) are not always consistent with CCP.[39] Imagine, once again, that a state wants to criminalize drug use among pregnant women because such drug use harms innocent fetuses and/or violates the dignity of the fetuses. Add to this that the reason for this criminalization is that this kind of drug use violates a moral constraint against harming or violating the dignity of innocent fetuses. To make things simple, imagine the state is very small, with a few hundred citizens. If this kind of criminalization increases the number of fetuses that will be harmed in society S at time T_2 by just one fetus (say, five fetuses are harmed per year), compared to non-criminalization in S at time T_1 (where four fetuses are harmed per year), even the moderate non-consequentialist would accept criminalization, which would be inconsistent with CCP. However, by following CCP and not criminalizing drug use by pregnant women, we permit the violation of this moral constraint to happen at T_1 in order to prevent more violations of the same, or a similar, moral constraint at T_2. However, this is morally unacceptable according to all deontologists (both absolute and moderate), as they believe that we should not violate one moral constraint (actively or passively) in order to ensure that two similar constraints are not violated. This observation speaks against non-consequentialist theories of criminalization. However, if the criminalization of conduct C would have catastrophic consequences for the well-being of thousands of people and no one would benefit from the criminalization of C there is room for non-consequentialist like e.g. Duff, that C should not be criminalized (see Sect. 4.4.4).

Non-consequentialists could object to CCP by arguing that if the non-criminalization of rape, for example (compared to its criminalization) would

[37]For a study showing that the criminalization of drug use among pregnant women leads to more pregnant women using drugs because criminalization and stigmatization prevent them from seeking help from health care staff, see Farr (1995).

[38]That versions of harm principles and offence principles, at the center of the discussion in Chaps. 2 and 3, are consistent with CCP should be obvious, as adherents of both types of principle would claim that the state should only criminalize kinds of conduct C that harm or at which people take offense, if we can thereby prevent or minimize that occurrence of C.

[39]As legal moralism is usually formulated in a context that makes it clear that it is not a branch of consequentialism, especially not of a utilitarian principle of criminalization, I take for granted that adherents of legal moralism are not consistent with CCP.

reduce the number of rapes by only one rape, it would follow from CCP that rape should not be criminalized. The problem with this implication of CCP—if, for example, you were a retributivist—would be that rapists would then not receive their deserved punishment. I believe there are at least two answers to this objection. One is that it is very unlikely that the non-criminalization of rape would reduce the number of rapes or the total amount of well-being. The other is that if rape is not criminalized by the state, we cannot say that rapists deserve state punishment; and we cannot say this if we accept (as most retributivists do)[40] that it is a necessary condition of state punishment that the person accused has violated the law.

6.7 Conclusion

I hope to have given a detailed and critical specification of UPC, the utilitarian principle of criminalization. Further, I have argued that critics of UPC like Douglas Husak and Victor Tadros have not given UPC a fair trial, and *en route* I have tried to defend UPC against certain objections. Finally, I have argued that UPC is attractive as a principle of criminalization because, unlike non-consequentialist theories of criminalization, it is consistent with the counterproductive criminalization principle. I would like to emphasize that I have not argued that UPC is the best principle of criminalization in the field. Instead, the aim has been to present a *soft* defence of UPC, the purpose of which is to show that UPC has not always been given a fair trial and, therefore, should not be dismissed. UPC is better than its poor reputation suggests.

Let me end this book with a few comments about the implementation of UPC. There is no doubt that it is not in any way self-evident or easy for decision-makers to apply UPC to the real world. There are often very few data or competing empirical claims about what the effect or impact of criminalizing a kind of conduct C amounts to when it comes to measuring the well-being caused by criminalization. However, just because a principle is difficult to apply because of either lack of empirical data or conflicting data does not, of course, mean that we should reject the principle. Instead, we should, as mentioned by Dan Priel, for example, try to make an effort to obtain the relevant data so that we can make better-informed decisions about which kinds of conduct C the state ought to criminalize.[41]

[40]See e.g. Duff (2018), p. 15.
[41]Priel (2018).

References

Andenaes J (1966) The general preventive effects of punishment. Univ Pa Law Rev 114 (7):949–983
Bentham J (1781) The principles of morals and legislation. Prometheus Books, New York
Broome J (2004) Weighing lives. Oxford University Press, Oxford
Bykvist K (2010) Utilitarianism: a guide for the perplexed. Continuum Publishing, London
Chiao V (2016) What is criminal law for? Law Philos 35(2):137–163
Doris JM, Plakias A (2008) How to argue about disagreement: evaluative diversity and moral realism. In: Sinnott-Armstrong W (ed) Moral psychology, vol. 2, The cognitive science of morality: intuition and diversity. MIT Press, Cambridge MA, pp 303–331
Duff A (2018) The realm of criminal law. Oxford University Press, Oxford
Edwards J (2017) Criminalization without punishment. Legal Theory 23(2):69–95
Farr KA (1995) Fetal abuse and the criminalization of behavior during pregnancy. Crime Delinquency 41(2):235–245
Feinberg J (1986) Harm to others. Oxford University Press, Oxford
Fried B (2012) The limits of a nonconsequentialist approach to tort law. Legal Theory 18 (3):231–262
Haidt J, Bjorklund F (2008) Social intuitionist answer six questions about morality. In: Sinnott-Armstrong W (ed) Moral psychology, vol. 2, The cognitive science of morality: Intuition and diversity. MIT Press, Cambridge, pp 181–218
Harsanyi JC (1975) Can the maximin principle serve as a basis for morality? A critique of John Rawls's theory. Am Polit Sci Rev 69(2):594–606
Hart H (1968) Responsibility and punishment. Oxford University Press, Oxford
Husak D (2008) Overcriminalization. Oxford University Press, Oxford
Kagan S (1998) Normative ethics. Westview Press, Boulder
Lippert-Rasmussen K (1999) Moral status and the impermissibility of minimizing violations. Philos Public Aff 25(4):333–349
Lippert-Rasmussen K (2005) Deontology, responsibility, and equality. Museum Tusculanum Press, Copenhagen
McCloskey HJ (1957) An examination of restricted utilitarianism. Philos Rev 66(4):466–485
Moore M (1997) Placing blame: a theory of the criminal law. Oxford University Press, Oxford
Norcross A (1997) Comparing harms: headaches and human lives. Philos Public Aff 26(2):135–167
Priel D (2018) Criminalization, legitimacy, and welfare. Crim Law Philos 12(4):657–676
Rachels J (2007) Punishment and desert. In: Lafollette H (ed) Ethics in practice. Blackwell Publishing, New Jersey, pp 510–518
Rawls J (1999) Theory of justice, revised edition. Oxford University Press, Oxford
Ripstein A (2006) Beyond the harm principle. Philos Public Aff 34(3):215–245
Scanlon T (1998) What we owe to each other. Harvard University Press, Cambridge
Schönherr J (2018) Still lives for headaches: a reply to Dorsey and Voorhoeve. Utilitas 30 (2):209–218
Simester AP, Sullivan GR (2000) Criminal law: theory and doctrine. Hart Publishing, Oxford
Tadros V (2011) Harm, sovereignty, and prohibition. Legal Theory 17(1):35–65
Tadros V (2013) The ends of harm. Oxford University Press, Oxford
Tadros V (2016) Wrongs and crimes. Oxford University Press, Oxford
Zamzow JL, Nichols S (2009) Variations in ethical intuitions. Philos Issues 19(1):368–388

Appendix: What Is Well-Being?

Introduction

In Chap. 2, our point of departure was the following formulation of being harmed by another person. A person P1 is harmed by another person P2 doing C if and only if P1 is made worse off in terms of well-being, because of C. But what is *worse off* (in terms of well-being) a variation from, and what constitutes *well-being*? In Chap. 2, we dealt with the first part of the question, namely, the baseline problem of harm. In this appendix, however, we shall deal with the second part of the question, namely, what is well-being?

Any plausible moral theory or public policy concerning criminalization will either assume or imply that the well-being of individuals matters morally. As was argued in Sect. 6.2, it would be absurd to deny that our moral assessment of acts and policies depends, at least in part, or indirectly, on their effect on the well-being of individuals. But again, what is individual well-being? What does it mean to say that a life goes well (or badly) for an individual? This appendix entails a defence of a theory of well-being that can be called 'welfare hedonism'. Welfare hedonism is the view that well-being consists solely of the presence of pleasure and the absence of pain experienced by an individual.[1] A central critique of welfare hedonism that can be found in the literature argues that it is not all kinds of pleasurable experiences that contribute to the well-being of an individual.[2] Wayne Sumner takes centre stage in this discussion and argues instead that well-being consists of *authentic happiness*.[3]

---

[1]For different versions of hedonism, e.g. psychological hedonism and ethical hedonism, see Kagan (1998), p. 31. For different versions of welfare hedonism, see Feldman (2004, 2010), Crisp (2006) and Tännsjö (1998).

[2]See also e.g. Sen (1987) and Hawkins (2008).

[3]Sumner has not changed his views on these matters since his 1996 book. See e.g. Sumner (2000), Sumner (2004), p. 44 and Sumner (2006).

T. Søbirk Petersen, *Why Criminalize?*, Law and Philosophy Library 134,
https://doi.org/10.1007/978-3-030-34690-4

> The theory I shall defend does not simply identify well-being with happiness; additionally, it requires that a subject's endorsement of the conditions of her life, or her experience of them as satisfying or fulfilling, be authentic. The conditions for authenticity, in turn, are twofold: information and autonomy. Welfare [or well-being] therefore consists in authentic happiness.[4]

In Sect. A.2, I shall describe the two requirements that Sumner and others place on authenticity: information and autonomy. I shall also seek to convey the motivation for these requirements. In Sect. A.3, I discuss some challenges to this kind of critique of welfare hedonism.

I offer the present critical assessment because, since Sumner presented his theory of well-being in *Welfare, Happiness and Ethics*, his position has attracted some attention in the philosophical literature.[5] This is not hard to explain. Sumner is an established, highly regarded moral philosopher, and one of the relatively few philosophers who have treated the concept of well-being at book length.[6] Furthermore, his theory is original and involves subtle responses to well-known problems for standard theories of well-being such as the desire-theory account and welfare hedonism.

Requirements for Well-Being: Experience, Information and Autonomy

Experience and Information

First of all, we should note that Sumner's theory can be called a *subjective* theory of well-being, in the sense that for a state of affairs to make me better off (or worse off), it has to enter into my experience.[7] In accepting this *experience requirement* (ER),

---

[4]Sumner (1996), p. 139.

[5]See e.g. Vallentyne (1997), Sobel (1998) and Eggleston (1999), for reviews of Sumner's book. Apart from a very short critique of Sumner's theory made by Vallentyne, the reviews do not entail any criticism of Sumner's own theory of welfare. For a critical discussion of Sumner's critique of desire-based theories of well-being, see Bykvist (2002). For a critique mainly on Sumner's distinction between subjective and objective well-being, see Bognar (2010). For a critique of Sumner's theory that is different from mine, see Tupa (2010). Tupa argues, e.g., that Sumner's theory of happiness supports a desire-based theory of well-being rather than Sumner's own version of a mental state theory. See also Feldman (2010), pp. 191–194 and Petersen (2009) for a critical discussion of Sumner's autonomy requirement.

[6]Bradley (2011), Griffin (1986), Bykvist (1998), Brülde (1998), Feldman (2004, 2010) and Egonsson (2007) are also members of this exclusive club.

[7]Sumner (1996), pp. 139 and 172. Sometimes the label 'subjective theory of well-being' is also used to cover preference theories of well-being (see Sumner 1996, p. 113), although some preference theories do not incorporate an ER, i.e. do not make experience a necessary condition of well-being; see e.g. Griffin (1986). And sometimes the variety of welfare hedonism at issue is not classified as a subjective theory but instead as an objective theory; see e.g. Brülde (2007a).

Sumner and others enter the company of subjective theories of well-being, including welfare hedonism.[8] But what separates his theory from welfare hedonism is that, in order to count as well-being, an experience needs, for Sumner, not only to be pleasurable but also *authentic*. For welfare hedonists, ER functions as a necessary and sufficient condition for well-being.[9] For Sumner, it is only a necessary condition. Let us turn to the *information requirement* (IR). Sumner imposes this requirement because he believes that welfare hedonism is vulnerable to challenges based on several types of counter-example. One of these is the well-known case of:

> **The Deceived Businessman**
> Imagine a man who, at the end of his life, thinks he has achieved everything he wanted in life: his wife and family love him, he is a respected member of the community, and he has founded a successful business. Or so he thinks. In reality, he has been completely deceived: his wife cheated on him, his daughter and son were only nice to him so that they would be able to borrow the car, and other members of the community pretended to respect him for the sake of the charitable contributions he sometimes made. For some time his business partner has been embezzling funds from the company, which will soon go bankrupt.[10]

Taken at face value, welfare hedonism would imply that the life of the deceived businessman has gone very well—indeed better than most lives—in respect of well-being. However, to Sumner this assessment is unconvincing,[11] and many observers would probably agree that this life is not the kind of life that the businessman would really want, or that we would want for ourselves or for our loved ones. So welfare hedonism must be wrong. The worry, one might say, is that the businessman's own evaluation of his life does not reflect the way his life *really* is, as he is not informed about the deception.[12]

So Sumner is motivated to formulate a theory of well-being that (1) accepts ER as a necessary condition, but (2) does not generate the supposedly wrong answer in cases like that of the deceived businessman. As we already know, Sumner's theory places two kinds of restriction on the scope of experiences constitutive of well-being. One of these is the information requirement. Sumner does not give a short definition of this requirement. However, the following quotation points out some of its central features:

> ... what we are seeking is an adequate subjective theory of welfare, one on which the subject's point of view on her life is authoritative for determining when that life is going well *for her*. By connecting welfare with happiness we have interpreted that point of view as an

---

[8]Sumner (2000), p. 19.

[9]At least if we talk about pleasurable experiences.

[10]See Kagan (1998), pp. 34–35 for an example like this.

[11]Sumner (1996), p. 98.

[12]For a philosopher who believes that bitter truth is preferable to comfortable delusion when it comes to theories of well-being, see Griffin (1986), p. 9.

> endorsement or affirmation of the conditions of her life. When that endorsement is based on a clear view of those conditions, we have no grounds for questioning or challenging its authority: in this respect, the individual is sovereign over her well-being. But when it is based . . . on a misreading of those conditions then its authority is open to question, since it is unclear whether or not she is endorsing her life *as it really is*. Where someone is deceived or deluded about her circumstances, in sectors of her life which clearly matter to her, the question is whether the affirmation she professes is *genuine* or *authentic*. In order for a subject's endorsement of her life to accurately reflect her own priorities, her own point of view—in order for it to be truly *hers*—it must be authentic, which in turns requires that it be informed.[13]

From this passage and others,[14] it would appear that IR amounts to this:

> **The information requirement**
> In order for a person P to have well-being, it is necessary that the experiences P has in sectors of her life (which clearly matters to her) are not based on false beliefs.

In other words, whatever happiness you experience, it must not be caused by false beliefs if it is to count as well-being for you. It is clear from the quotation that the subject need not be informed about everything concerning her life in order to make a proper assessment of her well-being. The information need only concern 'sectors of her life which clearly matter to her'. But given this description of what kinds of information are relevant, we must also ask: how well informed must an autonomous person be if her experience of happiness is to count as well-being? According to Sumner, a person is well informed when no new information will make her evaluate her life *differently* (i.e. better or worse) than she would in a situation in which she did not have the information.[15]

What, exactly, is Sumner's response to the case of the deceived businessman? Did the businessman acquire welfare? According to IR, the obvious answer is that he did not have welfare because he was uninformed—assuming, of course, that the businessman is autonomous and thus satisfies another of Sumner's requirements for welfare. However, if the businessman is informed about the deception and now seeks to make a retrospective evaluation of his life during the deception, it is, according to Sumner, an open question whether he now believes that he had welfare then. As Sumner says: 'When we reassess our lives in retrospect, and from a superior

[13] Sumner (1996), p. 160.

[14] It is clear that the information and autonomy requirements are regarded by Sumner as *necessary* requirements for well-being: 'For the happiness theory, the minimal wherewithal for having welfare is being a subject who is capable of being satisfied or unsatisfied by the conditions of one's life. In the case of paradigm human subjects with complex cognitive capacities, more is necessary as well: their judgments about the quality of their lives must be authentic.' (Sumner 1996, p. 178).

[15] Ibid., p. 160. Compare also Egonsson (2007), pp. 38–42, for a critical discussion of IR focusing on what it is to be 'well-informed' and, in particular, how one becomes so.

epistemic vantage point, *there is no right answer to the question of what our reaction should be*—that is surely up to us.'[16]

So, if the businessman is informed about the way in which he has been deceived, there are, according to Sumner, two obvious ways in which he can evaluate his life.[17] One possibility is that he will re-evaluate the life he had during the deception and claim: 'I believed that my life was going well, but I can see now that it was all an illusion or a farce played out by unscrupulous actors. Therefore, I now believe that my life did not go well.' If this is the businessman's response, it will follow that he did not, given IR, enjoy well-being when he was deceived. Another possibility is that, in re-evaluating his life, he will simply confirm his earlier evaluation. He might say: 'Well they cheated me, but my life was great anyway.' So whether or not the businessman had well-being, and indeed how much he had, depends on the way in which he *decides* to evaluate his life when he is properly informed about it.

More importantly, however, Sumner seems here to introduce a condition for judging well-being in retrospect. For he makes it clear that the businessman who has become aware of his own deception can *decide* to assess the period of deception either as one containing well-being or as one containing no well-being at all. So it is not only *authentic experiences* that count when it comes to the estimation of well-being *in retrospect*, but also what the person in question *decides when informed now about the past.* So in order to get a clearer view of Sumner's theory, we have to add:

> **The condition for judging well-being in retrospect**
> If an autonomous person P assesses his life in retrospect and is informed now about matters in the past that he did not know about in the past, P can *decide now* whether or not he had well-being *then.*

Note that this condition is a requirement not for possessing well-being, but *evaluating* it in certain situations. Let me now turn to the autonomy requirement, before embarking on a critical discussion of Sumner's theory.

Autonomy

Sumner endorses the *autonomy requirement* (AR) in response to objections to welfare hedonism differing from the one just described. Some philosophers reject welfare hedonism because it generates the verdict that a slave or a hopeless beggar might experience a life containing as much, or more, well-being than a free person with a high level of well-being. According to Sumner (and others, such as Sen),[18] we should deny that such experiences count as well-being. Sumner formulates his point like this:

---

[16]Sumner (1996), p. 159.
[17]Ibid., pp. 160–161.
[18]Sen (1987), pp. 45–46.

> Why are we reluctant to take at face value the life satisfaction reported by 'the hopeless beggar, the precarious landless labourer, the dominated housewife, the hardened unemployed or the over-exhausted coolie'? Presumably because we suspect that the standards which their self-assessments reflect have been artificially lowered or distorted by processes of indoctrination or exploitation. ... The problem is not that their values are objectively mistaken but that they have never had the opportunity to form their own values at all. They do not lack enlightenment ... they lack autonomy. Let us say, then, that (self-assessed) happiness or life satisfaction counts as well-being only when it is autonomous.[19]

It would appear from this passage that the autonomy requirement amounts to something like this:

> **The autonomy requirement (AR)**
> In order for a person P to have well-being, it is necessary that the experiences P has in sectors of her life that really matter to her are not the product of, for example, coercion, indoctrination or exploitation.

In other words, self-assessments of happiness accurately report well-being *only* when there is good reason to believe that they have *not* been influenced by such things as coercion or indoctrination. Undue influence of this sort can be exerted on the subject during the process in which she is *forming* her values. Once the subject has done that, it can be exerted on her ambition, or effort, *to live according to these values*. Sumner does not fully develop AR. He does not, for example, specify what he takes to be the best account of the nature of autonomy. However, he believes that when such a theory is worked out, the implication for his theory of well-being will be clear.[20]

The autonomy requirement points towards the answer philosophers like Sumner and Sen want in cases like that of the hopeless beggar, namely, that such people's self-assessments are not really their own and therefore do not give an accurate measure of well-being. In other words, their self-assessments of their lives should not be taken as genuine records of their well-being. However, where there is evidence that the subject in question is autonomous, and where the subject is also suitably informed, we should treat the subject's experiences of her own life as an authoritative guide to her level of well-being.[21] It is important to note that IR and AR can be taken as necessary requirements for well-being if, and only if, the individuals in question *are capable* of being informed or of being autonomous. Suppose we accept that small children and animals are not autonomous. It is clear, however, from Sumner's text that they would still be welfare subjects:

> For the happiness theory [i.e. Sumner's theory of well-being as authentic happiness], the minimal wherewithal for having welfare is being a subject who is capable of being satisfied or unsatisfied by the conditions of one's life. In the case of paradigm human subjects with complex cognitive capacities, more is necessary as well: their judgments about the quality of

[19] Sumner (1996), pp. 166–167.

[20] Sumner (1996), p. 171.

[21] Ibid.

> their lives must be authentic. Where these more sophisticated skills are absent, the *sine qua non* is the baseline ability to experience one's life, in the living of it, as agreeable or disagreeable. The most primitive form of this ability is the capacity for enjoyment and suffering, or for pleasure and pain. If we call this capacity sentience then we may say that on the happiness theory the class of core welfare subjects is populated by all sentient creatures.[22]

In essence, then, Sumner's theory of well-being seems to amount to the following. ER is a necessary requirement for well-being no matter what kind of individual you are (animal, child or adult). However, if besides the capacity to experience such things as pleasure or pain, you have the capacity to be informed and/or to be autonomous (as animals and young children arguably do not), IR and AR are also necessary conditions for well-being.

Together, these three requirements seem to give a sufficient condition for well-being for rational adults. On the one hand, if you, as an autonomous and well-informed person, experience pleasure, you enjoy or accrue positive well-being. On the other hand, if you, as an autonomous and well-informed person, experience pain, you accrue negative well-being. But as has already been hinted, something is missing from this picture. When it comes to a retrospective evaluation of situations like that of the deceived businessman, the businessman can, when he is informed about the deception, *decide* that his life involved well-being even when he was being deceived.

Some Challenges

Let us now turn to a critical discussion of these requirements. I begin by presenting some problems with using the case of the deceived businessman as a counterexample to welfare hedonism. Then I present a case designed to show that neither IR nor AR are obviously plausible. Following this, I want to spell out a shortcoming with Sumner's theory that is raised by both requirements. Finally, I present a problem arising from the fact that Sumner combines his theory of well-being with welfarism. The latter is the view that only welfare/well-being matters from a moral point of view.

One may be less than fully convinced that the case of the deceived businessman shows welfare hedonism to be wrong. In this paragraph, I deploy some of Fred Feldman's ideas in order to query the implications of this well-known counterexample to welfare hedonism.[23] The reason many people would not accept welfare hedonism—and, say, be prepared to swap lives with the businessman, or at least accept that he has a good life—might be that people have difficulty *imagining* that such a life can be great. If everybody were deceiving us, we would *usually* find out;

---

[22]Ibid., p. 178.

[23]Feldman (2004), pp. 41–43.

we would probably find out by accident, or because people in real life are not that good at acting, or because we are suspicious by nature. At any rate, when we find out, we will be pained to learn that our family and colleagues have deceived us, especially if we had readily made the assumption that they loved us. Moreover, such a life would certainly be miserable. But the businessman does not know anything about the deception. He only experiences pleasure in his life, so from his perspective, it does not seem right to claim that his life does not contain well-being. The same kind of reasoning can be used to weaken the objection to welfare hedonism raised by the case of the hopeless beggar by pointing to difficulties in imagining what the life of a happy beggar would be like. The central point here is that some people's intuitions concerning the strength of these cases may be coloured by issues that have little or nothing to do with well-being, but testify to a lack of imagination. Even if people's intuitions are not distorted by such a lack of imagination, they may, as we shall see, be distorted by other facts.

As I see it, the apparent force of the case of the deceived businessman may also derive from the fact that we do not know anything about what preferences or ideas the businessman has regarding the information that could make him re-evaluate his life. Let us imagine a case in which the businessman does not want to be informed about certain important parts of his life—for example, because he does believe that it is not a good idea to put *his present and pleasant experiences at risk* (they might cease to be available in light of new information). If this were the case, I would imagine more people—especially those in favour of a preference theory of well-being—would be reluctant to deny that the life of the businessman contains well-being when it comes to important parts of his life.

Second, I want to present a case designed to throw doubt on the idea that IR and AR are necessary requirements for well-being. I am well aware of the fact that people have different intuitions when confronted with examples like that of the deceived businessman and the one that I will present in the following. So in this area I believe that we should not expect a knock-down argument involving, say, a compelling counterexample. My hope is merely that the following case can at least point in a certain direction and make us sceptical of both requirements. Examples designed to show that an individual cannot have positive well-being at the time he is non-autonomous or deceived about reality are plentiful. Remember the cases of the deceived businessman and the hopeless beggar.[24] But note that it would also follow from IR and AR that an individual cannot have *negative* well-being in a period during which he is non-autonomous or deceived (or through his own failing, mistaken) about reality. Let me give one example that might turn your intuitions away from these two requirements.

---

[24]Of course, once the businessman is informed about the deception or the hopeless beggar has become an autonomous person, Sumner and Sen can say that such persons can now decide that their lives during the deception or during the period of being non-autonomous did (or did not) contain positive well-being.

> **The fear and discomfort of a fake threat**
> You are on your way to a shop. Suddenly, a person stops right in front of you and puts a gun to your head. You are therefore paralyzed by fear. He says that he will kill you when he has counted to 10. He begins to count and you have never felt worse in your life. When he reaches 10 you think that's it. But instead the person walks away without firing the gun. What you did not know was that the gun was not a real gun but a toy one. If you had been aware of this fact, you would not have been so miserable and you would just have walked away when the gun was pointed at your head. So you were not informed about facts that would have made you experience this important situation differently.[25]

According to Sumner, we cannot say that you had negative well-being at the time when the person pointed the gun at your head. To know that, you need to be informed about the relevant facts. You will only then be able to decide whether or not you had negative well-being during the hold up. But it seems unconvincing to claim that, at that moment at which you experienced some of the worst moments of your life, you did not experience negative well-being. Furthermore, if you will *never* know these vital facts, you will never know if you had negative well-being during the hold up. In fact, it appears that none of us know if our lives, right now, contain well-being. Again, this is not an adequate use of the word 'well-being'. Remember that Sumner says 'the best theory about the nature of welfare [or well-being] is the one which is most faithful to our ordinary concept and our ordinary experience.' The same kind of objection can be raised against the autonomy requirement. Feldman, for example, asks us to imagine a person who has been brainwashed by a religious minority into living according to some very demanding rigid values.[26] The person is terribly dissatisfied with his life, as it is impossible for him to behave in such a way as to satisfy these values. Moreover, as we have seen, according to Sen and Sumner, the life of such a person does not contain negative well-being, since he is not autonomous. But again, one could claim that this does not seem right, as the values with which he has been indoctrinated make him experience the worse time of his life.

Third, IR and AR face what I shall call a '*shortcoming concerning assessment authority over time*'. Using Sumner's distinction between happiness (pleasant experiences) and well-being, let us assume the following: between t1 and t2 (that is, over period A) you enjoy intense happiness, but your evaluation is non-authentic (because you lack information about parts of your life that really matter to you and because you are not autonomous). In this situation, following Sumner, we must deny that you are experiencing genuine well-being, although you believe that you are. Assume also that between t2 and t3 (period B) you enjoy a great deal of well-being and thus are able to evaluate your life in an authentic way (you are well-informed and autonomous). Furthermore, in period B you have got hold of some information X

[25] In order to add the autonomy requirement to the case, imagine that the fake threat is experienced by a non-autonomous being.

[26] Feldman (2010), pp. 191–194.

which makes it clear to you that in period B, you would judge that you *did not have well-being* in period A. Imagine, for example, that you find out that your business partner in period A had stolen money from you. Assume, furthermore, that from t3 to t4 (period C) you again enjoy a great deal of well-being and thus are able to evaluate your life in an authentic way. In that period, you are also well aware of the information X concerning period A. However, because you are older and have other values, you believe, during period C, that you *did have well-being* in period A. And so you could go on switching back and forth between the claims: 'In A, I did not have well-being,' 'In A, I did have well-being,' 'In A, I did not have well-being,' and so on. I see at least one problem with this. If we accept Sumner's requirements, which of the *authentic* assessments made in B and C is authoritative? Sumner's theory of well-being does not explicitly answer that question. This is *not* to say that we should abandon IR or AR because of this observation. My point is just that the two requirements need to be specified so that it allows us to compare well-being assessments over time where all the requirements for well-being are satisfied. According to one interpretation, Sumner could say that in B, your assessment of A is authoritative compared to your assessment in A. In addition, in C your assessment of A is authoritative compared to your assessment in A and B. So the well-being for you in period A can change *relative* to your evaluations of period A in periods B and C.

Finally, taken together, Sumner's theory of well-being and his commitment in his book *Welfare, Happiness, and Ethics* to welfarism generate moral problems. In what follows, I will present a case in order to make this point clear. However, before that, let me say a few words about welfarism. Welfarism is a view about *the value of welfare* (or well-being), whereas Sumner's theory of welfare is a view about *the nature of welfare* (or well-being). Welfarism says that welfare is *all* that matters from a moral viewpoint. In other words, according to welfarism welfare is the only moral factor we should be concerned about when determining what acts are morally right or wrong. Utilitarians are well-known adherents of welfarism, as they typically believe that the only factor that matters morally is the maximization of welfare. Let me begin with the following case:

> **The Hospital Visit**
> By making a visit to the hospital, you can benefit just one of two people you know, A or B, as you only have time to visit one of them. A and B have equal levels of well-being before your visit. They are both terminally ill and both will die in about three weeks. If you visit A, you will make him very happy. However, you do not like A, and if you visit him it will be because you would be critical of yourself if you did not. If you visit A, you will *not* tell A that you do not like him, and it is clear that A will believe you are visiting him because you like him. It is also clear that *if* A knew that you were only visiting him to avoid a bad conscience and was aware that you did not like him at all, A would claim that your visit did not bring him well-being. So, if you visit A, you will deceive him, but he will be very happy. If, on the other hand you visit B, he will enjoy your visit somewhat, but it will only make him slightly better off in terms of well-being, because he

already knows that you do not like him and that you visit him for the sake of your own conscience. So, visiting B does not involve deception and only makes B slightly better off in terms of well-being.

Now IR (the case could also be constructed to imply AR by saying that A was non-autonomous, whereas B was autonomous), combined with Sumner's commitment to welfarism,[27] suggests that, from a moral point of view and assuming that things are otherwise comparable and equal, you should only take B into account. This is because, under these commitments, B is the only person whose well-being will be changed by your visit. Person A will be very happy if you visit him; but he will not accumulate well-being, because what makes him happy is the result of a deception that would, if it were revealed, make him evaluate your visit negatively. Sumner's combined views imply that, other things being equal, one ought only to be concerned with the alternative that makes one person slightly better off in respect of well-being instead of also being morally concerned with the alternative that makes one person very happy. That does not seem right.

To deal with this case, someone like Sumner could hold that increases in well-being count, from a moral point of view, for *more* than comparable increases in happiness, but that increases in happiness (although it is not well-being) always have *some* moral weight. However, it is clear that if Sumner followed this strategy, he would be in a position, in cases like the hospital visit, to say that one should also take into account the happiness of person A; for he could then say that, from a moral point of view, we should indeed make an effort to increase happiness. However, if this is Sumner's strategy, we need a rationale for attaching less *moral* value to uninformed and non-autonomous happiness than we attach to informed and autonomous well-being; and it seems to me that any rationale for this asymmetry is doomed to fit poorly with Sumner's thinking. He has to give up his *welfarism* and argue that happiness caused by false beliefs or experienced by non-autonomous persons (though not identical to welfare) is a morally relevant factor *next* to well-being.[28] Therefore, well-being is not all that matters morally. Alternatively, he has to give up his *theory of well-being* and argue that a person's happiness, which might be caused by false beliefs, does contribute to the well-being of that person. One could here argue that a certain amount of authentic happiness counts for more well-being than a comparable and equal amount of unauthentic happiness, but that unauthentic happiness, in a non-instrumental sense, does make some contribution to well-being.[29] But if one accepts this suggestion, one would also have to give up the view that the information and autonomy requirements are necessary requirements for well-being.

It is, of course, true that the problem here with these moral challenges need not be Sumner's theory of well-being. The problem may be welfarism. However, my

---

[27]In Sumner (1996), he defends both welfarism and his theory of well-being.

[28]A moral factor is that which determines the moral value of an act. For this definition of a moral factor, see Kagan (1998), p. 17.

[29]This possibility is mentioned by Sumner (1996), p. 161 and by Brülde (2007b), p. 369.

objections point, at least, to an internal problem with Sumner's overall view of the nature and value of well-being *and* to an indirect (moral) problem with Sumner's theory of well-being when it is combined with welfarism.

Conclusion

Sumner and Sen deliver what appear to be the right answers in certain cases that are often used as counterexamples to theories of well-being (like welfare hedonism) in which the experience requirement functions as a necessary and sufficient requirement for well-being. However, in their effort to construct a plausible account of experience-based welfare, they impose requirements on experience that can certainly be queried.

In this appendix, I have tried to explain why a well-known case like that of the deceived businessman need not support the information requirement in the way that Sumner and others believe it does. I have also introduced a case that makes both the information requirement and the autonomy requirement seem less attractive. Furthermore, I attended to what I believe is a shortcoming in Sumner's theory of welfare (namely, that it is unclear which of any later and authentic assessments are authoritative when it comes to the evaluation of a person's well-being over time). Finally, I have attempted to show that, in combination with welfarism, Sumner's requirements rather implausibly imply that, for instance, other things being equal, we should only be concerned with the alternative that makes one person slightly better off in respect of well-being, instead of also being morally concerned with the alternative that makes one person very happy.

References

Bognar G (2010) Authentic happiness. Utilitas 22(3):272–284
Bradley B (2011) Well-being and death. Oxford University Press, Oxford
Brülde B (1998) The human good. Acta Universitatus Gothoburgensis, Gothenburg
Brülde B (2007a) Happiness and the good life. J Happiness Stud 8(1):1–14
Brülde B (2007b) Happiness theories of the good life. J Happiness Stud 8(1):15–49
Bykvist K (1998) Changing preferences. A study in preferentialism. Acta Universitatis Uppsaliensis, Uppsala
Bykvist K (2002) Sumner on desires and well-being. Can J Philos 32(4):475–490
Crisp R (2006) Reasons and the good. Oxford University Press, Oxford
Eggleston B (1999) Review of Sumner's welfare, happiness and ethics. Int J Philos Stud 7 (2):270–272
Egonsson D (2007) Preference and information. Ashgate, Farnham
Feldman F (2004) Pleasure and the good life. Oxford University Press, Oxford
Feldman F (2010) What is this thing called happiness? Oxford University Press, Oxford
Griffin J (1986) Well-being: its meaning, measurement and moral importance. Clarendon Press, Oxford
Hawkins J (2008) Well-being, autonomy, and the horizon problem. Utilitas 20(2):143–168
Kagan S (1998) Normative ethics. Westview Press, Boulder

Petersen TS (2009) What is it for a life to go well (or badly)?: some critical comments on Wayne Sumner's theory of welfare. J Happiness Stud 10(4):449–458
Sen A (1987) On ethics and economics. Basil Blackwell, New Jersey
Sobel D (1998) Sumner on welfare. Dialogue Can Philos Rev/Revue canadienne de philosophie 37 (3):571–577
Sumner LW (1996) Welfare, happiness and ethics. Oxford University Press, Oxford
Sumner LW (2000) Something in between. In: Crisp R, Hooker B (eds) Well-being and morality, essays in honour of James Griffin. Oxford University Press, Oxford, pp 1–19
Sumner W (2004) The hateful and the obscene: studies in the limits of free expression. University of Toronto Press, Toronto
Sumner LW (2006) Feldman's hedonism. In: Feldman F, McDaniel K et al (eds) The good, the right, life and death: essays in honor of Fred Feldman. Ashgate, Farnham, pp 83–100
Tännsjö T (1998) Hedonistic utilitarianism. Edinburgh University Press, Edinburgh
Tupa A (2010) A critique of Sumner's account of welfare. Utilitas 22(1):79–98
Vallentyne P (1997) Welfare, happiness, and ethics, LW Sumner. Econ Philos 13(2):330–337

Printed by Printforce, the Netherlands